THE
PSYCHOLOGY
BIBLE

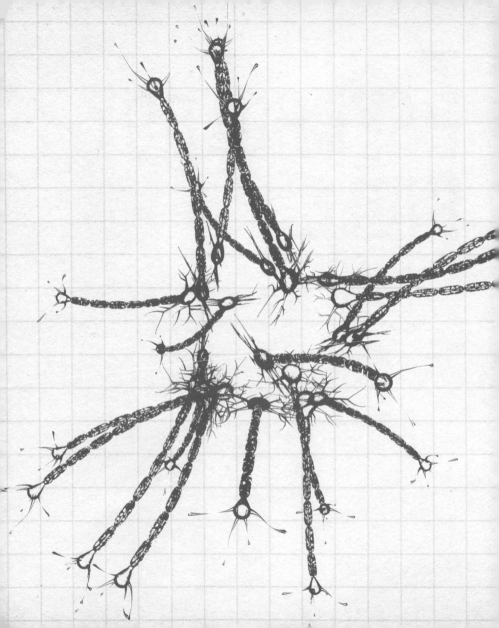

THE
PSYCHOLOGY
BIBLE

The definitive guide to the science of the mind

Sandi Mann, PhD

FIREFLY BOOKS

A FIREFLY BOOK

Published by Firefly Books Ltd. 2017

First printing

Publisher Cataloging-in-Publication Data (U.S.)

Names: Mann, Sandi, author.
Title: The psychology bible : the definitive guide to the science of the mind /
    Sandi Mann, PhD.
Description: Richmond Hill, Ontario, Canada : Firefly Books, 2016. | Includes
    index. | Summary: "An in-depth look into the brain's development on a
    psychological level, including an overview of well-known theories that are
    either debunked or applicable to our understanding of the human mind.
    Dr. Mann also explores the various types of psychotherapy available in
    modern medicine, which helps to remove prejudice and encourage people
    to find what works for them to achieve happiness and to feel rested" –
    Provided by publisher.
Identifiers: ISBN 978-1-77085-806-0 (paperback)
Subjects: LCSH: Psychology. | Psychology, Applied.
Classification: LCC BF145.M366 |DDC 150 – dc23

Library and Archives Canada Cataloguing in Publication

Mann, Sandi, author
    The psychology bible : the definitive guide to the science of the mind / Sandi
Mann, PhD.
Includes index.
    ISBN 978-1-77085-806-0 (paperback)
1. Psychology–Popular works. I. Title.
BF145.M35 2016 150 C2016-900573-9

Published in the United States by
Firefly Books (U.S.) Inc.
P.O. Box 1338, Ellicott Station
Buffalo, New York 14205

Published in Canada by
Firefly Books Ltd.
50 Staples Avenue, Unit 1
Richmond Hill, Ontario L4B 0A7

Printed and bound in China

DEDICATED TO DANIA AND ELISHA,
BOTH OF WHOM WOULD MAKE
BRILLIANT PSYCHOLOGISTS

First published by Cassell Illustrated, a division of
Octopus Publishing Group Ltd Carmelite House 50
Victoria Embankment London EC4Y 0DZ

COMMISSIONING EDITOR Leanne Bryan; **SENIOR EDITOR** Pauline
Bache; **COPY EDITOR** Alison Wormleighton; **ART DIRECTOR** Yasia
Williams-Leedham; **DESIGNER** Geoff Fennell; **PICTURE RESEARCH
MANAGER** Giulia Hetherington; **PRODUCTION CONTROLLER** Allison
Gonsalves; Dr Sandi Mann has asserted her right under
the Copyright, Designs and Patents Act 1988 to be
identified as the author of this work.

CONTENTS

INTRODUCTION

PSYCHOLOGY IS A TOPIC THAT FASCINATES AND ENTHRALS MOST PEOPLE — AND WHY NOT? AFTER ALL, IT IS ALL ABOUT PEOPLE SO IT IS NATURAL THAT WE WILL BE INTERESTED IN WHAT MAKES US TICK. PSYCHOLOGY IS ABOUT HOW WE THINK, FEEL AND ACT. IT IS THE STUDY OF HUMAN BEHAVIOR, THE PROCESSES THAT INFLUENCE THAT BEHAVIOR AND THE IMPACT OF OTHER PEOPLE, THE ENVIRONMENT AND A WHOLE HOST OF OTHER FACTORS.

THE STUDY OF PSYCHOLOGY HAS A LONG HISTORY (AS YOU WILL SEE ON PAGE 10), BUT IT IS AS RELEVANT TODAY AS IT HAS EVER BEEN. HUMANKIND FACES NEW CHALLENGES IN THE 21ST CENTURY, SUCH AS GLOBAL WARFARE, TERRORISM, COMPUTER-MEDIATED TECHNOLOGY, AUTOMATION, INCREASED LEISURE TIME AND THE RISE OF SOCIAL MEDIA — ALL OF WHICH IMPACT ON THE WAY WE THINK, FEEL AND BEHAVE. AT THE SAME TIME, WE STILL FACE MANY OF THE SAME ISSUES THAT HAVE ALWAYS AFFECTED HUMANS — GRIEF, BEREAVEMENT, BIRTH, CARE OF THE YOUNG, NUTRITION, EDUCATION AND GROWTH. THE STUDY OF PSYCHOLOGY CONTRIBUTES TO ALL OF THIS BY HELPING US UNDERSTAND HOW WE INTERACT WITH OUR WORLD AND HOW TO COPE BETTER WITH THE CHALLENGES WE FACE.

THIS BOOK WILL GUIDE YOU THROUGH SOME OF THE MOST IMPORTANT DEVELOPMENTS IN PSYCHOLOGICAL RESEARCH WHILE EXPLAINING HOW THEY IMPACT OUR LIVES TODAY. THE BOOK IS MADE UP OF FIVE DISTINCT PARTS, EACH OF WHICH COULD BE EITHER ENJOYED ON ITS OWN OR READ CHRONOLOGICALLY. WE BEGIN BY OUTLINING THE HISTORY OF PSYCHOLOGY AND THE VARIED DISCIPLINES AND PROFESSIONS THAT MAKE UP THIS BROAD FIELD; THIS IS USEFUL FOR ANYONE THINKING OF STUDYING PSYCHOLOGY AT A DEEPER LEVEL AND PERHAPS CONSIDERING IT AS A CAREER. PART 1 ALSO CONSIDERS THE MOST INFLUENTIAL

PEOPLE WHO HAVE CONTRIBUTED TO THE DEVELOPMENT OF PSYCHOLOGICAL UNDERSTANDING — INCLUDING NOT ONLY EMINENT PSYCHOLOGISTS, BUT ALSO ORDINARY PEOPLE WHO, FOR ONE REASON OR ANOTHER, HAVE ENDED UP AS VALUABLE CASE MATERIAL FOR PSYCHOLOGICAL INSIGHT. A BASIC GRASP OF THE BRAIN AND NERVOUS SYSTEM IS USEFUL TO UNDERSTAND PSYCHOLOGY, SO THIS IS INCLUDED, TOO.

PART 2 DISCUSSES THE MOST IMPORTANT THEORIES THAT HAVE SHAPED PSYCHOLOGICAL UNDERSTANDING OVER THE YEARS AND INCLUDES MOST OF THE REALLY IMPORTANT CONSTITUENTS THAT MAKE UP THE BUILDING BLOCKS FOR THE DISCIPLINE. FOLLOWING THIS, PART 3 FOCUSES ON THE PSYCHOLOGICAL EXPERIMENTS THAT HAVE CHANGED THE WORLD, FROM THE STANFORD PRISON EXPERIMENT TO MILGRAM'S SHOCK STUDIES. THE IMPACT OF THESE EXPERIMENTS, MANY OF WHICH WOULD NEVER BE ALLOWED TODAY FOR ETHICAL REASONS, ON TODAY'S SOCIETY IS EXPLORED. PART 4 MOVES INTO THE ARENA OF VARIOUS MENTAL-HEALTH CONDITIONS AND DISORDERS, INCLUDING THOSE AFFECTING CHILDREN. THIS IS FOLLOWED BY DISCUSSION OF THERAPEUTIC INTERVENTIONS, WITH A RANGE OF THERAPIES, FROM PSYCHOANALYTIC TO HUMANISTIC, EXPLORED. FINALLY, PART 5 ENDS WITH PRACTICAL ADVICE ON HOW TO USE PSYCHOLOGY FOR VARIOUS MEANS, FROM STOPPING SMOKING TO BEING A GREAT LEADER.

THIS BOOK IS A VOYAGE OF DISCOVERY INTO THE MIND THAT WILL ENLIGHTEN, ENTERTAIN AND EDUCATE. ENJOY THE JOURNEY!

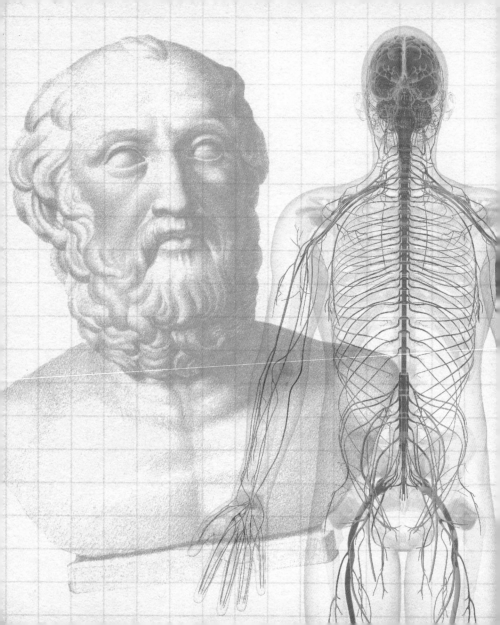

PART 1

PSYCHOLOGY & PSYCHOLOGISTS:

PSYCHOLOGY HAS A LONG AND ILLUSTRIOUS HISTORY, THROUGH WHICH ORDINARY PEOPLE HAVE HAD AS MUCH IMPACT ON THE SCIENCE AS THE PSYCHOLOGISTS THEMSELVES. IN ORDER TO UNDERSTAND THE DISCIPLINE OF PSYCHOLOGY WE MUST FIRST UNDERSTAND ITS ROOTS AND HOW PSYCHOLOGISTS WORK TODAY AND WORKED IN THE PAST.

WHAT IS PSYCHOLOGY?

THE HISTORY OF PSYCHOLOGY

Psychology today is defined as the scientific study of mind and behavior, but it dates back to around 550 BCE, when Ancient Greek philosophers developed theories of what they termed the *psukhē* (from which the first half of "psychology" is derived). The first use of the term "psychology" is often attributed to the German scholastic philosopher Rudolf Göckel (1547–1628), who published a work with "Psychologia" in the title in 1590.

Until the mid-19th century, the discipline of psychology was considered part of philosophy. French philosopher René Descartes (1596–1650) was very influential in what was regarded as the study of the soul. But in 1879 Wilhelm Wundt (1832–1920) established the first psychology research laboratory, in

IN THE EARLY DAYS *of trying to understand human behavior it was not clear whether the brain or the heart was the center for mental processses.*

Leipzig, Germany. Wundt was the first person known to refer to himself as a psychologist but other important early contributors include Hermann Ebbinghaus, a pioneer in the study of memory (see page 12), and Ivan Pavlov, who developed procedures associated with classical conditioning (see page 97).

Germany also became the leader in other branches of psychology, especially the use of the case study, led by the work of Sigmund Freud (see page 31), who pioneered the development of psychoanalysis. The study of psychology began to gather pace in the United States too, when Harvard physiology instructor (as he then was) William James opened a

IN 387 BCE PLATO SUGGESTED THAT THE BRAIN WAS THE MECHANISM OF MENTAL PROCESSES (ALTHOUGH LATER, IN 335 BCE, ARISTOTLE SUGGESTED THAT THE HEART WAS THE MECHANISM OF MENTAL PROCESSES).

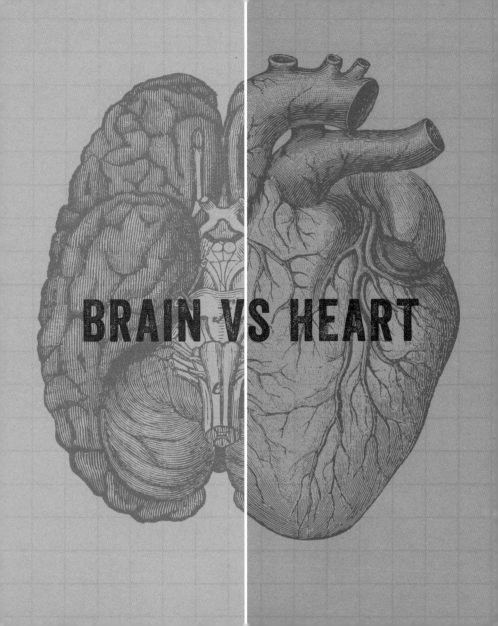

THE FORGETTING CURVE

Hermann Ebbinghaus (1850–1909) was a German psychologist who was one of the first researchers to study forgetting. He is known for his discovery of the "forgetting curve," which describes the exponential loss of information that one has learned. The sharpest decline occurs in the first 20 minutes and is significant throughout the first hour. The curve levels off after about one day. He is also well known for creating the concept of "nonsense syllables," three-letter sequences that did not make sense (such as DAX, BOK and YAT) so that real words would not interfere with his studies into memory. Unlike many researchers, Ebbinghaus worked primarily with one subject: himself. During his experiments, he memorized over 2,000 nonsense syllables. It was Ebbinghaus who first coined the term "learning curve" to describe how fast one learns information.

small experimental psychology laboratory. In 1890 he published *The Principles of Psychology*, one of the earliest and most influential psychology textbooks in the U.S. However, it was Britain that had the first scholarly journal dedicated to the topic of psychology — *Mind*, founded in 1876.

In 1892, 30 psychologists and philosophers, led by G. Stanley Hall (who was awarded the first American Psychology Ph.D), founded the American Psychological Association (APA). In 1896 the University of Pennsylvania was the site of the first psychological clinic, marking the birth of clinical psychology.

IN 1808 THE GERMAN PHYSIOLOGIST FRANZ GALL CLAIMED THAT PHRENOLOGY (THE STUDY OF THE SHAPE AND SIZE OF THE SKULL OVER RELEVANT PARTS OF THE BRAIN) COULD REVEAL INSIGHTS INTO PERSONALITY TRAITS.

The 20th century saw the formulation of behaviorism by John B. Watson (see below), which was developed further by B.F. Skinner (see page 29). Behaviorism, according to Watson, was the science of observable behavior. Only behavior that could be observed, recorded and measured, he said, was of any real value for the study of humans or animals. Watson conducted the controversial "Little Albert" experiment (see page 148) to prove that behaviors could be produced through conditioning, and he was at the forefront of the technique of behavior modification, which enabled children (and adults) to be trained using reward-and-punishment schedules.

The Psychological Society was established in the UK in 1901 (renaming itself the British Psychological Society in 1906). Meanwhile, in France, the first test of intelligence, the Binet–Simon Intelligence Scale, was developed, in 1905 (it was revised by American psychologists into the better-known Stanford–Binet IQ Test in 1916). The first psychological-test development company, Psychological Corporation, was launched in New York City in 1921; not only did it commercialize psychological testing but it also allowed testing to take place in businesses and clinics rather than only at universities and research facilities.

In 1952 the American Psychiatric Association published the first *Diagnostic and Statistical Manual of Mental Disorders* (*DSM*), marking the beginning of modern mental-illness classification (it has recently published the fifth edition). The American Psychological Association developed the first Code of Ethics for Psychologists the following year.

The final decades of the 20th century saw the rise of cognitive science, an interdisciplinary approach to studying the human mind.

THE REBELLIOUS J.B. WATSON

J.B. Watson (1878–1958) led a rather colorful life. He was arrested twice during high school (first for fighting with African–Americans, then for discharging firearms within the city limits). In 1920, Johns Hopkins University asked Watson to leave his faculty position because of publicity concerning the affair he was having with his graduate student (whom he later married and remained with until his death).

DIFFERENT PSYCHOLOGY DISCIPLINES

Over the years, various approaches to studying psychology have been developed.

BIOLOGICAL APPROACH: The biological approach has its origins with Charles Darwin (1809–82) and his theory of natural selection. This paved the way for the view that our minds and behavior are influenced more by biology (for example, genes and physiological structure) than by anything else. Such researchers took the view that in the nature–nurture debate (see page 20) nature wins; most behavior is inherited and has an adaptive (or evolutionary) function. Everything we do can be explained by biological processes rather than environmental influences; for example, the researchers explained abnormal functioning in terms of chemical imbalances in the brain rather than any other non-biological cause. All thoughts, feelings and behavior ultimately have a biological cause. Twin research and naturalistic observations formed much of the methodology in this approach, although lab studies were used, too.

PSYCHOANALYTIC/PSYCHODYNAMIC APPROACH: This approach originated with Sigmund Freud (see page 31), whose development of psychoanalysis was both a theory and a therapy. The psychodynamic approach to psychology sees events in childhood as having a significant impact on our behavior as adults. All behavior is thus

CHARLES DARWIN'S THEORY OF NATURAL SELECTION *argued that most mental processes had some evolutionary benefit to help us to survive and evolve.*

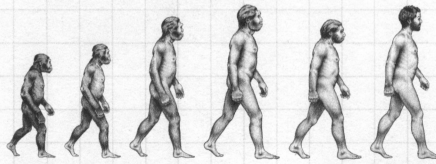

FREUDIAN SLIPS

Freudian slips are errors in speech, memory or physical action that are interpreted as occurring because of the interference of unconscious wishes or conflicts (thus seen as revealing a person's true thoughts). They are named after Sigmund Freud, who, in his 1901 book *The Psychopathology of Everyday Life*, described and analyzed a large number of seemingly trivial, bizarre or nonsensical errors and slips that he thought revealed much about the real motivations behind the person who made them (but he never actually called them Freudian slips). For example, substituting your father's name for your spouse's might suggest that, subconsciously, you see your spouse as a father figure — something that could be used by followers of psychodynamic approaches to explain marital discord.

A famous example of a Freudian slip occurred in 2014 when Pope Francis used the Italian word *cazzo* (which translates to "f***") instead of *caso* (which means "example") in a sermon. He quickly corrected himself but if you search for "Freudian slips" online, you will see many examples of celebrities' and politicians' slips that have now been immortalized via social media.

determined by the unconscious mind and childhood experiences; for example, a child startled by a lively dog might grow up to fear any unpredictable event. Most of the causes of our behavior are hidden within our unconscious mind and are therefore hard to access. To reach these processes, Freud developed psychoanalytic techniques, such as free association (where a patient is encouraged to say whatever comes to mind), dream analysis and slips of the tongue (otherwise known as Freudian slips – see page 15).

BEHAVIORIST APPROACH: This approach to studying psychology has its roots in the behaviorism developed by J.B. Watson and B.F. Skinner (see page 29). Early studies involved scientists watching rats, pigeons and cats trying to escape from boxes or to obtain food through a process of learning which behavioral responses would be most likely to yield results; it would happen by chance at first but the animal soon learned to produce the required response deliberately. This behavior, which could be "shaped" by reward-and-punishment regimes, could be applied to the human world, too. The behaviorist approach sees all human behavior as learned, through either classical or operant conditioning

MRI vs fMRI

One of the most common ways to view the internal structure of an organ without cutting it open is through the use of magnetic resonance imaging and functional magnetic resonance imaging, both of which use a powerful magnetic field and a computer to produce detailed pictures of organs, soft tissues, bone and virtually all other internal body structures. The two techniques, while similar to each other, differ in that an MRI largely views the anatomical structure while the newer fMRI views the metabolic function.

(see pages 97 and 98). The approach also utilizes only controlled studies and believes that only observable behavior (which can be measured) should be examined.

COGNITIVE APPROACH: The cognitive approach was developed in the mid-1950s out of dissatisfaction with the narrow emphasis on only observable behavior of the behaviorist approach. Cognitive perspectives hold that to understand people and their behavior we have to understand what is going on in their brains rather than just what we see them do. This perspective thus focuses on "mental" functions such as memory, perception, language, thinking, problem-solving and attention. Neuroscience is an approach within cognitive psychology that looks at what brain injury or disease can tell us about how the brain works; often this uses the case-study approach (see page 42 for examples) but also employs laboratory studies, perhaps involving brain-imaging techniques such as MRI (magnetic resonance imaging) scans.

EARLY BEHAVIORIST APPROACHES *took place by observing rats, pigeons or cats and watching how they learned new behaviors.*

HUMANISTIC APPROACH: At around the same time that the cognitive approach was developing, a humanistic perspective was emerging as a reaction to the behaviorist and psychoanalytical approaches, which were dominant at the time. The humanistic approach emphasizes individuals' inherent drive toward self-actualization, which is the process of realizing and expressing one's own capabilities and reaching one's potential. The focus is on the whole person, their thoughts and feelings, and the free will that governs their behavior — and directs them to be the best they can. Two of the most influential psychologists in the humanistic approach are Carl Rogers and Abraham Maslow (see pages 33 and 35). Humanistic therapies are discussed on page 253.

FREUD & DREAM ANALYSIS

In his book *The Interpretation of Dreams*, first published in 1899 (but dated 1900), Freud argued that dreams can reveal a lot about our repressed concerns, wishes and desires. Children's dreams, he argued, are simple manifestations of their desires based on the previous day's events (what he referred to as the "dream day") but adults' dreams are a little more complicated. Freud claimed that these occur when our defenses are weakened, although the dreams are distorted by the "latent" thoughts or attempts at censorship by the unconscious. This distortion disguises the real meanings (which are often wish fulfilment) of our dreams and his psychoanalytical dream-analysis technique is needed to uncover the real messages behind our dreams.

Psychoanalytical dream analysis involves identifying the distortions or "distorting operations" (what Freud called "dream-work") that have taken place to repress the wishes of the patient — and reversing them to uncover the "latent content." Freud distinguished between the "manifest content" of a dream (what the dreamer remembers) and the "latent content" (the underlying wish or meaning of the dream). The distorting operations he identified include:

CONDENSATION: This is where one dream object is used to represent several thoughts and ideas. For example, an animal in a dream might represent both a spouse and a lover.

DISPLACEMENT: The emotional significance that is attached to one object, place or person is separated and attached to an entirely different one that does not raise the dreamer's suspicions and causes the dreamer to self-censor their own dreams using defense mechanisms (see page 250). Thus, a dream about a house fire might actually represent a fear of loss of a loved one.

VISUALIZATION: This is where a thought or idea is transferred onto a visual image.

SYMBOLISM: This is similar to visualization, but here a symbol replaces an action, person or idea.

In addition, the dreamer is likely to try to make sense of their dream process and impose some sort of "secondary elaboration" on the story or events.

Freud's approaches paved the way for later "dream dictionaries" in which certain objects or events were supposed to represent particular meanings. Freud himself never really subscribed to this idea and while such dream analysis is quite popular today, it is not underpinned by psychological theory.

THE NATURE–NURTURE DEBATE

JUST HOW DO WE DEVELOP?
(AND ARE PSYCHOPATHS BORN EVIL OR DO THEY BECOME THAT WAY?)

One of the oldest debates in psychology concerns what exactly shapes our personality — and the relative influences of the environment (nurture) and our genes (nature). The term "nature and nurture" has been in use since at least the Elizabethan period and is thought to go back to medieval French. On the nurture side of the debate is the "blank slate" approach, first proposed by John Locke in 1690, which assumes that human behavior develops mainly from environmental influences (and thus denies the influence of hereditary components). This was the dominant view until the end of the 20th century when the pure behaviorist approaches of J.B. Watson and others gave a minimal role to genes. It began to change when identical twins separated at birth became the object of psychological research.

In the early 20th century, twins who needed adopting were routinely split up. This later provided an opportunity to study the relative influences of the environment and genes, since some of these identical twins who had the same genetic material were placed in differing environments (see page 50). Twin studies established that there was, in many cases, a significant heritable component to personality. By the 1990s, with the advances in genetic studies, the influence of heritability became easier to examine. In 2002 a book by Steven Pinker, called *The Blank Slate: The Modern Denial of Human Nature*, was instrumental in bringing about the shift away from the behaviorist purism of the 1940s–1970s.

It is now thought that an individual's personality (and even intelligence) is the product of both hereditary factors and the environment (such as upbringing, relationship with parents, social conditioning, nutrition and education). Family environmental factors, for example, may account for up to a quarter of the variance of IQ. With personality, studies have shown that identical twins reared apart are far more similar in personality than randomly selected pairs of people (and than fraternal twins, who share less genetic material than identical twins).

What about "evil people" then? Psychologists have long been preoccupied with this question, not least because of the implications for treatment and punishment. The answer is that, like other factors, psychopathy (which involves a lack of moral code, empathy and remorse) is probably the result of an interaction of nature and nurture. For example, a paper published in 2006 in the *Journal of Abnormal Psychology* entitled "Associations Among Early Abuse, Dissociation, and Psychopathy in an Offender Sample" suggests that at least some of the features of psychopathic personalities occur as a result of abuse ("nurture" factors). Other studies suggest a "nature" component to the condition. For example, a 1991 experiment found that psychopaths' brains react more slowly to emotionally charged words than non-psychopaths' brains do. Other studies found that fMRI (functional magnetic resonance imaging) images of psychopaths' brains reveal a thinning of the paralimbic tissue, which is thought to be responsible for feelings of empathy.

STUDIES OF TWINS *who have had different upbringings (for example through adoption) have been invaluable in helping us to understand how much of who we are is down to genetics and how much is due to environment.*

EVOLUTIONARY APPROACH: The premise of this approach is that the human brain is the way it is as a result of evolution, so the approach explains behavior by the evolutionary processes that shaped it. Any behavior that exists today thus has an adaptive purpose — in other words, it developed as a way to give us an advantage when it came to natural selection and survival of the fittest. Much behavior is therefore instinctual: it is based on innate impulses that we are born with. The evolutionary approach explains stress, for example, very well; this response was an adaptive emergency-response system that provided us with extra energy with which to "fight or take flight" and thus survive any predatory attacks. Nowadays, of course, the response does not serve us as well — it is, perhaps, a relic from our evolutionary past. The stress response is discussed in more detail on page 136.

COMPARATIVE APPROACH: This approach uses the study of animals to help with understanding human behavior. Charles Darwin was central in the development of comparative psychology. Towards the end of the 19th century, Douglas Alexander Spalding, who studied instinct and imprinting in birds (how baby birds become attached to a parent figure), was also a major influence. Particular areas of interest for comparative psychologists are heredity, adaptation and learning, and parenting behaviors, all of which are thought to shed some light on human behavior.

WHAT DO PSYCHOLOGISTS DO?

If psychology is the scientific study of mind and behavior, what exactly do psychologists do? People seem to think that we spend all our time "reading people's minds," but there is rather more to it than that. (Although, of course, we don't really mind-read, it can sometimes be useful if people think we do have that ability!) What we do depends on what sort of psychologist we are. Some of us spend our time doing research to increase our understanding of the human brain and how it affects behavior. Some of us treat patients who have mental-health disorders or conditions. Others work with children who have learning difficulties and still others might help devise campaigns encouraging people to adopt healthy behaviors, such as stopping smoking. Another group of psychologists work in business and organizations to help them operate more effectively, while yet another set of psychologists help athletes to perform better.

All of these types of psychologist will work using psychological models and principles about the human mind (developed and uncovered through years of research) to contribute in some way to individuals and to society. Some of the main psychology professions include the following:

ACADEMIC/RESEARCH PSYCHOLOGISTS: In order to develop the theories, models, principles and therapies that psychology practitioners use, we need people to do the research.

CASE STUDY: THE AUTHOR

I am a university-based Chartered Academic Psychologist — Chartered means that I am registered with the British Psychological Society and that my qualifications are recognized by them. I got to this position by doing my undergraduate degree in psychology, followed by my doctorate, in which I decided to research a very specific area of emotions — something called "emotional labor" (this is the work involved in managing or controlling emotions in the workplace). After gaining my doctorate, I obtained a job as university lecturer at England's University of Central Lancashire, where I am still based and where I teach subjects related to my main research areas, such as emotions, workplace issues and stress. I spend about half a day a week carrying out studies that further our understanding of some of these areas. (For example, I am currently researching boredom, which is a very commonly suppressed emotion.) Some universities allow their staff to spend longer on research. An important part of that research is trying to get it published in reputable journals so that everyone else can see and benefit from what I have found out.

Research psychologists usually are based in university research institutions and also teach undergraduate and postgraduate students. In fact, it is more commonly the other way around — academics (who teach) generally do research, too. An academic is a specialist in a particular area of psychology and will usually have a doctorate in that area. They will then spend their days teaching their specialist area and doing research (and supervising the research of others) to further our understanding of that field.

CLINICAL PSYCHOLOGISTS: This is probably the sort of psychologist with which people are most familiar. These psychologists provide therapy to depressed or anxious patients; however, they do a lot more than that. For example, they might assess people for psychological disorders, help patients with brain damage learn to adapt, diagnose children with developmental disorders or help people who have experienced trauma. Clinical psychologists may specialize in particular fields, such as the elderly, children or people with learning disabilities. They typically work within the health sector. To be a clinical psychologist, you would most likely do an undergraduate degree, followed by a year or two getting work experience as an assistant psychologist, then undertake a doctoral program. However, these requirements may differ according to the country you are in.

SPORTS PSYCHOLOGISTS *use research and theory to help athletes improve their performance.*

SPORTS PSYCHOLOGISTS: These professionals work with athletes and teams by applying psychological models and using techniques such as goal setting, visualization and relaxation that can help them perform better or cope with setbacks or the pressure of competing. They might be employed by sports teams, individual athletes, coaches, referees or sports associations and can also be involved in building team cohesion or helping with communication, such as between managers and squads. To be a sports psychologist, you would probably need to undertake a recognized master's degree after your undergraduate qualification.

OCCUPATIONAL PSYCHOLOGISTS: Often known as workplace, industrial or business psychologists, these people help employers, organizations and employees with a range of workplace issues such as workplace stress, bullying, leadership development, training, selection and assessment and ergonomics (how equipment fits human needs). To be a workplace psychologist, you would probably need to study a recognized master's degree after your undergraduate program. Workplace psychologists may be employed by large organizations or by occupational psychology consultancies, or they may be self-employed.

OCCUPATIONAL PSYCHOLOGISTS are experts at helping businesses get the most from their workforce, helping with organizational design and employee wellbeing.

HEALTH PSYCHOLOGISTS: This is a relatively new and emerging field that, in my view, probably developed as a response to the difficulty people were having in getting accepted on clinical training courses; many perfectly suitable candidates are turned down because of a lack of spaces and some of these turn to health psychology instead. There are many overlaps between clinical and health psychology, but health psychologists have a narrower range of skills, applying psychological methods to the study of behavior relevant to illness and healthcare. They might, for example, help devise campaigns to encourage people to eat healthily, stop smoking or undertake health screening. Another role is to work with patients with long-term conditions, to help them adapt to their illness and adhere to treatment or medication regimes. These psychologists often work in hospitals but may also work in universities. To be a health psychologist, you would probably need to do an undergraduate degree followed by a year-long master's degree.

FORENSIC PSYCHOLOGISTS: Otherwise known as criminal psychologists, these professionals usually work in criminal settings like prisons. They help with treatment and rehabilitation of offenders, and sometimes with helping prison staff to cope with stress or other aspects of their jobs. They may be involved in assessing whether offenders are suitable for release or parole or are a risk to the public (or to themselves). These psychologists might design and implement training programs for offenders, such as anger management, or generally help with improving prison regimes. To become a forensic psychologist, you would need to complete a master's degree after your undergraduate studies.

PSYCHOLOGISTS VS PSYCHIATRISTS

Psychiatrists are medical practitioners who have undergone extra training in psychiatric conditions. They prescribe medications to deal with mental-health problems but rarely undertake non-pharmaceutical interventions themselves like psychologists. Psychologists, on the other hand, do not prescribe medication. The two professions may work together — for example, a patient may be under the care of both practitioners, getting their medication from the psychiatrist (who will monitor its impact) and receiving their psychological interventions from the psychologist.

EDUCATIONAL PSYCHOLOGISTS: These psychologists work with children in educational settings and are often qualified teachers themselves. They assess children for learning, social or developmental problems, design and advise on interventions, help with behavior management or issues such as bullying, and advise on policy and input that a child or school may require. To become an educational psychologist, you would typically need to complete a teacher-training qualification after your undergraduate degree and then be accepted on a doctoral program (much of which involves placement activities).

EDUCATIONAL PSYCHOLOGISTS *assess children for a range of developmental conditions, then work with schools to devise intervention programs to help children access the curriculum and reach their potential.*

TOP TEN
MOST INFLUENTIAL
20TH-CENTURY PSYCHOLOGISTS

IN 2002, THE *REVIEW OF GENERAL PSYCHOLOGY* PUBLISHED A SURVEY OF THE HUNDRED MOST EMINENT PSYCHOLOGISTS OF THE 20TH CENTURY. THE JOURNAL'S "TOP TEN" ARE SHOWN HERE, IN ORDER OF INFLUENCE.

Sadly, no females enter the top ten or even the top fifty (owing, presumably, to lack of opportunities for women in days gone by). Elizabeth Loftus, whom we will see when learning about false memory on page 92, is the most influential female psychologist of the 20th century, at 58th place.

(list of most eminent psychologists of the 20th century courtesy of Review of General Psychology, 2002, vol. 6, No. 2)

1. B.F. SKINNER

Burrhus Frederic Skinner (1904–90) was an American psychologist and is commonly referred to as the father of behaviorism (see page 16), which sees behavior as a consequence of reinforcement rather than of thinking or emotions. Reinforcement is the primary process that shapes and controls behavior and it occurs in two ways, "positive" and "negative." Positive reinforcement is akin to reward and negative reinforcement to punishment. Skinner coined the phrase "operant conditioning" for this process of shaping and controlling behavior using reinforcement. For more about conditioning, see page 96.

Skinner is well known for his invention of the operant conditioning chamber, popularly known as the "Skinner box," with which he carried out his studies (see page 99). By combining positive reinforcement with punishment, such as electric shocks, he was able to control animals' behavior. This had a huge influence on the course of research into animal learning. It also enabled great progress in human applications that could be studied by measuring the rate, probability or force of a simple, repeatable response.

2. JEAN PIAGET

The Swiss developmental psychologist Jean Piaget (1896–1980) was the first psychologist to make a systematic study of cognitive development. Before his work, it was believed that children were just mini adults, but he was able to show that they thought in qualitatively different ways than adults do. His theory proposed discrete stages of development, marked by qualitative differences, rather than a gradual increase in abilities.

Although his theories were developed in the 1930s, they did not really become popular until the 1960s. By the end of the 20th century, Piaget was second only to B.F. Skinner as the most cited psychologist of the era.

3. SIGMUND FREUD

Sigmund Freud (1856–1939) was an Austrian neurologist (he qualified as a doctor of medicine at the University of Vienna in 1881) and is known as the father of psychoanalysis, which is a clinical method for treating mental-health problems through therapeutic techniques such as free association. (For more about these therapies, see page 246.) Freud believed that the unconscious mind consisted of three components: the id, the ego and the superego (see page 247). The id and the superego are constantly in conflict with each other and the ego tries to resolve the discord; if this conflict is not resolved, we tend to use defense mechanisms to reduce our anxieties. Psychoanalysis attempts to help patients resolve their inner conflicts.

Freud also developed theories about sexuality, such as the Oedipus complex, and about what dreams say about unconscious desires. He relied heavily on case studies to develop his theories, one of which involved Little Hans (see page 150). Before World War II, Freud, who was Jewish, fled Austria for Britain, and he died of cancer of the jaw (caused by his heavy smoking) in 1939. His daughter, Anna Freud, became a famous psychoanalytic therapist in her own right.

4. ALBERT BANDURA

Canadian-born Albert Bandura (b. 1925) is one of the few on this list still alive at the time of writing and is the most cited living psychologist. He is known as the originator of social learning theory (see page 101), which explains how we learn from other people and the construct of self-efficacy, which is the extent or strength of one's belief in one's own ability to complete tasks. He is also responsible for the influential 1961 Bobo Doll experiment (see page 158). Despite Bandura's great contributions to psychology, he actually fell into the area by chance; bored as a student, he took some psychology courses simply to pass the time.

5. LEON FESTINGER

The American social psychologist Leon Festinger (1919–89) is best known for his theories of cognitive dissonance (see page 133) and social comparison (see page 127). His social comparison theory led *Fortune* magazine to name him one of the ten most promising scientists in the United States. Oddly, at the start of his career he had no interest in social psychology — this became an interest much later on. Then in later life he abandoned his psychology career to pursue interests in archaeology. Nevertheless, Festinger is still considered one of the greatest social psychologists of all time.

6. CARL R. ROGERS

The American psychologist Carl Ransom Rogers (1902–87) was founder of the humanistic approach (or client/person-centered approach) to psychotherapy (see page 256), emphasizing the relationship between the client — who he did not refer to as a patient — and the therapist. Rogers was another psychologist who came to the profession late, having first explored both agriculture and religion as career options. His approaches emphasized the unconditional, positive regard that a therapist should show to a client and many of his ideals have been adopted across a range of therapies, not just the humanistic ones.

7. STANLEY SCHACHTER

The American social psychologist Stanley Schachter (1922–97) is best known for his development with Jerome E. Singer of the two-factor theory of emotion (see page 102) in 1962. This theory was the first to state that emotions have two ingredients — physiological arousal and a cognitive label that has to be given to that arousal for it to be labeled an emotion. Before this, there had been no role for cognition in the experience of emotions. The theory also led to the idea that emotion could be misattributed so that we might label arousal as an emotion incorrectly depending on what other information is available to us. While Schachter is best known for his work on emotions, he also researched obesity and addiction. He found, for example, that people of normal weight stop eating when they are full but that overweight people eat for reasons other than how full they are.

8. NEAL E. MILLER

Neal Elgar Miller (1909–2002) was an American experimental psychologist who, together with a colleague, developed a theory of motivation based on the satisfaction of psychosocial drives. He spent his career trying to map the physiological underpinnings of human drives like fear, hunger and curiosity, and made breakthrough discoveries, such as fear being a learned response or the fact that biofeedback techniques (whereby feedback about one's own biological processes or measures can be used to improve those processes) can allow people to control their own blood pressure. Most of his research was conducted using rats in labs, attracting controversy from animal rights groups.

9. EDWARD THORNDIKE

The American psychologist Edward Thorndike (1874–1949) is best known for his "law of effect." This states that responses that produce a reward are more likely to recur in that situation and responses that produce a punishment become less likely to recur. B.F. Skinner's theory of operant conditioning (see page 98) was built on the ideas of Edward Thorndike. Thorndike tested his ideas with the creation of a "puzzle box" in which he placed a cat who had to escape to reach the reward of food; using trial and error it soon learned what responses were needed to press the escape lever. The law of effect was used to account for the behavior of the cats in his experiments.

10. ABRAHAM H. MASLOW

Abraham Harold Maslow (1908–70) was an American psychologist best known for creating a "hierarchy of needs," a theory of motivation that is discussed on pages 108–9. He urged people to acknowledge their basic needs before addressing higher needs and ultimately self-actualization (self-fulfilment). Maslow also established the discipline of humanistic psychology which is discussed on page 17. In 1963 he turned down a request to be president of the Association for Humanistic Psychology because he felt that the organization should develop without a leader.

WHAT MIGHT YOU LEARN IF YOU WANT TO STUDY PSYCHOLOGY?

An undergraduate degree is an essential first step to all of the professional routes I have discussed so far. If you are considering such a course of study, it is useful to know what you might learn; this will also help you understand more about what psychology is.

While all psychology undergraduate degrees vary, most cover the following key areas:

DEVELOPMENTAL PSYCHOLOGY: This covers all aspects of how we develop across our lifespan, including adolescence and aging — but mostly concentrates on how children learn and develop in areas such as language acquisition, moral reasoning, intellectual development, attachment to carers, and personality and identity formation.

SOCIAL PSYCHOLOGY: This is concerned with how people are influenced by the presence of others (or even by the imagined presence of others). It covers areas such as attitude formation (and change), persuasion, minority influence, group dynamics, interpersonal attraction, prejudice and crowd psychology.

COGNITIVE PSYCHOLOGY: This is the study of mental processes including attention, creativity, language use, memory, perception, problem-solving and thinking.

INDIVIDUAL DIFFERENCES: As suggested by the name, this is concerned with those attributes that differ from person to person. It usually refers to aspects such as personality, intelligence, gender and age differences.

PHYSIOLOGICAL PSYCHOLOGY: This refers to the study of the physical elements that contribute to how we think, feel, perceive and behave. It thus involves the study of the brain, the nervous system and the hormone-secreting glands known as the endocrine system (see page 52).

ABNORMAL PSYCHOLOGY: This is the study of unusual or atypical behavior and thought patterns and tends to cover psychological conditions and disorders and mental-health problems. Nowadays it is called simply "clinical psychology" at many universities.

RESEARCH METHODS: Most psychology curricula will involve some sort of study into methods of research and how to carry out a scientific psychological study (see page 38).

TOOLS OF PSYCHOLOGY: HOW DO PSYCHOLOGISTS FIND OUT STUFF?

As already explained, the discipline of psychology relies on scientific study to expound our knowledge and further our understanding of the human condition.

The basic process for conducting psychology research involves asking a question, designing a study, collecting data, analyzing results, reaching conclusions and sharing the findings with the rest of the psychological community. A study always starts with a hypothesis or tentative prediction about a proposed relationship between two "variables." A variable is something that we can introduce or take away in order to see its effect on the outcome. For example, I might want to investigate how much praising my son improves his behavior; here the variable would be praise, and the hypothesis would probably be "praising my son will improve his behavior." This prediction, which is based on either previous research or some other logical reasoning, can then be tested. There are three main ways a prediction can be tested: through experiments, correlational research and observational methods.

WHY PSYCHOLOGY IS A SCIENCE

The aim of science is to create credible explanations (or theories) for phenomenon based on evidence. Psychologists arrive at conclusions about human behavior by observing, measuring and testing it using rigorous scientific methodology. These methods should be replicable and should have certain features to control for contaminants that might otherwise account for the findings in a study. This means that the psychologist can be reasonably sure that the conclusions follow from the proposed reason and not from other factors. Therapies and interventions can thus be based on these conclusions with reasonable safety.

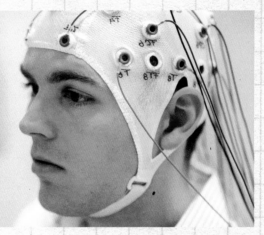

PSYCHOLOGY EXPERIMENTS *sometimes involve using equipment and technology to see what is happening in the brain under certain conditions.*

EXPERIMENTS

Once a psychology researcher has their hypothesis, they will need to test that with some kind of experiment. An experiment is what we do to test hypothesized relationships between variables. These experiments can be very complex, with many different variables, or they can be fairly simple cause-and-effect studies. Even a simple experiment will be made up of various components and should have a control group; this is a group that has not been subject to the experiment, so that comparisons can be made.

When the data from the simple experiment has been collected, the researchers will perform a number of statistical tests to determine whether any differences found between the control and the experimental group are statistically significant (or whether they could have occurred by chance). Statistical significance is established using statistical tests that estimate the likelihood of results occurring purely by chance; if the probability of those results occurring by chance is low enough, it is then assumed that they occurred as a result of the intervention rather than by chance — in which case they are statistically significant.

CORRELATIONAL RESEARCH

Not all psychology research is conducted by carrying out experiments. An alternative is to use correlational methods to look for relationships between variables. For example, if we wanted to examine the relationship between a child's age and their height, we would find a correlation such that as one rose, the other would too. Such correlational methods would not be appropriate for adults, however.

OBSERVATIONAL METHODS

This is where the researcher does not try to influence or change what is happening — but simply observes. There is thus no attempt at any intervention; the whole point of observational methods is that the researcher does not influence the proceedings in any way. This approach can be useful on occasions when it is not ethical to manipulate a variable (for example, we might want to measure aggression in children by observing them rather than by trying to do things to make them more aggressive) or when there is a need to minimize "demand characteristics" (whereby participants, deliberately or otherwise, provide the researcher with what they think they are looking for in an experiment).

There can, however, be the problem of "observer bias," in which the researcher

DOUBLE-BLIND STUDIES

A double-blind study is one in which neither the participants nor the experimenters know who is receiving a particular treatment. This prevents any bias that might be unintentionally caused by either the experimenter or the participants. (Without double-blind conditions, the experimenter can accidentally create "observer bias" by treating a group differently or inadvertently giving different signals to them as a result of knowing which treatment they are receiving. Similarly, the participants can unwittingly create "demand characteristics" if they guess — or are told — the purpose of an experiment, leading to their subconsciously changing their behavior to meet the expectations of the study.)

inadvertently sees and records what they are expecting to find. In addition, there is the whole issue of whether people react differently when they know they are being observed — this problem can sometimes be overcome by not informing the participants that they are being watched, perhaps by having the researcher join in with the activities they are observing.

Observational studies can be quite invasive in terms of privacy and there is also the issue of ethics with regards to covert observational methods. If the participants are being observed in ordinary circumstances (such as waiting for a bus) where anyone could observe them, then permission is usually not needed. In other circumstances, if getting agreement invalidates the study by producing bias, then it might be possible to get permission afterwards.

OBSERVATIONAL METHODS *can involve watching people or animals in natural settings, or, as in this picture, observing in a lab through one-way glass. Here Dr. Eckhard Hess, Associate Professor of Psychology at the University of Chicago, is at the control panel while watching the reactions of baby animals as he controls the light and sounds.*

ORDINARY PEOPLE WHO MADE GREAT CONTRIBUTIONS TO PSYCHOLOGY

This book is peppered with the work of eminent and influential psychologists, but many of their theories and findings would not have been possible without some of the ordinary people who inspired them. In the most part, these are people who had the misfortune to have lives (or, in some cases, deaths) that shed light on psychological phenomenon.

"HM"

HM was the pseudonym for Henry Gustav Molaison (1926–2008), an American who was known as the "man with no memory." He had suffered from severe epilepsy (see page 62) for many years and, at the age of 27, had undergone surgery to try to reduce the severity of his symptoms. This was performed by William Beecher Scoville, a Hartford neurosurgeon, and Henry was awake for the entire procedure. The operation involved the removal of a brain structure called the hippocampus, which lies within each temporal lobe (see page 54). The procedure was a success and Henry's seizures greatly improved, but sadly, the removal of his hippocampi had a severe effect on his memory. He could not remember anything that had happened since the operation, and he also suffered memory loss of the 11 years preceding the operation (for reasons that are still not clear).

The reason that HM inadvertently contributed so much to psychology was that, until his case, it was not known that the hippocampi in the temporal lobes of the brain were so crucial to memory. After HM, this type of operation for curing epilepsy was never carried out again — which was, of course, too late for poor HM.

HM's contributions to psychology continued for a further 55 years after his operation, during which time he willingly took part in a range of experiments at Massachusetts Institute of Technology. Through these, much of what we now know about memory was discovered. His post-surgery global amnesia meant that he could not learn or recall anything new, including, for example, names, faces and songs, at a conscious level. But he *could* learn new motor skills at a subconscious level — for example, when he hurt his leg, he was able to learn how to use a walking frame, even though he could not recall ever having used one before (such as on the previous day). His IQ remained normal and he was very happy and cooperative, never tiring of experiments because they were always new to him.

Henry's name (or his initials — his real name was only revealed following his death due to obligations toward patient confidentiality) has been mentioned in almost 12,000 journal articles, making him the most studied case in medical or psychological history. Even after his death he continued to contribute to psychology; his brain was dissected into 2,000 sections for ongoing research.

DAVID REIMER

David Peter Reimer (1965–2004) was a Canadian born biologically male but raised as a female following medical advice and intervention after his penis was accidentally destroyed during a botched operation in infancy. He was originally named Bruce and had an identical twin named Brian. At the age of 6 months, both boys had been referred for a routine operation to correct a minor problem with their penises that caused urination difficulties. Tragically, Bruce's penis was damaged beyond repair, after which Brian's operation was cancelled (his problem later corrected itself).

Their devastated parents took Bruce to Johns Hopkins Hospital in Baltimore to see John Money, a psychologist who was developing a reputation as a pioneer in the field of sexual development and gender identity, based on his work with intersex patients (whose gender was not clear from their genital organs). Money believed that gender identity developed mainly as a result of social learning and so could be changed by altering the way children were brought up. He advised that a vagina should be constructed for Bruce and he should be brought up as a girl. At the age of 22 months, Bruce thus became Brenda, resulting in what was to become the ultimate experiment in gender-identity investigations, especially as Reimer's twin, Brian, provided the perfect control.

Reimer would later claim that Money forced him to undergo bizarre sexual-

THE CASE OF DAVID REIMER *showed that gender was not something that could be learned or conditioned; raising a child to be the opposite gender will not make them so.*

orientation and learning interventions to encourage him into his new gender. These involved what Money called childhood "sexual rehearsal play," which he felt was required to ensure that Reimer became a healthy female adult. Money reported on the case (as "John/Joan") for many years in psychology journals and regarded the story as a success. He claimed that Bruce had adapted well to being Brenda and had adopted a female role successfully. The case was used to bolster support for his notions that gender could be learned, even for non-intersex children.

Sadly, however, these conclusions were later found to be untrue. In 1997 Reimer himself told his story to journalists and other sections of the media in order to prevent other children from having to undergo what happened to him. He rejected the claim that he "became" female in any way, and he repeated this in great detail in a book on his story, *As Nature Made Him: The Boy Who Was Raised as a Girl*. Indeed, by puberty he claimed to be so depressed and suicidal that he refused to see Money again. At this point it should be noted that Reimer did not know his own full history and had no knowledge that he was born male. When he was finally told the truth, he began to transition back to his original gender and became David at the age of 14.

David later married and was stepfather to three children. Tragically, he committed suicide at the age of 38. His twin, Brian, who had been diagnosed as schizophrenic, had previously taken his own life.

David Reimer left a legacy that has helped our understanding of what it is that makes us male or female (and of the fact that external genitalia are only one factor in this).

KITTY GENOVESE

Unlike most of the other examples in this section, Kitty Genovese led an unremarkable life and did not come to the attention of psychologists during her lifetime. It was her horrible death and the circumstances around it that led to her unwittingly making great contributions to psychological thinking.

Catherine Susan "Kitty" Genovese was born in 1935 in New York City, where she was living at the time of her untimely death. On 13 March 1964, she drove home from work in the early hours of the morning. After parking but before managing to reach her apartment, she was attacked by Winston Moseley, a 29-year-old married father of two, who stabbed her. Screaming, she attracted some attention from neighbors and Moseley ran away, leaving Kitty seriously injured. However, he returned ten minutes later and stabbed her to death.

What distinguished this murder from any of the many other random homicides in NYC was that Kitty's attack was allegedly witnessed by dozens of people — between 12 and 38 people were said to have witnessed at least some part of the murder — yet little or nothing was done to help her.

This lack of action by so many people led to a flurry of theorizing about what became known as the "bystander effect" (see right). The social psychologists John Darley and Bibb Latané started this line of research, showing that, contrary to common expectations, the presence of larger numbers of bystanders decreases the likelihood that someone will step forward and help a victim. The suggested reasons for this "bystander effect" include the fact that onlookers imagine that others will intervene, so their own input is not required ("diffusion of responsibility"); in addition, the onlookers see that others are not helping either, they believe others will know better how to help and they feel uncertain about helping while others are watching. The Kitty Genovese case thus became a classic feature of social psychology textbooks.

THE BYSTANDER EFFECT

In 1968 John Darley and Bibb Latané followed up interest in the 1964 murder of Kitty Genovese by demonstrating the existence of the bystander effect in a laboratory setting. In a typical experiment, an emergency situation was staged with participants who were either alone or among a group of other participants or accomplices. The researchers measured how long it took them to intervene (if indeed they did intervene).

These experiments found that the presence of others inhibits helping, often quite dramatically. For example, 70 percent of the people who were alone called out or went to help a woman whom they believed to have fallen, but when there were other people in the room only 40 percent offered help.

Darley and Latané suggested that bystanders might feel less personal responsibility to help if others are present (diffusion of responsibility). When there are no other people present, there is no one else to rely on, so greater personal responsibility is felt.

PHINEAS GAGE

Phineas P. Gage (1823–60) was another brain-injury victim whose condition contributed greatly to our understanding of the functional structure of the brain. In 1848, Gage, an American railway worker, was involved in a horrific accident that resulted in a metal tamping iron (a bar resembling a javelin) being embedded in his head; it entered on the left side of his face and came out at the top of his head.

Surprisingly, Gage remained conscious and, indeed, is alleged to have dryly commented to the doctor who attended to him, "Here is business enough for you." Gage survived both the initial trauma and the procedure to remove the iron. However, his personality was said to

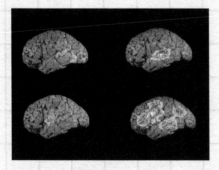

THE CASE OF PHINEAS GAGE *showed how different parts of the brain were responsible for different functions. The above shows how sections "light up" when stimulated.*

have undergone dramatic changes. These were changes that we now know to be consistent with the functionality of the damaged areas of his brain, particularly the frontal lobe (see page 54). Until Gage, it was not known whether different parts of the brain were responsible for specific functions, but this case study helped enlighten the scientific community about cerebral localization (in which functions are performed in certain structures of the brain).

GENIE — THE FERAL CHILD

Genie (b. 1957) was an American child reared in social isolation by an abusive father. Believing her to be mentally challenged, Genie's father (who later committed suicide before being brought to justice) decided to isolate her socially and kept her locked alone in a room. In 1970, she came to the attention of Los Angeles child-welfare authorities. For 13 years she had been bound in a crib with her arms and legs or to a child's toilet and had been forbidden to interact with anyone, and had been given very little food. One consequence of this isolation was that she had not learned to speak. Genie was of special interest to psychologists, who were able to examine, in a real case study, just how a lack of environmental stimulation can impact on development.

Psychologists who studied her found that within months of being rescued, Genie's nonverbal communication skills came on in leaps and bounds and she also began to pick up basic social skills. She developed some language skills, too, but never fully acquired a first language. This was used as additional evidence for Noam Chomsky's 1965 theory of language acquisition; it states that there is a critical period during which children acquire language and any language skills not learned during this period will never be as good. Chomsky suggested that children are born with a language acquisition device (LAD) that is primed to learn language during this critical period of development (for more about this, see page 120).

The study of Genie's brain also helped in the understanding of brain lateralization (how some neural functions, or cognitive processes, tend to be more dominant in one hemisphere than the other), especially its effect on language. The difference between Genie's abilities with regards to language and her competence in other areas lent support to the hypothesis that there were different areas responsible for cognition and for language acquisition. That Genie's nonverbal communication abilities were exceptionally good, suggested that nonverbal communication was qualitatively different from spoken language. Genie's main difficulty lay with carrying out functions that were thought to be mainly controlled by the right hemisphere, so this also added to new knowledge of brain functioning.

Genie spent a few years being rehabilitated in hospital and in foster homes (some of them turning out to be abusive) but never progressed to become "normal" in social skills, cognitive function, emotional expression, motor skills or many other areas. She later withdrew from contact with those who had been studying her. Her current whereabouts are unknown but she is thought to be residing in a residential home for adults with learning difficulties.

THE TWO "JIMS"

Jim Lewis and Jim Springer were identical twins raised apart from the age of 4 weeks. They came to the attention of psychologists when they were reunited at the age of 39 in 1974. They discovered so many similarities that they have been used as a case study for the nature-nurture debate ever since. They were similar not only physically (as are identical twins, that was to be expected), but also in a host of other ways that suggest a strong influence of genes as opposed to environment. For example, they had similar medical histories — both had early-onset heart disease. There were also a number of behavioral and personality similarities; they had similar smoking habits (including the same brand preference), they both enjoyed carpentry as a hobby, both endured the same type of headaches and their scores correlated closely on tests of personality traits and intelligence. Both Jims had at one time held part-time posts as sheriffs. Both married women named Linda, only to divorce and remarry — each to a woman named Betty. Both had sons named James Alan.

The two Jims contributed greatly to our understanding of the important role of genes in shaping personality. They became part of the Minnesota Study of Twins Reared Apart at the University of Minnesota, which is probably the best-known twin study that was able to take advantage of a period when twins put up for adoption were routinely split up. The University of Minnesota is still researching twins to this day but is unlikely ever again to have such a special case study as the two Jims.

THE HARDWARE OF PSYCHOLOGY

All psychological functioning originates from the nervous system (as indeed, all functioning does), so it is important for psychologists to understand how it works. The nervous system is made up of two main systems:

CENTRAL NERVOUS SYSTEM (CNS): This consists of the brain and the spinal cord.

PERIPHERAL NERVOUS SYSTEM (PNS): This contains the nerves, which transfer information between the central nervous system and the rest of the body. It is made up of two systems: the *somatic nervous system (SNS)* — responsible for functions within our voluntary control (such as movements, eating and talking) — and the *autonomic nervous system (ANS)* — responsible for functions we cannot consciously control (such as breathing, digestion and hormone production). Some functions of the autonomic nervous system are to do with making us more active at times of stress, such as speeding up the heartbeat or inhibiting the muscles of digestion; this is called the *sympathetic nervous system*. Others are to do with day-to-day activities when the body is at rest, such as slowing the heartbeat or stimulating the muscles of digestion; this is known as the *parasympathetic nervous system*.

CENTRAL NERVOUS SYSTEM

PERIPHERAL NERVOUS SYSTEM

THE CENTRAL AND PERIPHERAL NERVOUS SYSTEMS *work together to send and receive all the messages and signals that allow the human body and brain to function.*

THE BRAIN

The brain, which processes and interprets all the information sent from the spinal cord and the peripheral nervous system, is made up of three main areas: the forebrain, the midbrain and the hindbrain. The midbrain and hindbrain together make up the brainstem.

THE FOREBRAIN

This is the area responsible for multiple functions including language, thinking, information processing and motor function. The forebrain contains structures such as the *thalamus* (which moderates sleep and consciousness among other things), *hypothalamus* (which controls eating, drinking and sexual behavior), *amygdala* (which processes emotions) and *hippocampus* (which plays an important role in memory). Together these structures make up the *limbic system*, sometimes referred to as the "emotional brain." The forebrain also contains the biggest area of the brain, the *cerebrum* (also known as the *cerebral hemispheres* or *cerebral cortex*), which is folded so as to have more surface area and is divided into four lobes, each with different functions, as shown in the table:

LOBE OF THE CEREBRAL CORTEX	FUNCTION
Frontal lobe (containing the prefrontal cortex)	reasoning, planning, parts of speech, movement, emotions and problem-solving
Parietal lobe	movement, orientation, recognition and perception
Occipital lobe	visual processing
Temporal lobe	auditory processing, memory and speech

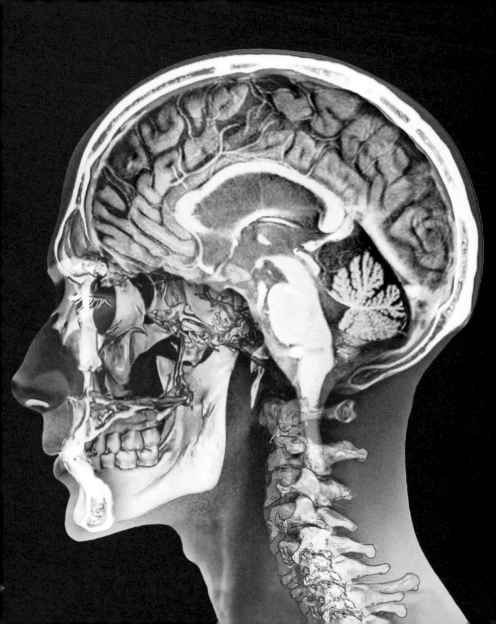

DOES SIZE MATTER?

Is size of brain important? Are people with larger or heavier brains more intelligent or do they have any other advantage? This is a difficult question as there are other factors that must also be considered. For example, there is a correlation between relative brain size and performance in intelligence tests in the animal kingdom. But body size has to be taken into consideration, too, since large animals need larger brains to monitor and operate their large organs. Bigger animals also have a higher number of nerve endings — all of which need monitoring and this needs a bigger brain. So body size needs to be factored out if we are to consider the impact of brain size. Once body size is taken out of the equation, we find that fish and reptiles have small brains, while mammal and birds have larger ones — and, mammals and birds do indeed perform better in intelligence tests than fish and reptiles.

Among mammals there is variation in brain size — horses, for example, have smaller brains than primates and dolphins, both of which are thought to be the more intelligent species. And, of course, humans are the primates with the biggest brains (they are about three times bigger than they should be for our body size) and we are clearly superior in many measures of intelligence.

As regards differences within the human race, there is no evidence that brain-size variation has any impact on intelligence. Actual brain size, of course, may not be the critical factor anyway, since the number of neurons in the brain may be more important — and may not be dependent on size. Weight might thus be a more interesting factor to consider, but the problem is that there is not much variation in the weight of the human brain — and weight may be affected by other factors apart from the number of neurons.

Albert Einstein, arguably one of the most intelligent humans in history, did not have a bigger or heavier brain than the average — but what he did appear to have was a higher interconnectivity of his brain neurons. Indeed, many scientists now believe that it is not brain size, weight or circumference that dictates cognitive ability, but a brain's underlying organization and synaptic activity.

THE MIDBRAIN

This is the portion of the brainstem that connects the hindbrain and the forebrain. The smallest region of the brain, the midbrain acts as a sort of relay station for auditory and visual information. The midbrain contains the *reticular activating system* (see page 87), which is the region through which nearly all information enters the brain.

THE HINDBRAIN

Extending from the spinal cord, the hindbrain contains structures such as the *cerebellum* and the *pons*. The *cerebellum*, which is associated with movement, posture and balance, is similar to the cerebrum in that it consists of two hemispheres and has a highly folded surface, or cortex. The pons is partly made up of tracts connecting the spinal cord with higher brain levels.

LEFT OR RIGHT BRAIN?

The theory of left- or right-brain dominance is based on the concept of lateralization of brain function, which suggests that different hemispheres of the brain control different functions, communicating via the *corpus callosum*. Each hemisphere controls the opposite side of the body. It has long been believed that different functions are localized within different hemispheres — for example, language is centered in the left hemisphere while the right hemisphere controls spatial information and visual comprehension.

This theory suggests that people have a dominance that is reflected in their abilities. For example, people who are "right-brained" are thought to be more intuitive, creative, thoughtful, subjective and better at reading emotions, while "left-brained" people are seen as being more logical, analytical, objective and better with numbers.

However, much of this is now known to be rather exaggerated. It is generally accepted today that communication across the corpus callosum means that both hemispheres can work together. There may be nuances that are localized in each hemisphere, but to say that the left is solely responsible for language is no longer considered to be true.

DISEASES OF THE CENTRAL NERVOUS SYSTEM: PARKINSON'S DISEASE & ALZHEIMER'S DISEASE

Parkinson's disease, named after the English doctor James Parkinson, is a degenerative disorder of the central nervous system that mainly affects the motor system. Parkinson published the first detailed description of the disease in "An Essay on the Shaking Palsy" in 1817. Symptoms include shaking, rigidity, slowness of movement and difficulty with walking and gait, and problems in thinking and behavior and dementia in advanced stages of the disease. Depression and sensory, sleep and emotional problems are other common symptoms.

Parkinson's is caused by the death of cells that generate dopamine, which is a neurotransmitter (see page 61). These cells are in a region of the midbrain called the *substantia nigra*. The cells in this region usually work by inhibiting motor processes, which stops them from becoming active when we don't want them to be active. When we do want a particular motor function to activate, the neurotransmitter dopamine acts to cause this inhibition to wane so that the necessary motor system can be activated. Thus a lot of dopamine activity will stimulate motor activity, while low levels of dopamine, which occurs in Parkinson's disease, mean that making a particular movement requires far more effort. This is why people with the disease have reduced ability for movement.

Treatment involves medications that result in more dopamine being produced. This may lead to excessive dopamine activity, which can cause overstimulation of the motor neurons, resulting in involuntary jerks and movements.

Alzheimer's disease accounts for 60–70 percent of cases of dementia worldwide and is a chronic neurodegenerative disease (involving degeneration of the nerve cells) that usually starts slowly and gets worse over time. The most common early symptom is short-term memory loss — difficulty in remembering recent events. As the disease advances, symptoms can include problems with language, disorientation (including easily getting lost), mood swings, loss of motivation, not managing self-care and behavioral issues.

This disease — named after Alois Alzheimer, the German doctor who first described it — is characterized by loss of nerve cells and synapses in the cerebral cortex and other regions.

During the course of the disease, proteins build up in these regions to form structures called "plaques" and "tangles." This leads to the loss of connections between nerve cells and eventually to the death of nerve cells and loss of brain tissue. People with Alzheimer's also have a shortage of some neurotransmitters in their brain.

Drug treatments attempt to counter these effects. For example, Acetylcholinesterase inhibitors are one set of medications that can be used to reduce the rate at which the neurotransmitter acetylcholine (ACh) is broken down, thereby increasing its concentration in the brain and combating the loss of ACh caused by the death of neurons.

MICHAEL J FOX *suffers from Parkinson's disease and has used his fame as a Hollywood actor to raise awareness for the condition and its effects.*

THE SPINAL CORD

This is a cylindrical bundle of nerves that runs down the middle of the spinal column from the brainstem to the peripheral nervous system. The spinal cord is surrounded by a clear fluid called *cerebral spinal fluid* (CSF), which acts as a cushion to protect the delicate nerves.

Spinal cord nerves relay information, via millions of nerve fibers from inside and outside the body, to the brain and back again. The nerves that connect the spinal cord to the body are referred to as the peripheral nervous system.

THE SPINAL CORD *contains millions of nerve fibers that relay information from our body to the brain and back again.*

THE NERVOUS SYSTEM

The basic units of the nervous system are *neurons* or *nerve cells*. They consist of *axons* and *dendrites*, which are able to conduct and transmit signals; axons transmit signals away from the cell body while dendrites, which are shorter than axons, carry signals toward the cell body.

Neurons communicate and send messages by transmitting electrical nerve impulses. While the electric impulses travel down the neurons, they do not jump across the synapses (gaps) between them; instead, neurons communicate across the gaps mostly by releasing chemicals called *neurotransmitters*. These are produced by glands such as the pituitary and adrenal glands. Neurotransmitters can be *excitatory* (exciting the neurons and stimulating the brain) or *inhibitory* (having a calming effect on the brain).

There are three kinds of neuron. *Motor* neurons transmit signals from the central nervous system (brain and spinal cord) to organs, glands and muscles. *Sensory* neurons send information to the central nervous system from internal organs or from external stimuli. *Interneurons* transmit information between motor and sensory neurons.

NEURONS are designed to conduct electrical impulses by releasing neurotransmitters to transmit messages across the nervous system.

EPILEPSY

One of the most common disorders of the nervous system, epilepsy is a neurological condition involving the brain that makes people more susceptible to having recurrent, unprovoked seizures. A seizure (known as a fit or convulsions) occurs in the brain when part of the brain receives a burst of abnormal electrical signals, temporarily interrupting normal electrical brain function. Anything that interrupts the normal connections between nerve cells in the brain can cause a seizure and in epilepsy this can be caused by an imbalance of neurotransmitters. One neurotransmitter that is of particular relevance to epilepsy is gamma aminobutyric acid (GABA), which normally helps prevent nerve cells from over-firing.

The symptoms of epilepsy are repeated seizures. There are different types of seizure, depending on the area of the brain affected. Partial seizures are where only a small part of the brain is affected, whereas generalized seizures are where most or all of the brain is affected. There are also other types of seizure.

Some severe seizures might damage the brain but most people with epilepsy do not suffer any short- or long-term damage. However, some people with epilepsy (depending on the kind of epilepsy they have and where the seizures occur) do report problems with memory, communication or language, which might result from seizures (or might result from the medication to control seizures).

PSYCHOLOGICAL ASSESSMENT

Unless you are studying psychology, much of the information on the previous pages will not be very visible in your day-to-day life; it is the "behind-the-scenes" work of the psychologist. For many people, their first or main contact with the psychology profession is when they have some kind of psychological assessment.

Psychological assessment refers to the tests that a psychologist might use to assess you or to find out if you have a particular condition and if so, how you are affected. Not everyone, however, who encounters psychological assessment has a "condition" at all. This section covers some of the main forms of assessment that you or members of your family might come across.

PSYCHOLOGICAL ASSESSMENTS IN THE WORKPLACE

Many people will have their first, and possibly only, encounter with psychological tests when they are applying for a job or at some other point in their working life. Psychological assessment in the workplace environment is often termed psychometric testing. The word "psychometric" comes from the Greek words for mind (*psukhē*) and measurement (*metron*), reflecting the fact that psychometric tests are a standard and scientific method used to measure individuals' mental capabilities and behavioral style, and thus their suitability for particular jobs or professions.

The most common psychometric tests measure either mental ("cognitive") ability or personality, although they may also measure aptitude, such as the ability to cope with stress. Many of these tests are designed by occupational psychologists (see page 26).

MENTAL/COGNITIVE-ABILITY TESTS

Measurement of cognitive, or mental, ability (otherwise known as intelligence testing) has always been important to psychologists, who for various reasons have found it useful to distinguish between people of different mental capabilities. Many jobs require a certain level of intelligence, although this has become less important with the advent of so many modern qualifications — if someone has a degree, for example, a certain level of intelligence can probably be assumed without the need for extra mental-ability testing.

Intelligence testing began its life with children in France. In the early 20th century, the French government was reforming education for children and wanted to know which children would benefit the most and which would need extra help. Psychologists Alfred Binet and Théodore Simon developed a battery of questions aimed at separating out the children likely to do well at school from

PSYCHOLOGICAL ASSESSMENTS IN THE WORKPLACE *are most commonly carried out for selection purposes.*

those who were less likely. The test they devised was known as the Binet–Simon Intelligence Scale (see page 13) and is generally recognized as the first intelligence test; it still forms the basis of measures of intelligence today.

The Binet–Simon Scale was brought to the United States, where psychologist Lewis Terman from Stanford University took Binet's original test and standardized it using a sample of American participants. This version, first published in 1916, was called the Stanford–Binet Intelligence

Scale and soon became the standard intelligence test used in the United States. It utilized a single measure of intelligence, which was known as the intelligence quotient or IQ. Some people felt, however, that this test relied too much on verbal ability and did not recognize that there are many forms of intelligence (see page 104). This led American psychologist David Wechsler to develop the Wechsler Adult Intelligence Scale (WAIS) in 1955, and this is still in wide use today, although it has been revised several times since that first version — the one in current use is WAIS-IV. There is also a version for children (see page 72).

RORSCHACH INKBLOTS

The Rorschach Inkblot Test is a personality test developed by Swiss psychologist Hermann Rorschach in 1921. In it individuals are asked to look at a series of inkblots and describe what they see — because the shapes were ambiguous, it was thought that a person would project their own individual personality onto them. In the 1960s, the Rorschach was the most popular "projective" test of personality, although it is rarely used today.

The idea that interpretation of "ambiguous designs" can be used to assess an individual's personality goes back to Leonardo da Vinci, who pointed out that some people can look at a stained wall and see landscapes, while others might see battles and still others might see animals. The reasoning behind this is that when we see an ambiguous, meaningless picture (in this case, an inkblot) our mind will attempt to impose some meaning on the image by "projecting" its personality onto it.

However, it should be noted that Hermann Rorschach originally developed the inkblots as a tool for the diagnosis of schizophrenia and never actually intended for them to be used as a general personality test. When, in 1939, the test began to be used as a projective test of personality, Rorschach expressed reservations that never went away.

Rorschach's scepticism came to be shared by others. Problems with the test include the fact that the testing psychologist could project their own views onto the inkblots when interpreting responses. For example, if the person being tested says that they see a dress, one psychologist might classify this as a sexual response, whereas another might classify it simply as clothing. Critics have also suggested that the Rorschach test lacks inter-rater consistency; two different testers might come up with two entirely different personality profiles for the same person.

A moratorium on its use was finally called for in 1999 by a psychologist named Howard Garb and very few psychologists would use it today as a personality test.

You probably will not come across the WAIS as part of a workplace assessment, however, because it is quite time-consuming and needs one-to-one input from someone qualified to use it. In selection procedures, having a test that can be used with many candidates at the same time, and that is not too time-consuming, is more efficient. The WAIS tends to be used more in clinical settings – for example, after a person has suffered a brain injury.

Workplace intelligence tests usually measure what psychologists call fluid intelligence and crystallized intelligence. Fluid intelligence, the ability to think

RORSCHACH INKBLOTS *were designed in the 1920s. It was thought that people's personalities could be analyzed by what they imagined the ambiguous shapes to be. The inkblots, however, are no longer used for this purpose.*

and reason abstractly and solve problems, is independent of learning, past experience and education. Crystallized intelligence, the ability to learn from past experiences and relevant learning and to apply this to a situation, is something that develops with experience. Tests that ask about knowledge (for which a person can prepare and study) test crystallized intelligence, whereas those that test problem-solving or decision-making skills test fluid intelligence and are much harder to prepare for in advance.

Examples of workplace intelligence tests that you might come across if you are going for a job include the following:

EMPLOYEE APTITUDE SURVEY: This measures verbal comprehension, numerical ability, visual pursuit, space visualization, word fluency, verbal reasoning, symbolic reasoning, manual speed and accuracy, numerical reasoning and visual speed and accuracy. It is available online.

WONDERLIC CONTEMPORARY COGNITIVE ABILITY TEST: Assessing the aptitude of prospective employees for learning and problem-solving in a range of occupations, the Wonderlic is available in 12 languages and

ETHICAL ISSUES OVER WORKPLACE TESTING

Some experts believe that modern psychometric testing suffers from potential ethical issues, such as the following:

- Some tests can be quite intrusive, as they may include questions about disabilities, sexual orientation, sexual practices, religious beliefs or ethnic background.

- Not all organizations understand how important it is that test results be confidential.

- What companies do with the results and how they are communicated to candidates can be a concern. (For example, candidates may be left thinking that they have a "bad" personality.)

- Some tests are inadequate or are not administered by qualified personnel.

- Some psychological tests may be biased against culturally disadvantaged groups or those with disabilities.

is often used in college, in entry-level jobs and in team-making efforts. It consists of 50 multiple-choice questions to be answered in 12 minutes and is available online.

Many occupational psychology specialists offer their own batteries of cognitive tests.

PERSONALITY TESTING

Common personality tests used in organizations include the Occupational Personality Questionnaire (published in 1984 by Saville & Holdsworth Ltd.), which measures 32 facets of temperament thought to be relevant in occupational settings, and 16PF (published by OPP), which is widely used and was developed from a statistical analysis that located 16 personality factors from a mass of personality measures. Another common test is the Myers-Briggs Type Indicator (MBTI), also published by OPP, which is designed to measure psychological preferences in how people perceive the world and make decisions. The MBTI asks the candidate to answer a series of "forced-choice" questions, leading to their being identified as one of 16 types. The basic test takes 20 minutes and at the end of it you are presented with a precise, multidimensional summary of your personality.

HOW TO SUCCEED AT PSYCHOMETRIC TESTS

- A good company should not spring any surprises on you, so you should receive a letter outlining exactly what tests you can expect — this will allow you to prepare mentally and practically (making sure you have your reading glasses for example).

- Prepare by doing practice tests beforehand.

- Read the instructions — make sure that you don't miss any questions, that you don't forget to turn the pages over, and that you write or mark the answers in the correct place on the scoring sheet.

- Don't try to fake it. Lying or trying to create an overly good impression will most likely be found out, as many tests have an inbuilt "lie detection" scale.

- Relax — usually psychometric tests form only a small part of the overall selection procedure.

TESTS OF MENTAL HEALTH

If you ever need to be seen by a clinical psychologist for mental-health issues (see Part 4 for more on these), you will most likely be asked to complete a questionnaire to assess your condition. Some common questionnaires that you might come across include the following:

BECK DEPRESSION INVENTORY (BDI): Created by Aaron T. Beck, this 21-question, multiple-choice, self-report inventory is one of the most widely used instruments for measuring the severity of depression.

BECK ANXIETY INVENTORY (BAI): Also created by Aaron T. Beck, this is a 21-question, multiple-choice, self-report inventory about how the patient has been feeling in the last week. The information is expressed as common symptoms of anxiety (such as numbness and tingling, sweating and fear of the worst happening) and is used to measure the severity of an individual's anxiety.

BECK HOPELESSNESS SCALE (BHS): This 20-question self-report survey, also developed by Aaron T. Beck, was designed to measure the three components of hopelessness: negative feelings about the future, loss of motivation to do anything and low expectations of improvement.

EDINBURGH POSTNATAL DEPRESSION SCALE (EPDS): Postnatal depression is a common mental-health condition that affects around a tenth of women. The EPDS is a brief self-rating scale (containing just ten questions) and has been shown to be a good way for health practitioners to identify patients at risk. Items on the scale are similar to general symptoms of clinical depression, such as guilt, sleep difficulties (not caused by being disturbed by the baby), low energy, anhedonia (inability to get pleasure from previously enjoyable activities) and suicidal ideation (thoughts that can suggest a likelihood of committing suicide).

GENERAL HEALTH QUESTIONNAIRE (GHQ): A psychometric screening tool to identify minor psychiatric disorders, this comprises a number of questions (there are versions with 12, 28, 30 or 60 questions), each with a f4-point scale for responses.

PERCEIVED STRESS SCALE (PSS): This was developed to measure the degree to which we appraise situations in our lives as stressful. Items were designed to assess how unpredictable, uncontrollable and overloaded the respondents find their lives to be. The scale also includes a number of direct queries about current levels of experienced stress.

STATE-TRAIT ANXIETY INVENTORY (STAI): A psychological inventory developed by Charles Spielberger, this is based on a 4-point scale and consists of 40 questions on a self-report basis. It measures two types of anxiety — state anxiety (anxiety about an event) and trait anxiety (anxiety level as a personal characteristic).

ANXIETY AND STRESS can be measured with specially designed questionnaires. These allow the therapist to see where the problems lie, how severe they are and how they might be treated.

TESTS FOR CHILDREN

If you are a parent who is worried about your child's development, you might encounter various types of psychological assessment, such as cognitive assessment (to test mental abilities). These may be carried out by either an educational psychologist or a clinical psychologist. Common tests in these circumstances include the following:

WISC TO TEST COGNITIVE/MENTAL ABILITY: The Wechsler Intelligence Scale for Children, Fourth Edition (WISC-IV) is, like the adult version (see page 65), an individually administered, comprehensive clinical instrument for assessing the intelligence of children aged from 6 to 16. It assesses verbal comprehension, perceptual reasoning, working memory and processing speed, as well as general intellectual ability. Subtests include block design, similarities, digit span, picture concepts, coding, vocabulary, letter–number sequencing, matrix reasoning, comprehension and symbol search. Supplemental subtests include picture completion, cancellation, information, arithmetic and word reasoning. It is thus a good way to identify any possible deficits in a particular area.

CONNERS COMPREHENSIVE BEHAVIOR RATING SCALES (CONNERS CBRS) TO ASSESS ADHD SYMPTOMS: Attention deficit hyperactivity disorder, or ADHD, is a developmental condition (see page 233). Conners CBRS is not available to the general public and is not a diagnostic tool (there is no diagnostic test for ADHD) but it can be used as part of the diagnostic process. There are three Rating Scales; one is designed for parents, another is for teachers and a third asks adolescents to rate their own behavior.

AUTISM DIAGNOSTIC OBSERVATION SCHEDULE (ADOS) TO TEST FOR AUTISTIC SPECTRUM DISORDER TRAITS: This is a semi-structured assessment of communication, social interaction and play (or imaginative use of materials) used to assess children suspected of being on the autistic spectrum (see page 228). The examiner provides a series of opportunities for the child to show social and communication behavior relevant to the diagnosis of autism and then observes and assigns the child's responses to predetermined categories. The child usually enjoys the experience and sees it as playing games with the examiner.

TESTING CHILDREN to track their development has a long history and allows parents and educators to access the right help or input if the tests suggest this is required.

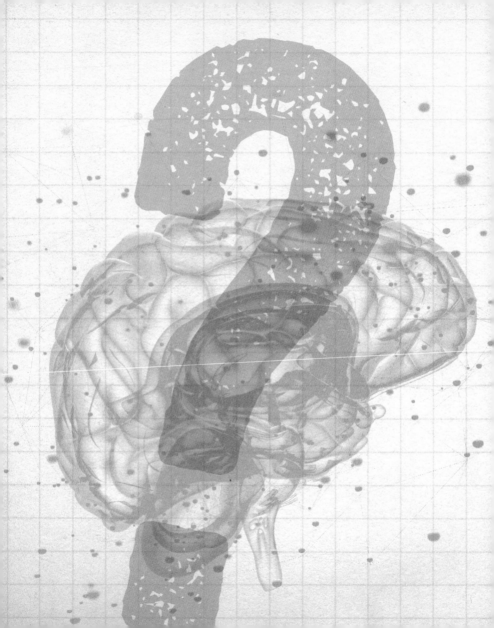

PART 2

THEORIES THAT HAVE SHAPED SOCIETY

MUCH OF WHAT WE KNOW AND UNDERSTAND ABOUT HUMAN BEHAVIOR AND THOUGHT HAS BEEN THE RESULT OF VARIOUS PSYCHOLOGICAL THEORIES THAT HAVE EMERGED SINCE SCIENTISTS FIRST BEGAN TO STUDY THE HUMAN MIND. HERE WE LOOK AT SOME OF THE MOST INFLUENTIAL THEORIES THAT HAVE HELPED US UNDERSTAND THE HUMAN PSYCHE.

THEORIES OF PERCEPTION

Perception is the process of making sense of our environment. Psychologists have long realized that seeing, hearing, smelling, touching and tasting are not simply physical processes of sensation; we have to make sense of those sensations, too. This is how we know that objects that are far away have not shrunk — they just appear smaller — or that a coin seen from a side angle is still round. Perception is how we make sense of words instead of seeing them as individual letters or how we see someone as a whole person rather than a collection of body parts. Some of the main theories that try to account for how we perceive or make sense of our environment are outlined below.

GESTALT THEORY OF PERCEPTION

Gestalt psychology attempts to understand the world by viewing elements of it as organized, structured wholes rather than the sum of their constituent parts. The Gestalt theory of perception, which was developed in the 1930s–1940s, suggests that we are constantly trying to organize objects so that we can understand the

THE GESTALT THEORY OF PERCEPTION *explains that we try to make sense of the world by looking for coherent patterns or shapes. So some of us might immediately see an elephant when we look at this cloud.*

WE KNOW THAT THE EIFFEL TOWER *is not really this small; we use the principle of invariants to work this out.*

seen as belonging together; and the Principle of Good Continuation states that we prefer continuous figures rather than separate ones (so we will see an X as a letter rather than four separate lines). Gestalt perception also explains why we have a tendency to see faces in clouds and other random shapes (see page 78).

GIBSON'S THEORY OF DIRECT PERCEPTION

The American psychologist James Gibson (1904–79) was one of the most important 20th-century psychologists in the field of visual perception. The question driving Gibson was, "How do we see the world as we do?" He answered this with, among other theories, his (1966) theory of "affordances." These are qualities of an object or environment that tell us what opportunities or actions certain things might offer us (for example, dark shade affords an opportunity to get out of the sunshine; a knob suggests the action of twisting; a cord indicates pulling; a thick cushion signals the availability of sitting comfortably). The affordances give us cues, helping us to make sense of what we see. Gibson believed that "sensation is perception" and that we don't need to work at analyzing what we see, which is why his approach is called direct perception.

whole from just a part of them. This led to a variety of "principles" to explain how we carry out this "organization." For example, the Principle of Proximity states that things that are closer together will be seen as belonging together; the Principle of Similarity states that things that share visual characteristics, such as shape, size, color, texture, value or orientation, will be

FACE PAREIDOLIA

(OR WHY JESUS APPEARS IN TOAST)

The phenomenon of seeing faces in random shapes — such as famous people in toast, heads in clouds or ghosts in photographs — is known as face pareidolia. It is part of our attempt to make sense of the world and to see connections between random shapes, dots or lines. In fact, we are hard-wired to recognize faces, so this is why spotting them in random patterns is so common. And because famous faces are imprinted in our minds, reports of spotting Jesus, the Virgin Mary or Elvis in the most unlikely places are not uncommon. For example:

- In 1994 Diana Duyser, from Florida, "saw" the Virgin Mary in her toast. She preserved the holy bread for ten years before auctioning it on eBay where it sold for about $28,000.

- In 2009 the Allen family of Ystrad, Wales, spotted the face of Jesus on the underside of a Marmite lid.

- In 2002 some 20,000 Christians traveled to Bangalore to pay homage to a chapati with the image of Christ burnt on it, with many visitors offering prayers to the holy bread.

- In 2012 a chicken nugget shaped like George Washington sold for more than $8,100 on eBay.

- In 2013 JC Penney sold out of a teapot after its resemblance to Hitler was noted on the social news site Reddit.

All of these demonstrate "top-down" processing, in which we use higher interpretive processes to make sense of visual stimuli.

FACE PAREIDOLIA *led to staff at the Posh Pizza shop in Brisbane, Australia, discovering the face of Jesus on a three-cheese pizza. It became known as the "Cheesus Pizza."*

Gibson also believed that we are able to make sense of what we perceive because of environmental cues that he called "invariants." These are the elements of our optic array (what our eyes are perceiving at any given instant), which although they appear to be constantly moving, we interpret as being static, regardless of our actions. Thus even though objects may appear to grow or shrink, we see them as unvarying in size or "invariant."

GREGORY'S TOP-DOWN THEORY OF PERCEPTION

British psychologist Richard Gregory (1923–2010) disagreed with Gibson's "bottom-up" approach to perception, in which we don't have to work to analyze what we perceive. Instead, Gregory believed that we have to process sensory information in order to understand it; hence his 1970 theory was called a

THE NECKER CUBE: WHICH IS THE FRONT?

The Necker cube is an optical illusion of an ambiguous box, first published in 1832 by the Swiss crystallographer Louis Albert Necker. Our brains can flip between two different perspectives so that we can see the front of the box in two different places. According to Richard Gregory, this is because we are trying to decide between two alternative hypotheses to make sense of the visual image we see. The actual image, of course, remains static — it is the brain, and thus "top-down" processing, doing the flipping.

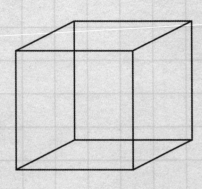

"top-down" theory of perception. For Gregory, perception is merely a hypothesis (suggested explanation) in which we make inferences about what we see using prior knowledge and past experience. Although our hypotheses are usually correct, sometimes we get it wrong — which can explain how visual illusions work, especially those that are ambiguous like the Necker cube (see left).

THEORIES OF PAIN PERCEPTION

Compared with our understanding of other forms of perception, the perception of pain is less understood. Pain does not seem to be simply about sensation, since the same pain sensation seems to be able to cause different perceptions of the degree of pain to different people. Three of the best-known pain theories are discussed here, although none of them fully explains pain perception:

SPECIFICITY THEORY: According to this theory, which was one of the first modern theories to explain how we perceive pain (developed in 1895 by the Austrian physiologist Maximilian von Frey), specific pain receptors (such as those for hot, cold or

RUBBING OR SOOTHING *an injured arm can lessen the pain by interfering with the pain messages going to the brain.*

pierced skin) transmit signals to a "pain center" in the brain and this center produces the perception of pain. While it is likely that there are different nerve fibers for pain transmission, this theory does not account for the differences in pain perception between different people.

PATTERN THEORY: This approach, developed by Goldschneider in 1920, holds that there are patterns of pain signals rather than specific ones and that the brain interprets these patterns as various types of pain. High levels of stimulation are required to sense something as pain rather than simply as a sensation (for example, the pain of being slapped as opposed to the sensation of being caressed) and this activation threshold (the strength at which the stimulus is just perceived) can differ from person to person.

GATE CONTROL THEORY: The gate control theory, which was developed in the 1960s by Ronald Melzack and Patrick Wall, attempts to explain the "top-down" brain influences on pain perception as well as the effects of "bottom-up" stimuli in moderating the sensation of pain. This theory suggests that there is a "gate," or control system, in the spinal cord through which all information regarding pain must pass before reaching the brain. Sometimes other sensations might block the gate and stop the pain sensation from getting through. This would explain why rubbing a scraped knee or banged elbow really does make the pain go away — the nerve signals from the rubbing can interfere at the spinal cord level with the signals transmitting the painful sensations from the scraped knee or banged elbow. In other words, the tactile messages can block or attenuate the pain messages from getting through the control center. This is because when there is pain somewhere, such as in the hand or foot, the pain signal travels along a peripheral nerve until it arrives at the spinal cord for transmission to the brain. However, at the spinal cord level there may be many different types of sensations (such as touch, vibration and heat) coming in from around the body, all of which will "compete" for transmission to the brain. (For advice on how to make a painful procedure less uncomfortable, see page 272.)

PHANTOM PAIN

The term "phantom pain" was first coined by the American neurologist Silas Weir Mitchell in 1871 and refers to feeling pain or discomfort from a part of the body that is no longer present (for example, as a result of amputation). It is thought that the majority of amputees (around 80 percent) experience phantom sensations at some time of their lives, yet little is known about what causes them. Scientists used to believe that the pains were "psychological" but experts now acknowledge that these are real sensations somehow produced by the spinal cord and brain.

Some theorists believed that phantom pain was caused by a neuroma (a benign or occasionally malignant tumor on a nerve-cell sheath), formed from injured nerve endings at the site of the amputation. Neuromas were thought to fire abnormal action potentials in which the electric responses of nerves are changed so that they send messages when they shouldn't. However, most researchers now believe that the pain does not originate from the site of the amputation but that it is a response to mixed signals from the brain. After an amputation, areas of the spinal cord and brain lose input from the missing limb, but the brain adjusts to this loss in unpredictable ways. This can trigger the body's most basic message that something is not right — pain.

It is possible that the brain is able to remap the part of the body's sensory circuits that relates to the missing limb, assigning it to an entirely different part of the body (often the face, surprisingly). In other words, because the amputated area is no longer able to receive sensory input, the information is referred elsewhere — from a missing arm to a still-present cheek, for example. So when the cheek is touched, it is as though the missing arm were also being touched. Because this is yet another version of confused messages, the result can be pain.

THEORIES OF ATTENTION

Perception is only as good as the information that we attend to; if we do not notice or attend to a stimulant, we cannot perceive it. There are a couple of influential theories that help to explain why we attend to some stimuli and not to others, and what it is about aspects of the environment that catches our attention.

BROADBENT'S FILTER MODEL OF ATTENTION

Donald Eric Broadbent (1926–93) was a British psychologist who pioneered theories to explain selective attention (the act of attending to some parts of a stimulus while not noticing others). Many theories of selective attention have assumed that there is some kind of filter or bottleneck preventing some information from getting through. In 1958 Broadbent argued for the existence of a filter device, called a sensory buffer, located between the system that registers incoming information and the short-term memory storage. By being allowed to pass through the filter, incoming information is selected for further processing on the basis of its most important characteristics. Because we have only a limited capacity to process

DONALD BROADBENT BECAME INTERESTED IN SELECTIVE ATTENTION WHEN DURING HIS TIME IN THE ROYAL AIR FORCE HE OBSERVED COMMUNICATION DIFFICULTIES THAT OFTEN AROSE FROM PSYCHOLOGICAL CAUSES, SUCH AS ATTENTION AND MEMORY, RATHER THAN FROM PHYSICAL CAUSES RELATED TO EQUIPMENT OR TECHNOLOGY.

information, this filter thus prevents the information-processing system from becoming overloaded. The inputs not initially selected by the filter remain briefly in the sensory buffer and if they are not processed they disappear rapidly.

THE COCKTAIL PARTY PHENOMENON

We are probably all familiar with being at a noisy party and trying to have a conversation with someone next to us. It is actually surprising how we manage to filter out all the background noise in order to focus on what our conversational partner is saying. However, if someone across the room suddenly mentions our name, our attention switches and we hear it — even though we might have had absolutely no sensation of having heard a single other word of the conversation from across the room. This is known as the "cocktail party effect" after being observed by Colin Cherry in 1953. Clearly, we must have been processing the stimuli around us at some level if we can hear our name.

DO WE NOW HAVE THE ATTENTION SPAN OF A GOLDFISH?

According to scientists, the use of smartphones and other devices in today's society has left humans with an attention span shorter than a goldfish. Researchers for Microsoft studied the brain activity of participants in Canada using electroencephalograms. They found that the average human attention span has fallen from 12 seconds in 2000, which is around the time the mobile revolution began, to 8 seconds in 2015. This is slightly less than the attention span of goldfish, which is 9 seconds. This reduction in ability to focus is thought to be due to our increasing reliance on the fast-moving and fast-changing world when viewed through our devices.

TREISMAN'S ATTENUATION MODEL OF ATTENTION

UK-born Anne Marie Treisman (b. 1935) is a selective-attention expert with different views from Broadbent. She maintains in her "attenuation model" that the filter that Broadbent referred to does not eliminate stimulation but attenuates it (or turns down its volume) so that it is still available for further processing. Thus if there are several competing sounds in a room (such as the television, children bickering and a baby crying), we are able to, in effect, turn down the volume of all the noise except the one we are attending to (or want to attend to). This would explain why if we heard our name among a sea of noise, we would pick up on that. It also explains the "cocktail party phenomenon" (see page 85). To get through the filter, items have to reach a certain threshold or level. All the selected/attended-to material will reach this threshold. Some sounds will always have a reduced threshold, for example your own name or words like "help" and "fire" — this explains why we will hear these against a background of noise.

CENTER OF ATTENTION

The reticular activating system, or RAS, is the brain's attention center. The system consists of a number of ascending and descending circuits that connect the brainstem to the forebrain (see page 57) and it is responsible for "switching on" the brain, taking us from sleep states to states of high alertness and attention. The RAS sifts through all incoming information and decides what is important and what is not. If the RAS is damaged (as it is located at the back of the head, it is specially vulnerable), the patient can fall into a coma. Unusual activity of the RAS has been associated with attentional disorders such as ADHD and chronic fatigue syndrome. Some drugs can affect the functioning of the RAS; anesthetics, for example, work by switching off parts of it.

THEORIES OF MEMORY

Memory is at the heart of everything; how we talk, walk, learn and feel. What we call memory is actually a three-stage process involving:

1. **Encoding of information (laying down the memories)**
2. **Storage of that information**
3. **Retrieval of those memories**

Most theories of memory are concerned with how we store information for later retrieval. Here we look at three important theories of memory. (For tips on how to improve your memory, see page 277.)

ATKINSON & SHIFFRIN'S MULTI-STORE MODEL

According to this model, proposed by Richard Atkinson and Richard Shiffrin in 1968, there are three primary types of memory storage systems:

SENSORY MEMORY: This is the storage system that occurs as the initial stage in the memory process, but sensory information is "stored" for only a very short time — less than half a second for visual stimuli and 3–4 seconds for auditory — because it is "raw" (unprocessed).

SHORT-TERM MEMORY (STM): Also known as working memory, this is where active processing happens; information can be held here for around 20–30 seconds. Our short-term memory capacity is very limited, too (see right). We can keep the information here longer if we rehearse (repeat) it. Otherwise, the data will be lost unless we pay further attention to it (by thinking about it) to allow it to pass to the next stage — long-term memory.

LONG-TERM MEMORY (LTM): This has an almost infinite capacity and information in long-term memory usually stays there for the duration of a person's life. However, that does not mean people will always be able to remember something in their long-term memory, as they may not be able to retrieve it.

7 PLUS OR MINUS 2

Short-term memory has a very limited capacity: George A. Miller (1920–2012), when working at Bell Laboratories, conducted experiments demonstrating that it can only store about seven pieces of information, plus or minus two pieces (the number can be written as 7±2). The title of Miller's famous paper on this was "The magical number 7±2." We can attempt to increase the capacity of short-term memory using a method called chunking, whereby we combine small bits of information into bigger chunks — but we can still recall only around seven such chunks.

TRY THIS:

Here is a list of numbers — look at each set for a few seconds, then cover them up and write down what you can recall. Try "chunking" as the strings get larger.

687	9752712
3095	968473582
98462	984746352417
847256	374652830372525

Most people should manage the first five lists easily but will start to struggle after that. Anyone who can recall the final string is a memory genius!

BADDELEY & HITCH'S MODEL OF WORKING MEMORY

A number of problems became apparent concerning the characteristics of Atkinson and Shiffrin's model of short-term memory (see page 88) and in 1974 Alan Baddeley and Graham Hitch developed an alternative model of short-term memory, which they too called working memory. They suggested that the STM was made up of several subsystems, each having a specialized function. Of particular interest was the "central executive" subsystem which essentially acts as a sensory store, channeling auditory information to the "phonological/articulatory loop" (for auditory information) or to the "visuo-spatial sketchpad" (for visual and spatial information). In 2000 Baddeley expanded the model by introducing a third area, the "episodic buffer" (which links information across domains – such as the visual sphere – to form integrated units of visual, spatial and verbal information and chronological ordering).

As an example of this in action, imagine that you are out for dinner and the bill arrives. It is $35.50 and there are three of you. How much should each of you pay? (Do this in your head!)

Calculating this involves your working memory. For example, you might divide 30 by 3 first — and hold 10 in your memory while you then divide 5 by 3, and then divide 50 by 3. You will need to recall the answers from each bit of the sum so you can add them together. All this involves your working memory, which acts like a kind of workspace or virtual blackboard.

(If you managed this easily then you have a good functional working memory. But if you struggled, don't worry — your working memory might be limited by your ability to manipulate numbers.)

THE MASTER & THE SLAVES

The elements of Baddeley and Hitch's 1974 working memory model (previous page) can be likened to a particularly controlling master (the "central executive") ordering and directing "slaves" — in this case, the phonological/articulatory loop and the visuo-spatial sketchpad of our working memory. The central executive completely controls the actions of these systems. The "slaves" cannot do anything without their master's say-so. It is the central executive, for example, that decides what to pay attention to and what to prioritize, such as auditory input over visual. Like any boss, the central executive delegates much of the groundwork, such as data collecting, to its staff and takes on a supervisory role in coordinating these activities.

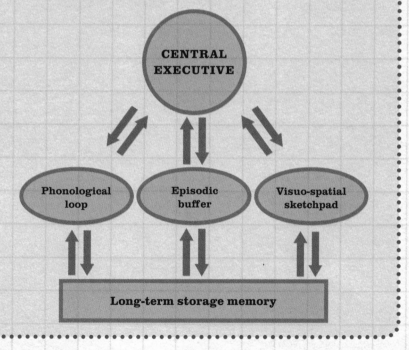

CENTRAL EXECUTIVE

Phonological loop

Episodic buffer

Visuo-spatial sketchpad

Long-term storage memory

FALSE MEMORY

Psychologists are interested not only in how we remember and forget things that have happened, but also in how we appear to recall things that never happened (known as false memories).

In 1974, psychologist Elizabeth Loftus conducted an experiment whereby participants were randomly assigned to watch videos of car accidents, in which separate videos showed collisions at 20 mph (32 km/h), 30 mph (48 km/h) and 40 mph (64 km/h). Afterwards, participants filled out a survey in which they were asked, "About how fast were the cars going when they smashed into each other?" The question was always the same, except the verb used to describe the collision varied between smashed, bumped, collided, hit or contacted. If actual speed in the video was what determined the estimates of speed given by the participants, it could be assumed that they would give lower estimates when they saw the lower-speed collisions. However, the results suggested that it was the word that had been used to describe the collision (such as smashed or contacted) that predicted the participant's estimate of the speed, rather than the speed itself.

This experiment shows that the phrasing of a question can create false memories. Even the smallest adjustment in wording a question can create a false memory. For example, asking someone if they had seen "the" stop sign, rather than "a" stop sign, causes the respondent to presuppose that there was a stop sign in the scene they are trying to recall — and they are thus more likely to "remember" seeing it. Similarly, asking "what shade of red was her dress?" assumes that the dress was red and so people will "remember" its being red. Asking someone "how tall was the gunman?" rather than "what was his height?" will lead to greater estimates of height. All this shows how easily memories can be manipulated. (For more on false memory, see page 176.)

CRAIK & LOCKHART'S LEVELS OF PROCESSING MODEL

This model of memory storage assigns a more important role to long-term memory than previous models, in particular with regard to the processing that takes place there. Where the multi-store model (see page 88) suggests that information is transferred from short-term to long-term memory through the process of repetition, this model suggests that it is the depth or level at which we process information that

TEST YOUR WORKING MEMORY

Here is a test of the capacity of your working memory. Write the answers to these sums then, when you get to a word, read it out and go to the next sum:

67 + 87 =

JACKET

897 + 45 =

WATER

76 — 23 =

LETTER

732 + 64 =

ANIMAL

456 + 498 =

HAIRGRIP

65 + 8 + 23 =

ENGINE

23 + 56 + 29 =

PHONE

76 — 43 =

NOTEPAD

Now cover up the list: how many words can you recall? If you can recall five or more of the words, you have a very efficient working memory. But don't worry if you can't recall many — not many people can.

determines its place in long-term memory and also how well we recall that information. In other words, thinking about something — for example, thinking about an event or considering solutions to a related problem — will help us remember it even without rehearsing it (repeating the words or event in our mind).

Fergus I.M. Craik and Robert S. Lockhart suggested in 1972 that memory processing can operate at different depths of analysis, some more complex than others. They referred to this as elaborate semantic processing. They also proposed that the method of learning is important in later recall. For example, organizing items into categories helps this, as does making items distinctive in some way; in addition, items with which more information is associated can be recalled better.

TIP-OF-THE-TONGUE PHENOMENON

We all are familiar with that frustrating feeling when the word we want is on "the tip of our tongue" but we just cannot retrieve it. This is different from simply forgetting something — with the tip-of-the-tongue phenomenon, we feel strongly that we have only forgotten it temporarily and that it will come back to us (which usually happens when we stop trying to recall it). Often we can remember features of the word, such as its first letter or what it sounds like, or even a word that means the same. The phenomenon occurs irrespective of gender, age or educational level. Monolinguals, bilinguals and multilinguals all experience it and so do deaf people using sign language.

One explanation is that something blocks, interferes with or prevents the retrieval of the target word even though we know it is there. Or it could be that there are weak connections between various elements of the word. Words contain several types of information, including letters, sounds and meanings, which are held in separate parts of memory but are connected. When you try to think of a word, you generally start with the meaning. If the connection between that meaning and the sound information is not strong enough, the sound information won't be activated sufficiently to allow you to retrieve all of it.

THEORIES OF LEARNING

Learning is defined as a relatively lasting change in behavior as a result of experience. Learning has its roots in behaviorism, a psychological approach initially developed by American psychologist John B. Watson, which was concerned with behaviors that could be observed and measured (as opposed to internal, mental processes that could not be measured) — Watson devised the Little Albert experiment that is discussed on page 148. His theory was based on the idea that all behaviors are acquired through the conditioning that occurs when we interact with our environment. Two types of conditioning are identified — classical conditioning and operant conditioning — and these form the basis of all learning according to the behaviorist perspective.

IVAN PAVLOV *and his colleagues at the Military Medical Academy in 1914, observing the dogs that would lead to the development of the theory of classical conditioning.*

THEORY OF CLASSICAL CONDITIONING

Classical conditioning is also called Pavlovian conditioning after the scientist who first observed it. Ivan Petrovich Pavlov (1849–1936) was a Russian physiologist known primarily for his use of dogs as research subjects. Pavlov, originally interested in salivation responses in dogs, discovered that when a buzzer was sounded just before food was presented, the dogs, which would initially salivate when the food was presented (a natural response), would later come to associate the buzzer with the presentation of the food and salivate when the buzzer was sounded even without food. This he termed "conditioning" — the dogs had been conditioned to salivate when they heard the buzzer. It is popularly believed that Pavlov always signaled the occurrence of food by ringing a bell. However, his writings record the use of a wide variety of stimuli, including electric shocks, whistles, metronomes, tuning forks and a range of visual stimuli, in addition to the ring of a bell.

Classical conditioning, then, is a learning process in which an association is made between a previously neutral stimulus (in other words, one that did not provoke a response) and a stimulus that naturally evokes a response.

CLASSICAL CONDITIONING IN ACTION

(OR WHY I CRAVED MARS BARS IN A CERTAIN LECTURE THEATER)

When I was an undergraduate psychology student, I took a module in the psychology of advertising. One of our seminars involved choosing a print-ad campaign, bringing it to the class and analyzing it. I chose Mars Bars and during the two-hour class that I spent thinking about Mars Bars, I began to really crave one, as you do when you think about delicious chocolate. However, the following week, even though we had moved on to an entirely different topic, as soon as I stepped into the classroom, I wanted a Mars Bar. This happened in every subsequent class. I ate a lot of Mars Bars that semester, proving that even knowing the mechanism behind conditioning does not make a person immune to it.

THEORY OF OPERANT CONDITIONING

While classical conditioning involves making an association between involuntary automatic behaviors (such as salivation) and a stimulus (such as a bell), operant conditioning involves applying reward or punishment after a behavior; it focuses on strengthening or weakening voluntary behaviors. Unlike classical conditioning, which is passive (the participant does not have to actively do anything), operant conditioning requires the learner to actively participate and perform some type of action in order to be rewarded or punished.

Most people associate operant conditioning with B.F. Skinner (see page 29), but his theories were based on the work of Edward Thorndike who famously used a "puzzle box" to study animal behaviors in the late 1890s. The puzzle box, as discussed on page 35, consisted of a cage in which a cat was placed and from which it had to work out a way to escape in order to obtain its reward (food). The box contained a lever that, when pressed, opened a door. The cat would flail around

THORNDIKE *devised a special cage in which a cat could be observed while it learned how to escape.*

until it happened to press the lever accidentally. This would occur for a few trials until the cat realized that there was a connection between its pressing the lever and the door opening. Then it would learn to press the lever to escape quickly every time it was placed in the box. This led to Thorndike's law of effect, stating that any behavior that is followed by pleasant consequences is likely to be repeated and any behavior followed by unpleasant consequences is likely to be stopped.

Around half a century later, Thorndike's work provided a framework for Skinner to develop his principles of operant conditioning. Skinner used a smaller version of Thorndike's puzzle box, called the operant conditioning chamber, or Skinner box (1948). The box had a lever (for rats) or a disc in one wall (for pigeons). If the animal pressed on this, food would be delivered to it and responses reinforced in this way increased in frequency. Four types of conditioning were identified:

POSITIVE REINFORCEMENT: When a behavior is strengthened (more likely to continue) because we receive a reward for doing it — for instance, a child who is naughty and gets attention for it, which they enjoy, is more likely to be naughty again.

NEGATIVE REINFORCEMENT: When a behavior is strengthened because it causes something unpleasant to stop — for example, if we are cold, we put on a sweater and thus learn to dress warmly to avoid feeling cold.

WE WRAP UP *to remove the uncomfortable feeling of being cold; this is negative reinforcement because we learn to do something (wrap up) in order to stop something unpleasant (being cold).*

PUNISHMENT: When a behavior is weakened (less likely to continue) because something unpleasant happens when we do it — for instance, a dog who gets punished for soiling the house learns to stop doing this.

EXTINCTION: When a behavior is weakened because we no longer get reinforcement for it — for example, if we stopped being paid for working, we would stop going to work.

WRITING "LINES" is punishment because it is a negative event that follows behavior that is undesirable (to adults at least).

There are also various schedules of reinforcement that can be applied. For example, reinforcement can be given each time an act is performed (continuous reinforcement) — which is most effective when we want to teach a new behavior — or only sometimes (partial reinforcement). In partial reinforcement, the reinforcement could be organized to occur after a certain amount of time (for example, every two minutes), which is referred to as fixed-interval reinforcement or after a random and unpredictable amount of time, known as variable-interval reinforcement. An alternative form of partial reinforcement is ratio-based, which means that it is the number of times the behavior is performed that is key; fixed-ratio reinforcement comes after a certain number of acts are performed whereas variable-ratio reinforcement occurs after a random and unpredictable number of acts are performed.

It takes longer to learn behaviors with partial schedules, but the learned behaviors last longer after the reinforcement ceases — they are said to be resistant to extinction.

SOCIAL LEARNING THEORY

Bandura's social learning theory of 1977 (see page 32) takes a different perspective from the behaviorist view of learning outlined so far. The Canadian–American psychologist Albert Bandura suggested that people can learn from each other through processes unrelated to conditioning, such as observation or imitation (often referred to as modeling). Unlike Skinner, Bandura saw humans as active information processors who are able to think about the relationship between their behavior and its consequences. These cognitive processes, he said, are an important element of observational learning. Because the social learning approach takes into account the cognitive factors that mediate between stimuli and responses, it addresses one of the biggest criticisms of behaviorism: its neglect of thinking or cognitive processes. Bandura developed his social learning theory partly through his famous studies using the Bobo doll, which are explained in more detail on page 158.

PSYCHOLOGICAL THEORIES
THEORIES OF EMOTION

Several theories of emotion have been proposed over the years to attempt to account for what happens when we experience an emotion. One of the most popular theories is the two-factor theory of emotion.

SCHACHTER & SINGER'S TWO-FACTOR THEORY OF EMOTION

We met Stanley Schachter in the list of top ten influential 20th-century psychologists on page 34. Schachter and Jerome E. Singer's two-factor theory of emotion, also called the Schachter–Singer theory, states that the experience of emotion is based on two factors: physiological arousal and cognitive labeling. Prior to this 1962 theory, it had been considered that emotions were purely physical sensations and that the role of mental processes was limited. Some early theorists even held that different emotions were associated with different patterns of physiological arousal — and this is how we distinguish between them. However, according to the two-factor theory, when an emotion is felt, a physiological arousal occurs (which might not differ between emotions and, indeed, might not even differ from the arousal we feel for non-emotional reasons) and the person uses the immediate environment to search for emotional cues to label the physiological arousal.

Thus, if we feel physiological arousal (such as feeling sweaty and breathless) and we have an explanation for it that is non-emotional (we have just run for the bus), then we will not label that arousal as an emotion. In the absence of a ready explanation (if we have not run anywhere), we will look for one and we might label it as fear. Schachter and Singer tested this with their famous suproxin study, outlined on page 170.

LOVE OR FEAR?

In 1974 the psychologists Donald G. Dutton and Arthur P. Aron tested the two-factor theory by having male participants walk across two different sorts of bridges. One was a scary suspension bridge, which was very narrow, rocked when walked upon and was suspended above a deep, fast-flowing river. The second was lower, more stable and wider and it crossed a gentle part of the river.

At the end of each bridge an attractive female experimenter met the participants and gave them a survey to fill out, with a number to call if they had any questions. The study showed that the men who walked across the scary bridge were most likely to call the woman, asking for a date. This was thought to be because they experienced physiological arousal on the scary bridge (namely, increased heart rate, faster breathing and sweating) through fear, but when they saw an attractive female, they latched on to her as an explanation for the symptoms they were experiencing. They misattributed the real reason to a more convenient or more available explanation, as suggested by the two-factor theory.

THEORIES OF INTELLIGENCE

A number of theories have been proposed to account for what intelligence actually is and what its basic elements are. (For tips on improving your IQ, see page 275.)

SPEARMAN'S TWO-FACTOR THEORY

Charles Edward Spearman (1863–1945), an English psychologist known for his work in statistics, proposed his two-factor theory of intelligence in 1904. In it he argued that there were two types of factor that make up intelligence: a general factor (which he called g) as well as other specific factors such as verbal, mathematical and artistic skills. The general factor is an innate and universal ability, whereas specific factors are learned — but both factors are thought to correlate with each other, such that people high in one are likely to be high in the other.

A LEAD VIOLINIST *is, according to Spearman, likely to have general intelligence in addition to specific musical ability.*

GARDNER'S THEORY OF MULTIPLE INTELLIGENCES

In his 1983 book *Frames of Mind: The Theory of Multiple Intelligences*, Howard Gardner (b. 1943) claimed that humans have several different ways of processing information and that these are relatively independent of one another (rather than related, as previous researchers had believed). Since 1999, Gardner has identified eight intelligences and he believes it is possible to shine in one but not others:

MUSICAL–RHYTHMIC: This area has to do with abilities around sounds, rhythms, tones and music.

VISUAL–SPATIAL: This area deals with spatial judgment and the ability to visualize in one's imagination.

VERBAL–LINGUISTIC: People with high verbal–linguistic intelligence display an ability with words and languages.

LOGICAL–MATHEMATICAL: This area has to do with logic, abstractions, reasoning, numbers and critical thinking.

BODILY–KINESTHETIC: The core elements of the bodily–kinesthetic intelligence are control of one's bodily motions and the capacity to handle objects skilfully.

INTERPERSONAL: Individuals who have high interpersonal intelligence are characterized by their sensitivity to others' moods, feelings, temperaments and motivations, and their ability to cooperate in order to work as part of a group.

INTRAPERSONAL: This area has to do with introspective and self-reflective capacities.

NATURALISTIC: This area deals with nurturing and relating information to one's natural surroundings.

THE BELL-SHAPED CURVE

The Bell Curve: Intelligence and Class Structure in American Life, by American psychologist Richard J. Herrnstein (who died before the book was released) and American political scientist Charles Murray, is a 1994 book that attempts to explain the variations in intelligence in American society. The book's title comes from the depiction on a graph of the bell-shaped normal distribution of intelligence quotient (IQ) scores in a population. It illustrates how most people's IQs will be centered around the middle, with fewer at the upper and lower ends. The central premise of the authors was that human intelligence is substantially influenced by both inherited and environmental factors.

Many of the arguments put forward by the authors were controversial, particularly with regard to the suggestion that lower IQ scores for African–Americans were due in some way to genetics. The book also argued that the average genetic IQ of the United States is declining, owing to the tendency of the more intelligent to have fewer children than the less intelligent and large-scale immigration to the United States of those with supposed low intelligence. The authors recommended the elimination of welfare policies that encouraged poor women to have babies since they were deemed more likely to produce children with lower IQs.

The controversies led to many commentaries, reviews, books and counter-arguments being published in the 1990s about the ideas expressed in the book. A more recent response was Richard Nisbett's 2009 book *Intelligence and How to Get It*. In it Nisbett argued that the differences in IQ scores were largely as a result of socioeconomic factors and that when controls were introduced for these the differences between ethnic groups largely disappeared.

THEORIES OF MOTIVATION

Motivation is what inspires us to do what we do. Theories of motivation can be classed as either content or process theories. Content theories are concerned with identifying people's needs and strengths, and looking at *what* motivates a person, whereas process theories try to identify *how* motivation is initiated and sustained, such as factors that determine how much effort people will put into attaining a goal. Probably the best known of the content theories are Maslow's theory of hierarchical needs and Herzberg's two-factor theory. The best known of the process theories is arguably Vroom's expectancy theory. All three theories are discussed here.

THEORIES OF MOTIVATION *can help us understand how and why people are motivated (or otherwise) to achieve their targets and goals.*

MASLOW'S THEORY OF HIERARCHICAL NEEDS

We met Abraham Maslow in Top Ten Psychologists on page 35. His theory of motivation, proposed in 1943 (and expanded upon in 1954), suggested that we have various needs, or motivators, and that these can be arranged into a hierarchy. At the bottom of the hierarchy are the most basic needs and at the top are the "highest" needs. A pyramid is often used to illustrate these five levels of needs, although Maslow never used this format himself.

The four lowest levels of the hierarchy of needs contain what Maslow called "deficiency needs": physiological needs, safety and security needs, social needs such as friendship and love, and self-esteem. If these deficiency needs are not met, we will feel anxious and tense. Maslow claimed that these basic needs must be met before the individual will strongly desire (be motivated by) the high-level need for self-actualization.

1. Physiological needs are the physical requirements for human survival, including food and water. We cannot function properly until these needs are met — how often are we driven from our desks at work in search of food before we can carry on?

2. Once our physical needs are met, we will be motivated by safety needs. In today's developed world this relates less to safety from war or famine than to security in such areas as our jobs, savings accounts and insurance policies.

Safety needs

Physiologial needs

Self-actualization needs

Self-esteem needs

Social needs

3. After our safety needs have been met, we will be driven to fulfil our social needs — the urge to belong, affiliate and be loved by friends, family and romantic partners.

4. Next comes the need for self-esteem, which we may be motivated to meet through undertaking hobbies, volunteer work or other activities.

5. Finally, at the highest level, is the need for "self-actualization," or fulfilling our potential — being the best parent possible, the best artist or whatever means the most to us.

MOTIVATORS & HYGIENE FACTORS

According to Herzberg's two-factor theory, motivators are to do with the intrinsic conditions of a job and will give positive satisfaction when present. They include:

- Challenging work
- Recognition
- Responsibility
- Opportunity for meaningful tasks
- Involvement in decision-making
- Sense of importance to the organization

Hygiene factors do not give positive satisfaction as such. Instead, dissatisfaction results from their absence. They are mainly extrinsic to the work itself. They include:

- Status
- Job security
- Salary
- Fringe benefits
- Work conditions
- Health insurance
- Good annual leave

HERZBERG'S TWO-FACTOR THEORY

Sometimes known as Herzberg's motivation-hygiene theory, this is another content theory, but aimed at the workplace. Frederick Irving Herzberg (1923–2000) was an American psychologist and one of the most influential names in business management. He added a new dimension to Maslow's theory by suggesting a two-factor model of motivation, where there are two different sets of characteristics that influence satisfaction at work. One set of factors or job characteristics leads to satisfaction at work when they are present, while the absence of another, separate set of job characteristics, leads to workers feeling unhappy at work. Satisfaction and dissatisfaction, he said, were thus independent of each other rather than one rising while the other falls. Those factors whose presence leads to satisfaction are called motivators while those whose absence causes dissatisfaction are called hygiene factors.

VROOM'S EXPECTANCY THEORY

Although there are a number of process theories, the best known is probably Vroom's expectancy theory, also known as his valence-instrumentality-expectancy theory. Victor Harold Vroom (b. 1932), a business school professor at the Yale School of Management, proposed this theory in 1964 to help explain why people might choose one course of action over another. The theory explains that people will be motivated to do something by the following factors:

- **EXPECTANCY** (If I try really hard, I can do the job.)

- **INSTRUMENTALITY** (If I do the job well, I will be rewarded.)

- **VALENCE** (I really want the reward.)

Motivation will be low if (a) we do not believe that hard work will make much difference to how well we do, (b) we feel that even if we do really well we will not get the reward, or (c) we feel that the reward is not all that desirable.

THEORIES OF CHILDREN'S DEVELOPMENT

The way children develop from helpless babies to fully functioning adults can appear to be nothing short of miraculous and developmental psychologists have long been fascinated with how these tremendous changes are achieved. Some of the most influential theories explaining parts of child development are outlined here.

ATTACHMENT THEORY

Any parent will know that newborn babies are not born devoted to their own parents; it comes with time. For the first few weeks or even months, a baby is happy as long as their basic needs are met — they don't care who feeds and changes them, as long as someone does. This can be a little disheartening for a new mother (and sometimes father) as she watches her precious baby being just as happy with a random stranger as with the person who gave birth to them.

But new parents should make the most of that "pre-attachment" stage because suddenly, at around 8 months, a baby will start demonstrating a strong and exclusive preference for their primary caregiver, to the extent that they will be distraught when that person leaves the room for a moment. This is *attachment* and it refers to the deep emotional bond between a child and their primary caregiver. Providing an explanation of how this parent–child relationship emerges, attachment theory originates in the work of the British psychologist John Bowlby, which began in 1958.

A number of stages of attachment, based on the baby's age, were outlined by Bowlby:

UP TO 3 MONTHS: Indiscriminate attachments. At this stage most babies respond equally to any caregiver and do not cry or fuss when left with a stranger.

AFTER 4 MONTHS: Preference for primary caregiver (for example, mother) and secondary caregiver (for example, father) is expressed but the baby will accept food and care from anyone.

AFTER 7 MONTHS: Special preference for the primary caregiver. The baby shows fear of strangers ("stranger fear") and distress when separated from the object of their attachment ("separation anxiety").

AFTER 9 MONTHS: Multiple attachments occur whereby children will bond with a range of "special" people such as grandparents or nursery staff.

If a child does not develop these attachments for some reason (such as inconsistent care, loss of primary caregiver or having multiple carers), this may cause problems for the child's relationships in later life.

Other psychologists later added more to our understanding of what influences attachment in children, including a classic comparative psychology study using monkeys looked at the effects of maternal deprivation and related them to deprivation in children. These experiments (known as "Harlow's Monkeys") are outlined on page 154.

AFTER ABOUT 9 MONTHS OF AGE *attachment to specific people is normal. This explains the "clingy" stage that babies and toddlers go through.*

In the 1970s, the American–Canadian psychologist Mary Ainsworth expanded greatly upon John Bowlby's original work with her "strange situation" studies. In these studies, she placed children and their mothers in rooms with strangers (with whom the child was subsequently left alone).

Ainsworth used these studies to identify three major styles of attachment:

ATTACHMENT IN ANIMALS

Austrian Konrad Lorenz's imprinting theory of 1935 suggested that newly hatched goslings follow the first moving object they see during a critical period of 12–17 hours after hatching. Known as imprinting, the process suggests that attachment is innate (programd genetically rather than learned). This imprinting is independent of feeding and if it does not occur within the critical period it will not occur at all.

Lorenz was able to get newborn goslings to imprint on him by ensuring that he was the first thing they saw when they hatched. He then mixed these goslings with another batch who had imprinted onto their mother, putting them in a box and then releasing them. While the goslings that had imprinted on their mother waddled off after her, "his" goslings duly followed him; they preferred to be around him throughout their development and even as grown geese. Lorenz won the 1973 Nobel Prize in Physiology and Medicine for his experiments on animal behavior.

TRY THIS:
THE STRANGE SITUATION

If you have a child between the age of about 1 and 3 years, you can try a version of Mary Ainsworth's strange-situation experiment. You will need to recruit a friend who is not known to your child. Go to their house and let your child play and explore while you are with them. Note their behavior. A securely attached child will use you as a base from which to explore — they will show you things and return to you every so often. They may interact with the "stranger."

Now leave the room. If your child gets very distressed, return (we don't want to upset your child with this experiment). If they seem okay, stay outside for a few minutes (but abandon the experiment if they get upset) and ask your friend to note what happens in your absence. Now return and see what response you get; a securely attached child will be very happy to see you (but don't worry if they don't respond in this way — many secure and happy children do not always behave according to the theory!).

SECURE ATTACHMENT: The child shows distress when the mother leaves and joy when she returns, turning to her for comfort.

AMBIVALENT–INSECURE ATTACHMENT: The child is extremely distressed when the mother leaves but may push her away when she returns.

AVOIDANT–INSECURE ATTACHMENT: The child does not seem bothered by the mother's leaving or return and on her return does not turn to her for comfort.

PIAGET'S THEORY OF COGNITIVE DEVELOPMENT

Jean Piaget, whom we first met on page 30, was responsible for developing ground-breaking theories that changed the way the development of children's mental and intellectual capacities was viewed. Piaget showed the world that children are not simply underdeveloped versions of grown-ups.

Children, he claimed, were like scientists, constantly experimenting with the world in order to make sense of it. Two processes, he said, allow them to develop their intellectual understanding of how things work. The processes work on the assumption that children are forever creating and testing theories about how the world works, such as that things fall down when dropped. These processes are:

ASSIMILATION: This is the first process, when children are faced with a new way of doing something or some new information, which they then try to fit with an existing theory. Thus, they might try dropping different objects and finding that they all fall to the ground, they assimilate those experiences into their theory of gravity (obviously, they don't call it that!).

ACCOMMODATION: If, however, someone then gives the child a helium-filled balloon and they attempt to drop it but find that it does not fall to the ground, the child needs to alter their existing theory of gravity to accommodate the fact that some things do not fall to the ground. This process is called accommodation.

Piaget theorized that children use accommodation and assimilation to progress through the following four stages of cognitive development:

TRY THIS:
PEEK-A-BOO

When you play peek-a-boo with a young baby, you are able to test their grasp of object permanence. Every time you "disappear" (such as behind a curtain or blanket), a child in the sensorimotor stage will think you have gone and will thus be surprised when you pop back up again. An older child, who has grasped the fact that just because they can't see you doesn't mean you have gone, will not show such surprise and the game of peek-a-boo will no longer have the same appeal.

1. THE SENSORIMOTOR STAGE: This stage begins at birth and continues until about age 2. The key skill learned at this time is what Piaget called "object permanence" and refers to a child's realization that objects stay the same even when the child cannot see them. Thus, a young baby who is shown a ball that is then covered with a blanket believes the ball to have gone. The baby does not look for it — if they cannot see it, it is no longer there. An older child will lift the blanket to find it — they know that the ball is still there even though they cannot see it. This is object permanence. To try this experiment on your own child to see if they have grasped object permanence yet (see left).

2. THE PREOPERATIONAL STAGE: Between 2 and 7 years of age, the child develops from being an egocentric thinker, who can only see their own point of view, to a less egocentric one, who realizes that other people see things differently. The egocentric thinker assumes that, for example, if they like something, other people do as well and that if they can see something, others can too.

TRY THIS:
IS YOUR CHILD IN THE EGOCENTRIC STAGE?

You can perform your own experiment like Piaget did to see if your child is still an egocentric thinker. Use a toy town set with features such as houses, shops and hills. Put a doll or figure in a place where it has a very different view of the scene than does your child. Ask your child what the doll can see. An egocentric thinker will describe what they can see, not appreciating that the doll would have a totally different vantage point. An older child will have no problem describing the view from the doll's point of view, realizing that it will differ from their own.

3. THE CONCRETE OPERATIONAL STAGE: Between 7 and 11 years, the child learns concrete operations that are characterized by the ability to "conserve." This is the ability to understand that a certain quantity of small items like buttons or marbles will remain the same despite adjustment of the size or shape of their container. (See exercise below.)

4. THE FORMAL OPERATIONAL STAGE: By the age of 11 years, children have generally entered the formal operational stage. This is when they can think in the abstract — in other words, they can use their imagination and creativity to manipulate ideas and concepts in their heads.

TRY THIS:
CAN YOUR CHILD CONSERVE?

Show your child a short, flat glass filled with water. Take a long, thin glass and pour the water into it. Now ask them which has the most water. A child who has not yet grasped conservation will say that the taller glass has more water in it, while a child who can conserve will know that both glasses have the same amount.

There are variations of this experiment you can try. Put some buttons in two small equal piles. Spread out one pile and then ask your child which pile has the most buttons — the pile that is not spread out or the one that is. A child who can conserve will know that they both have the same amount of buttons even though the spread-out pile looks bigger. You can try this with a piece of clay, too — if your child thinks a long thin sausage contains more clay than the same piece in a squat lump, then they have not yet grasped conservation.

TRY THIS:
IS YOUR CHILD IN THE FORMAL OPERATIONAL STAGE?

Give your child the following puzzle: Yasmin is taller than Charlie and Charlie is taller than Harry. Who is the tallest?

If your child can work this out in their head, then they are in the formal operational stage; if they need to draw pictures in order to decide, then they are not quite there yet!

THEORY OF LANGUAGE DEVELOPMENT

It has long been recognized that children do not learn to speak in the same way that adults learn a new language. In most cases, children seem to pick up their mother tongue without any difficulty at all, yet an adult trying to master a foreign tongue may struggle and is never likely to gain completely fluent mastery in the same way.

What, then, accounts for the seemingly magical way that children learn to speak? It used to be assumed that they learned to associate words and meanings and that when they made the connections correctly — by imitating what they heard — they would be rewarded (by getting the desired object or praise). This is the behaviorist approach to language development, which was first put forward by B.F. Skinner (see page 29).

However, Skinner's account was later criticized by Noam Chomsky (b. 1928), the world's most famous linguistic expert. Chomsky argued that language acquisition cannot simply rely on the environment providing children with enough language to emulate. They could never acquire all the tools needed for processing an infinite number of sentences on that basis.

Instead, Chomsky proposed the theory of universal grammar. This states that the reason children so easily master the complex operations of language is that they have innate knowledge of certain principles that guide them in developing the grammar of their language. In other words, children are born with an ability to learn language; according to Chomsky, they have a "language acquisition device" deep-wired in their brains that enables this. It provides children with the ability to learn the basic rules of grammar that are common in all languages.

Later theorists proposed that there is a "critical period" in which language is acquired in children and if the child is not exposed to a language in that period, they will never fully master it. The sad case study of Genie, the "feral" child (see page 48), is used as evidence for this theory. Other proof lies in the fact that children can pick up more than one language during the critical period (usually before puberty), but if learning a foreign language is left until after the critical period, they are unlikely ever to be fully bilingual or multilingual.

CHILDREN ARE PREDISPOSED to learn language during a critical period in their development, according to linguist Noam Chomsky.

BILINGUALISM

If learning one language seems an unbelievable accomplishment for such young brains, what about those children who master two or even more languages? Worldwide, it is estimated that there are as many bilingual children as there are monolingual children. Bilingual children are thought to have many advantages over their monolingual peers. For example, bilingual children are better able to focus and ignore distractions, are more creative and are better at problem-solving than monolinguals. Knowing more than one language seems to make the brain more flexible.

There are two ways that children learn a second language:

- When both languages are learned simultaneously from birth. The child might learn to speak slightly later than a monolingual child but goes through exactly the same developmental stages — somehow managing to pick up two or more languages in roughly the same time that it takes monolinguals to learn one. Children in these situations are able to differentiate between the two languages easily and they often speak one language to one parent and a second language to the other (or one at home and one out of the home). In this situation, both languages are "first" languages.

- When the languages are learned sequentially. In other words, the second language is introduced some time later than the first (usually after the age of 3 years), such as when the child moves to a different country. In this situation, the later language (or languages) is the child's second language.

The ability to become bilingual is influenced by the amount of input (how long the child is exposed to the second language) and also by the separation of input (whether one parent speaks one language and the other the second, which is thought by some to prevent confusion).

THEORIES OF SOCIAL PSYCHOLOGY

Humans are social animals, preferring to live and interact in groups rather than alone. Fitting into these groups and feeling that we belong is important to us — so much so that our attitudes, thoughts and behavior are often strongly influenced by the people around us. Social psychology is all about how we feel, think or behave when in the company of other people, compared with when we are alone. Being in the presence of others can sometimes have quite dramatic effects and a number of classic psychological theories have attempted to explain how, when and under what conditions these influences are strongest.

HAWTHORNE EFFECT

This is a phenomenon whereby people change the way they act when they are being observed. The effect was first noted by researcher Henry A. Landsberger in the 1950s when he analyzed a series of experiments that had previously been conducted in the 1920s and 1930s at a Western Electric factory, the Hawthorne Works, outside Chicago. The factory bosses commissioned a study using two groups of employees to see how working conditions affected worker productivity. Productivity seemed to improve when the level of light was increased and other positive changes were made to working conditions, while it stayed the same or diminished when the light levels were unchanged or when they went back to normal. What was of particular interest was that productivity increased whenever levels of light were introduced. Other positive changes, such as the cleaning or relocation of work stations, also resulted in increased productivity. Even changes that resulted in conditions going back to how they were at the start seemed to improve productivity.

Landsberger concluded that it was not the changes in the environment that were responsible for the increased productivity. Rather, the motivating factor seemed to be the fact that the workers were being observed and were thus receiving extra attention.

THEORY OF MINORITY INFLUENCE

Traditionally, it was assumed that a minority would always have a tough time trying to convince a majority to change their views. Yet we now know that minorities can in fact exert a disproportionate influence on the majority, far greater than their number should predict. There are many examples in history of minority influence leading to widespread change (such as the Suffragettes' campaign for women's rights or the American civil rights movement). Even a lone dissenter can be a catalyst for change. Rosa Parks, for example, the African-American woman who refused to move from her seat to the "black" seating area of the bus.

In 1969 the Romanian-born French psychologist Serge Moscovici (1925–2014) developed a theory to explain how a minority group is best able to influence the majority. In experiments similar to the Asch studies (discussed on page 145), participants were asked to state the color of various slides. While the slides were obviously blue or green, Moscovici had minority accomplices state the wrong color to see whether they might influence the majority.

ROSA PARKS *famously refused to move from her seat on a bus in Alabama in 1956 — an act of defiance that led to an uprising for civil rights and racial equality in America.*

TRY THIS:
TEST A MINORITY INFLUENCE

You can try your own test of minority influence at home or at work. Tell a group of friends a joke that has a bemusing (and thus unfunny) punchline. For example, "A police officer pulls over a man and says, 'Do you know how fast you were going back there?' The man replies, 'No, but I know where I am.'"

Have a "stooge" primed to laugh uproariously and then see how many others join in. Try this with a different group, but this time have two stooges. Do more people join in the laughter, even though they clearly have not got the joke?

Moscovici found that if the minority is consistent (sticking to their views), committed (risking negative effects such as ridicule by holding their views but they still stick to them) and persuasive (able to put across their arguments well), it can greatly increase their chances of influencing the majority. Minorities who appear to be acting out of strong principles or moral justification also hold greater sway with the majority. Minorities can win over majority members by appearing to have as much in common with them as possible (other than the dissenting view). We are more influenced by people who seem to be like us than by those who do not. In addition, the bigger the minority, the stronger their influence, up to a point.

These theories of minority influence could help explain how minority terrorist organizations are able to grow in influence. The members are highly committed to their cause, which they promote as being just; they use sophisticated propaganda techniques to make their message persuasive; they appear to make great personal sacrifices for their cause; and they often appeal to common denominators between them and the majority (such as religion or attitudes toward a certain social group). And of course, as the minority grows, they exert even more influence, because others believe that so many people cannot be wrong.

GROUP POLARIZATION

Psychologists have long been fascinated by the impact on the quality of a group's decision-making that individuals within the group have. Until the 1960s it was generally thought that a group opinion corresponded roughly to the average of the opinions of the members of that group. This view was influenced by research on conformity (see page 145) that suggested that group members were likely to end up with similar responses when asked to make estimates of judgments.

In 1961 James Stoner (who was actually a student at the time) changed all that. He created an experiment in which he asked individuals to make some judgments about a number of hypothetical dilemmas. Each dilemma was such that it involved making a choice between two courses of action, one of which (with the more desirable outcome) involved a higher degree of risk than the other. The participants had to decide what level of risk was acceptable to persuade them to make a particular choice. Next, the individuals were put into groups and were asked to reach a unanimous decision on each of the dilemmas they had considered individually. Stoner found that the group

TRY THIS:
TEST FOR GROUP POLARIZATION

Test for group polarization with a group of friends, using this hypothetical dilemma. Without conferring, decide on the level of risk (1 is the highest risk) you each find acceptable privately, then work out the average score. Now get together and reach a group consensus. Is this more extreme than the average of individual scores? Repeat the exercise individually — have the individual averages gone back to pre-group levels?

THE DILEMMA: An electrical engineer may either stick with their present job at a modest but adequate salary or take a new job offering considerably more money but no long-term security. What chance of success (that the new job would bring security) would you advise the engineer is acceptable if they try the riskier alternative?

1. 1 chance in 10 that the new job will bring security

2. 3 chances in 10

3. 5 chances in 10

4. 7 chances in 10

5. 9 chances in 10

6. I would not recommend this alternative no matter how high its likelihood of success.

decisions were nearly always riskier than the average of the decisions made by the individual group members prior to the discussions.

In many subsequent studies, it became clear that the so-called "risky shift" was actually a "shift to extremity" and that groups may also make more cautious or conservative choices than individuals. It thus became better known as a polarization phenomenon. Where individuals' pre-discussion decisions were cautious, the groups became more cautious; where the individuals' pre-discussion decisions were initially risky, the groups shifted even further in that direction. And it was found that these shifts became internalized, so that when the individuals went back to the dilemmas alone, their individual answers post-discussion were more extreme (in the direction of the group discussion).

There are two fascinating theories that could account for group polarization:

SOCIAL COMPARISON THEORY: Each of the dilemmas that have to be considered will be associated with various social values (such as caring for others, being adventurous or being kind). Making a decision about what course of action to take will thus reflect the importance of that social value to the person making the decision. It is human nature to perceive ourselves as closer to our social ideals than others are — we like to think of ourselves as kinder, more thoughtful, more adventurous and so on, than most people. However, once the group discussion gets under way, some of the participants in Stoner's experiments will realize that there are others who appear to be further along the socially valued pole (kinder, more considerate, more adventurous) than they are themselves.

The outcome of this social comparison is that they will then shift their opinions further in that direction in order to present themselves in an even more socially desirable light. The net result is that the group decision is more extreme than the average of the individual positions.

PERSUASIVE ARGUMENTS THEORY: This approach suggests that the main reason for group polarization is availability of information and arguments during the group discussion. In any discussion there is unlikely to be exactly the same number of arguments for and against a decision; rather, there is likely to be a bias in one direction. Each individual when on their own may not have access to all these arguments and viewpoints, but once the discussion gets underway, all this different information comes out into the open. Each learns more of the arguments supporting the dominant view (and perhaps one or two extra arguments against). These additional arguments thus convince group members to shift their opinion even further in that direction.

GROUPTHINK

Coined by the social psychologist Irving Janis in 1972, the term "groupthink" describes the poor decisions that can occur within groups. Janis devised the theory after analyzing poor political decisions made in the United States that had disastrous consequences (see pages 129 and 130). He wanted to know why, when so many experienced and knowledgeable minds were involved, such poor decisions were made.

Groupthink is believed to occur primarily because members of a group feel under pressure to conform to the majority view — even if they fundamentally disagree. In a group situation, especially where the group is very cohesive or where there is a very directive and powerful leader suggesting an opposing path, people find it hard to stand up for what they believe is correct. Members tend to keep quiet rather than risk the embarrassment of opposing everyone else. The consequences of this inhibition are:

ILLUSIONS OF INVULNERABILITY: Because no one is confident enough to put opposing views forward, the group is under the illusion that their decided course of action is the correct one and will lead only to success.

This means that groups are more likely to take risks or to ignore any possibility of things going wrong.

RATIONALIZING: This is where members ignore warning signs and rationalize their decisions without reconsidering their beliefs. Because they believe everyone is on board, they feel it is perfectly rational simply to accept the assumptions they have made even when the warning bells might be ringing.

STEREOTYPING: This refers to negative stereotyping of people outside the immediate group. Thus, if someone (say, an expert or technician) outside the decision-making group raises concerns about the safety of the proposed course of action — as happened in many of the decision processes outlined on the right — the group members are likely to discount those views on the basis that the dissenting person is not an expert, knows nothing, or has ulterior motives.

SELF-CENSORSHIP: People who might have doubts hide their fears or misgivings.

"MINDGUARDS": Some members of the group act as self-appointed censors to stop dissenting information or views reaching the group.

EXAMPLES OF POOR DECISIONS FROM GROUPTHINK

- The decision made by President John F. Kennedy and his advisers to launch the Bay of Pigs invasion of Cuba in 1961.

- The decision made by President Lyndon B. Johnson and his advisers between 1964 and 1967 to escalate the war in Vietnam.

- The decision made by President Richard M. Nixon and his advisers to cover up the Watergate break-in in 1972.

- The decision made by NASA in 1986 to launch the *Challenger* space shuttle (which exploded after take-off, killing all seven crew members) — see page 130.

- The decision made by NASA in 2003 to launch the space shuttle *Columbia* (which exploded over Texas upon re-entering the Earth's atmosphere, killing all seven crew members).

- The collapse of Swissair, a Swiss airline company, in 2001. Swissair is alleged to have suffered two symptoms of groupthink: the belief that the group, which was doing well, was invulnerable and the belief in the morality of the group.

- The UK-based companies Marks & Spencer and British Airways were also thought to be victims of groupthink in the 1990s. The main symptom was the illusion of invulnerability, as both companies underestimated potential failure because of years of profitability and success. During 1998–9 the price of Marks & Spencer shares fell from 590p to less than 300p and that of British Airways from 740p to 300p.

GROUPTHINK & THE CHALLENGER DISASTER

The direct cause of the *Challenger* explosion, which killed all on board, including a civilian — and was shown live on TV — was technical (faulty O-rings). But many commentators suggest that groupthink was the real reason the shuttle was allowed to take off, because the problem with the O-rings was known.

It later emerged that engineers at Morton Thiokol, the contractor responsible for building the solid rocket boosters, had vigorously opposed the launching of *Challenger*, but their warning had been disregarded by management. The engineers were concerned that the abnormally cold temperatures that January morning in 1986 would affect the O-rings and they repeatedly raised these concerns. But the mission had already been cancelled because of bad weather and, as far as NASA was concerned, another cancellation because of the weather was unthinkable — it was under enormous pressure to launch and to increase public interest in the space program, as it had been waning.

Prior to lift-off, Thiokol representatives recommended not launching until the temperature reached 53° F (12° C), but the forecast did not show temperatures reaching this baseline for several days. The chief engineer was put under enormous pressure to give the go-ahead to launch, despite his concerns. He was ordered to "take off his engineering hat and put on his management cap," suggesting that organizational goals should take priority over safety considerations. Others who raised objections about launching were threatened with expulsion from the decision-making group. Despite awareness of the problem with the O-rings, staying on schedule was seen as more crucial and the engineer reluctantly gave the go-ahead to launch.

ILLUSIONS OF UNANIMITY: Since no one is prepared to disagree publically with the prominent view, the group believes that everyone is in agreement and feels the same way.

DIRECT PRESSURE: Anyone who does try to dissent has pressure put on them and those who question the group are often seen as disloyal or traitorous.

Groupthink is most likely to occur when there is great pressure to make a decision or the group is under stress, when there is a strong, powerful leader and when the group is insulated from the outside world. These conditions were met during the fateful decision to launch the *Challenger*, as discussed on page 130.

TRY THIS:
REDUCE GROUPTHINK

The next time you are part of a group that needs to make an important decision (whether at work or elsewhere) take the following steps to ensure that you don't get caught out by groupthink:

1. Appoint a "devil's advocate" whose job is to look for flaws in arguments and assumptions made.

2. If there is a leader (or you are the leader), they should keep a low profile so as not to influence the proceedings.

3. Encourage dissenting views — ask people to look for what might go wrong with the proposed plan.

4. Bring outside experts in — and listen to them.

5. Once the decision is made, hold a "second-chance" meeting a bit later on, to provide an opportunity to rethink and to express doubts.

THEORIES OF ATTITUDES

Psychologists have long been interested in how people form their attitudes — and how they might be encouraged to change them. Attitudes are thought to be made up of three components:

AFFECTIVE COMPONENT: Feelings/emotions.

BEHAVIORAL COMPONENT: The way our attitudes influence how we act or behave.

COGNITIVE COMPONENT: Belief/knowledge.

Because attitudes so often predict behavior, it is obviously important to understand how attitudes are formed and how they can be changed. The marketing and advertising industries are particularly keen to understand this, since attitudes drive consumer behavior.

THEORIES RELATING ATTITUDES TO BEHAVIOR

Two theories are considered useful in helping to understand the relationship between attitudes and behavior:

THE THEORY OF REASONED ACTION: This theory was developed by Martin Fishbein and Icek Ajzen in 1975 in an attempt to explain how our attitudes might predict the chances of our carrying out a certain behavior or action. The theory claims that our behavioral intentions to act are influenced by our attitudes toward that behavior (which might be positive or negative) and by "subjective norms," which refers to the views that other relevant people (such as family, friends and colleagues) might have toward our performing that behavior. For example, Samir might really enjoy smoking, but he is aware that his family disapprove of his doing this — both aspects will interact and impact on his intent to smoke or not.

THE PHENOMENON OF COGNITIVE DISSONANCE

Sometimes, when behavior does not match attitudes, people may actually change their attitudes to fit with their behavior. In 1957 the American psychologist Leon Festinger identified the phenomenon of cognitive dissonance, in which a person experiences psychological discomfort through holding beliefs or attitudes that conflict with behavior; in order to reduce this tension, they may change their attitudes.

As an example of this, imagine that you just bought a new phone. The very next day a brand-new phone is released that looks so much better. But it is too late — you already have a new model and have spent ages inputting all your data and getting the settings exactly how you like them. You now hold two conflicting "cognitions": that you have a new phone and spent ages setting it up and that you now realize there is a better phone out there. This conflict — cognitive dissonance — is uncomfortable. You can resolve the conflict either by taking the phone back and getting the new phone instead (which is too much hassle) or by changing your cognitions about the attributes of the new model versus the one you have. To do this, you look for reasons to convince yourself that your phone is better after all: the screen size better suits your needs, the battery life is longer, the new model is too cumbersome. This way, you reduce the conflict by bringing the two dissonant cognitions together. Now you are happy again — yes, there is a new model but that's okay as you have convinced yourself that your phone is better for you.

THE THEORY OF PLANNED BEHAVIOR:

Proposed by Icek Ajzen in 1985, this theory evolved from the theory of reasoned action, with "perceived behavioral control" added to the mix of factors that influence intention to act in a certain way.

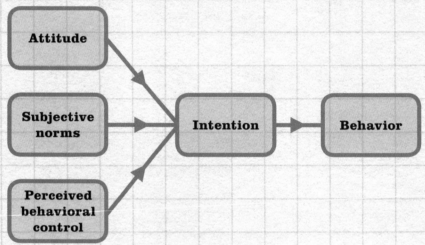

Perceived behavioral control refers to perceptions that a person may have of their ability to perform the target behavior. Thus, Sadie might want to lose weight (intention) because she believes being overweight is unhealthy (attitude). This intention might be influenced by other people such as her friends — if they are all gorging on ice cream, it might be harder for Sadie to resist (subjective norms). In addition, if Sadie believes that she is unlikely to have the willpower to go on a diet, perhaps because she has tried and failed many times in the past (perceived behavioral control), this will also adversely affect her intention to eat more healthily — and thus she will be more likely to indulge in fatty and sugary treats.

THE ELABORATION LIKELIHOOD MODEL OF PERSUASION

Attitudes can, of course, be changed and advertisements, marketing and health promotion messages aim to do just that. The elaboration likelihood model (ELM) of persuasion, developed by Richard E. Petty and John Cacioppo in the mid-1980s, describes how attitudes form and change. The model proposes two major routes to persuasion that can lead to changes in attitude or beliefs: the central route and the peripheral route.

With the central route, persuasion is likely to result from a person's careful and thoughtful consideration of the merits of the information in the persuasive message. The resulting attitude change will be relatively enduring and resistant to being changed back. The central route is used when the person receiving the message has the motivation as well as the ability to pay attention and think about the message and its topic. Thus, someone who is keen to, say, lose weight, stop smoking or try a new brand of make-up will be very receptive to the central route of persuasion.

Much of the time when we are trying to change attitudes, the people we are trying to persuade have little or no interest in being persuaded or have less ability to pay attention and process the message. Persuasion here needs to take the peripheral route, which results from how the message or the messenger makes them feel, rather than deep processing (which involves really thinking about the meaning behind the message). Thus, factors like the credibility or attractiveness of the sources of the message, or the quality of the message, can have greater influence than the actual quality of the arguments (as in the central route). This is why ads often feature celebrities or scientists in white coats. In other words, here we might be influenced more by whether we like the speaker than by the actual arguments they make. Change involving the peripheral route is likely to be temporary.

Reaching people via the central route, then, is far more conducive to lasting change in attitudes and many health campaigns attempt to do just this. One of the best ways of motivating people to take the central route is to try to make the message personally relevant to them, for example, by having the speaker be just like them (in age, gender, appearance) — this is why ads for butter or milk might feature "ordinary" housewives. Fear can also be effective in making people pay attention, which is the reason that many health campaigns rely on graphic images or concepts. (However, this can backfire if the fear is too strong, as it can stimulate the fight-or-flight response — see below.)

FIGHT-OR-FLIGHT

First described by the American physiologist Walter Cannon in 1915, the fight-or-flight response is a psychological phenomenon that occurs in response to an acute stressor: when we encounter a sudden source of stress, our body triggers a response designed to help us cope.

The response is designed to give us extra energy in the areas that matter most, especially the limbs (to enable us to run away or to stay and fight). This is why, when under severe stress, people can sometimes perform superhuman feats, like lifting a car off a trapped child. In order to transport this extra energy (in the form of blood glucose) around our body, hormones such as adrenalin are released that make our hearts pump faster to get the blood quickly to its destination. Our breathing also becomes faster and shallower in order to get oxygen quickly into our lungs. This is why, after we have had a fright, we feel shaky and breathless, with a racing heart.

The problem with the fight-or-flight response is that it is designed for occasional, short-term stressors. Nowadays, we are often under long-term stress and so are in fight-or-flight response quite often and for long periods. This causes a range of symptoms that can have adverse effects on health, such as raised blood pressure or stomach problems (as blood is diverted away from non-essential functions when we are stressed). For more about the fight-or-flight mechanism, see page 191.

QUIZ:
WHICH ROUTE SHOULD YOU USE TO PERSUADE SOMEONE?

Imagine that you want to persuade someone to do something — for example, to buy a particular product, watch a particular film or eat at a certain restaurant. Should you use the central route or the peripheral route? This quiz will help you find out!

Are they interested in the area (for example, are they asking for help choosing a film or product?) or are you trying to "cold sell" (they are not looking for information on what you are trying to persuade them about — for example, they are not planning to visit any restaurant soon)?

ARE THEY INTERESTED?

Are they paying attention to you?

YES

Do you have time to make a case?

YES

Do they feel that your message is relevant to them? (This is more likely to happen if they are interested in the area — there is no point trying to persuade them to choose one sports shirt over another if they hate sports.)

YES

Choose central route: make logical arguments and present all the facts and information.

TRYING TO COLD SELL

Are they distracted?

YES

Do you have to make your points very quickly?

YES

Is your message personally relevant to them? (For example, are you telling them about a restaurant that is not too far from where they live?)

NO

Choose peripheral route: don't bother with sound arguments; instead mention more superficial aspects such as a celebrity who has endorsed the product.

PART 3

PSYCHOLOGY EXPERIMENTS THAT CHANGED THE WORLD

AS DISCUSSED ON PAGE 39, THE METHOD USED TO ADVANCE PSYCHOLOGICAL KNOWLEDGE MOST OFTEN IS THE EXPERIMENT. SOME OF THE MOST INFLUENTIAL THEORIES OF HUMAN BEHAVIOR WERE DEVISED THROUGH SOME INGENIOUS EXPERIMENTS, MANY OF WHICH COULD NEVER BE CARRIED OUT TODAY FOR ETHICAL REASONS (SEE PAGE 183). A NUMBER OF THE BEST-KNOWN EXPERIMENTS ARE OUTLINED IN THIS SECTION.

THE EXPERIMENTS

THE STANFORD PRISON EXPERIMENT

On August, 14, 1971 psychology professor Philip Zimbardo began an experiment that is still the focus of psychological teaching, research and discussion today. Conducted at Stanford University in California, it was designed to see what would happen to people if they were given power over others — would they abuse that power? Would ordinary people become brutal and sadistic, as happened in many real prisons? How far would they take it? Could it be used to explain abuse in prisons? At the same time, Zimbardo was also interested in what changes people undergo when they are faced with authority — do they become obedient or do they rebel? One of the key aims of the study was to shed light on how much people's behavior is caused by inherent personality traits and how much by the environment they are put in.

The whole experiment was set up to resemble a prison situation in a basement at Stanford University's psychology building and Zimbardo and his team made the conditions as realistic as possible. Twenty-four male students were selected, from an initial pool of seventy-five, as being the most psychologically stable, and were randomly assigned roles of prisoner or guard for what they were told would be a period of up to two weeks. They received $15 per day.

From the start, Zimbardo designed the experiment in order to induce disorientation, depersonalization and deindividuation (loss of a person's sense of individuality and personal responsibility) in the "prisoners." The guards were not allowed to harm the prisoners physically but were permitted to control them, take away their privacy, leave them bored and frustrated, take away their individuality (for example, referring to prisoners only by number), and remove all their power or control over their situation. The guards were kitted out with batons, mirrored sunglasses (to prevent eye contact) and other uniform items.

To make the situation as real as possible, the local police department were recruited to help out and they "arrested" the prisoners at their homes and "charged" them with armed robbery. They then subjected them to full booking procedures, such as fingerprinting and mug shots. Then the process of deindividuation really began: when the prisoners arrived at the prison, they were stripped naked, deloused, had all their personal possessions removed and locked away, and given identical and uncomfortable prison-issue clothes.

Almost immediately the guards settled into their roles and started treating the prisoners with disdain, belittling them and subjecting them to petty rules and orders. They gave them boring and pointless tasks to do and generally dehumanized them. By the end, some punishments handed out were fairly brutal, such as making the prisoners use buckets as toilets (which they were not allowed to empty), having to be naked, making them sleep on concrete floors, and locking them in dark cupboards.

And the prisoners? They, too, quickly adapted to their new roles, undertaking prisoner-like behavior such as becoming overly interested in the prison rules, telling

IN THE STANFORD PRISON EXPERIMENT *props were used to make the "prison" setting as realistic as possible.*

PRISONERS AND GUARDS *both soon took on their expected roles in the experiment.*

tales on other prisoners (in order to try to gain the guard's approval, as they were so dependent on them), and becoming more and more submissive toward their powerful guards (who in turn, became more and more assertive and controlling).

The experiment was halted after six days when Christina Maslach, a recent Stanford Ph.D (later to become an eminent psychologist in her own right, as well as marrying Zimbardo), visited the "set" and was appalled by what she saw.

But the study did demonstrate that decent people will readily conform to the social roles they are expected to play, especially when there are strong stereotypes governing the expected behavior. None of the "guards" had previously demonstrated any sadistic traits, so the experiment seemed to suggest that the environment, rather than personality, was key in creating their brutal behavior. Could this even explain the actions of the suicide bombers who flew into New York's Twin Towers or those of the American torturers at Iraq's infamous Abu Ghraib prison?

The famous study was partly replicated in 2002 by British psychologists Alex Haslam and Steve Reicher for the BBC (which they called *The Experiment*). The BBC Prison Study is now taught as a core study on some UK A-level Psychology syllabi.

MILGRAM'S SHOCK STUDIES

Still on the subject of obedience to authority, if you were told to administer an electric shock to another person, what would you do? Refuse? What if the person ordering you to do this were an eminent psychologist in a white coat — and they are telling you that you must do this? Most of us probably think we would not obey and, indeed, it is likely that in today's society, where there is less emphasis on blindly following orders (perhaps as a result of experiments like those described in this section), we wouldn't. But in 1961 times were different and, following Milgram's shock studies, they would probably never be quite the same again.

The Milgram experiment was designed to investigate obedience to authority figures and was conducted by American psychologist Stanley Milgram (1933–84). The series of experiments were designed to understand how willing people would be to obey someone in authority who ordered them to take action that would appear to inflict pain on others. Milgram's work was reported in 1963 in an article published in the *Journal of Abnormal and Social Psychology*, while his 1974 book, *Obedience to Authority: An Experimental View*, expanded on the experiments and findings.

When the experiments first commenced in the summer of 1961, it was three months after the start of the trial of the infamous German Nazi Adolf Eichmann in Jerusalem. U.S.-born Milgram — who had Jewish immigrant parents and acknowledged that if his parents had not emigrated from Prague, he might have been one of Hitler's victims — wanted to know if Eichmann and his accomplices were just following orders, as was often claimed. He designed his experiment to see if ordinary people could be made to inflict pain on others if ordered to by someone in authority.

The study was made up of a "teacher" and a "learner." The teacher was the experimental subject whose behavior Milgram was interested in, while the learner was an accomplice who would pretend to feel pain at the supposed electric shocks the teacher was told to administer.

The teacher was given a list of word pairs for the task and they were told to read the first word of each pair and four possible answers to the learner. The learner then had to press a button to indicate which of the four options they had selected as the answer. If the learner gave the wrong answer, the teacher was ordered to administer a "shock" to the learner, with the voltage increasing in 15-volt increments for each wrong answer. If they gave the correct answer, the teacher would then read the next word pair from the list. The teachers believed that they were administering actual painful shocks. In reality, there were no shocks in Milgram's experiment.

After a few supposed increases in the level of shocks given, the learner began to bang on the cubicle wall, but the teacher was ordered to continue the study. After several times banging on the wall, the learner then started to complain about their heart condition. After this the learner became quiet.

At this point, many of the teachers who took part were clearly alarmed and wanted to check on the learner. Some wanted to stop the experiment, questioning its purpose. However, most continued after being assured by the white-coated experimenter that they would not be held responsible — and many resumed after simply being told that they must continue.

Before conducting the experiment, Milgram had surveyed Yale University psychology majors, psychiatrists and his colleagues, asking them to predict the behavior of the teachers. He found that most believed that very few subjects would be prepared to inflict the maximum voltage.

However, 65 percent of the subjects administered the experiment's final, (supposedly) massive, 450-volt shock, although many were clearly very unhappy doing so. The study showed how hard it is not to obey authority when ordered to do so, even when pain is apparently being inflicted.

Milgram's research has spawned countless spin-off studies among psychologists and has even entered into the realm of pop culture. It has inspired songs including Peter Gabriel's "We Do What We're Told (Milgram's 37)" and Dar Williams's "Buzzer"; a French television game — "Le jeu de la mort" (The Game of Death); episodes of the television shows Law and Order and Bones; a made-for-television movie with William Shatner; and the biopic The Experimenter, starring Peter Sarsgaard as Stanley Milgram.

PSYCHOLOGY EXPERIMENTS
ASCH CONFORMITY STUDIES

Imagine that you sign up for a psychology experiment at your local university. You meet the other participants and await instructions. You are to be given two cards — on one is a single vertical line and on the other are three straight, vertical lines of varying lengths, labeled A, B and C. Your task is to match the single line with the one of the three that is equal length — easy!

The study begins and each of the participants calls out the letter of the line that they think matches the single line. Your turn is last. There is always a line that is clearly the same length and you find the task easy. Suddenly, things start getting uncomfortable. On the third trial, you see that line C is exactly the same length as the target line, but the other participants call out A. You are puzzled — surely anyone can see that C is the correct answer. What do you do? Do you have the courage of your convictions and call out C or do you follow the crowd and go for A?

This was exactly what happened in Solomon Asch's famous 1951 conformity experiments, which changed the way we view conformity and group pressures. He based his line study on Muzafer Sherif's (1906–88) conformity study that used the

SOLOMON ASCH *was famous for his studies on conformity and group pressure — and in particular, what it took for individuals to stand firm in the face of an opposing majority.*

autokinetic effect (see page 147). Sherif found that people's estimate of movement on the dot of light could be influenced by the majority view. Asch wanted to replicate the study using judgments that were objective rather than subjective.

Asch (1907–96) was interested in the extent to which social pressure from a majority group could influence a person to conform.

Asch wanted to see how many people would conform when the answer was obviously wrong. To this end, each participant was placed in a room with seven others who the participants believed to be like them but were, in fact, accomplices of Asch and were primed to give the same wrong response each time.

Over the 12 trials with 50 participants, about 75 percent conformed (gave the obviously incorrect answer) at least once, while only 25 percent of participants never conformed. Afterwards those who conformed to the majority (but obviously incorrect) view were asked why they ignored the evidence in front of their eyes — most explained that they were fearful of being ridiculed by the others. They wanted to fit in (which became known as "normative influence") and in some cases they felt that the others must know something that they did not (termed

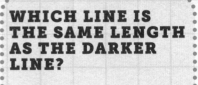

WHICH LINE IS THE SAME LENGTH AS THE DARKER LINE?

A B C

"informational influence"). Both these influences were thus shown to affect the likelihood of conformity.

Asch carried out variations of his original study in order to uncover other factors that might influence the extent to which people conform to majority influence. For example, he found that the presence of one other person in the group giving the correct answer caused a massive drop in conformity — having an ally is clearly a great protection against group pressures of the majority. He also found that if he made the lines more similar to the target line so that the task was harder, conformity increased, suggesting that when we are unsure, we look to others for guidance.

TRY THIS:
CREATE THE AUTOKINETIC EFFECT

In a dark room, very small movements of the eyes will make a pinprick of light appear to move, because the eyes lack a stable frame of reference — this is known as the autokinetic effect. To try this out for yourself, make a pinprick in a piece of card and then go into a completely darkened room. Put a flashlight against the card so that the light shines through the hole and onto the wall. Gaze at the wall — you will notice the pinpoint of light appearing to move.

THE CASE OF LITTLE ALBERT

The Little Albert experiment was published in 1920 by John B. Watson (who we met on page 16 in relation to behaviorism) and has been extremely influential in aiding our understanding of classical conditioning (see page 97). The aim of the study was to condition fear in a child by associating something that naturally caused anxiety (loud noises) with a previously neutral stimulus. This was to show how fears and phobias can be learned.

A 9-month-old baby called Albert, who was regarded as psychologically healthy, was recruited for this study from the Johns Hopkins University hospital where Watson worked. Watson established that the child was happy to play with a range of objects such as a white rabbit, a rat, a dog, a monkey, masks and cotton wool without any fear. For the experiment, he placed the baby on the floor and allowed him to play happily with a white rat. Whenever he touched the rat, Watson and his colleagues struck a metal bar with a hammer out of sight of Albert — naturally, this caused an extreme fear reaction, which was shown by his crying and distress.

After a while, Watson found that the white rat alone, without the loud noise, was enough to produce the fear response in Little Albert. The baby boy had associated the white rat (originally a neutral stimulus, now a conditioned stimulus) with the loud noise (an unconditioned stimulus) and was producing the fearful or emotional response of crying (originally the unconditioned response to the noise, now the conditioned response to the rat). This is the same kind of classical conditioning as Pavlov had used in his experiments with dogs (see page 97).

JOHN B. WATSON *was able to condition Little Albert's new fear of rats to be generalized to other furry objects, including rabbits and even a Santa beard.*

Little Albert seemed to generalize his fear to other furry objects so that when Watson sent a non-white rabbit into the room some days later, Albert also became distressed. He showed similar reactions when presented with a furry dog and a sealskin coat, and even when Watson appeared in front of him wearing a Santa Claus mask with a white cotton-wool beard.

Watson used his findings to expound on his theories of learning, but Little Albert was never desensitized from his fear. It is not known what happened to the child after his mother (who some say did not consent to the experiments) took him away from the hospital, although there have been many attempts recently to identify him. In 2009, psychologists Hall P. Beck and Sharman Levinson published an article in which they claimed to have discovered the true identity of "Albert B," claiming that it was a pseudonym for Douglas Merritte, the son of Arvilla Merritte, then a woman who appears to have been a wet nurse at the Harriet Lane Home on the university campus. Sadly, Douglas died at the age of 6 years of acquired hydrocephalus.

Other researchers later contested the claim that Douglas was Albert and instead suggested that a William Barger (known as Albert), who died in 2007 at the age of 87, was the real Little Albert. Barger seemed to meet many of the criteria identified from Watson's records — and he had a lifelong fear of dogs.

THE CASE OF LITTLE HANS

Like the case of Little Albert, that of Little Hans also revolved around a phobia — only this time it was not induced as part of an experiment. In fact, it was an attempt by Sigmund Freud, the father of psychoanalysis (whom we met on page 31), to treat Little Hans's apparent horse phobia that led to this infamous case.

In 1909 Freud published a summary of his treatment of Little Hans, in "Analysis of a Phobia in a Five-year-old Boy," in which he developed his theory of the Oedipus complex (see page 152), which he used to explain the little boy's anxiety around horses.

Freud never actually held any therapy sessions with Hans, but instead worked through correspondence with his father, who was a friend. Very familiar with Freud's theories, he had written to Freud because he considered that Hans might be of interest to him. Hans's father appeared to first contact Freud when the child was 3 years old and, according to the letters, developed an active interest in his "widdler" (penis) and also in those of other people; this led to his mother threatening him that if he were to continue to touch his penis, she would summon the doctor to come and cut it off.

When the boy was about 5 years old, Hans's father wrote to Freud that Hans was afraid that a horse might bite him. He lived in a busy street and had witnessed several frightening episodes involving accidents with horses. Because of his phobia, Hans became reluctant to leave the house. He seemed particularly to fear white horses with dark areas around the mouth that wore blinkers, which Freud concluded represented his father (who had a black moustache and wore glasses).

Freud's interpretation was that Hans was afraid that the horse (which represented his father) would bite (symbolism for castrate) him in order to punish him for his sexual feelings toward his mother. Hans's phobia of horses began to fade around the time of two significant fantasies that he had. In the first, Hans

had several imaginary children and claimed that the mother of these children was his own mother and that the grandfather of the children was his own father. In the second fantasy, Hans imagined that a plumber had somehow removed his bottom and penis and replaced them with larger versions. Freud

LITTLE HANS'S *fears all began with a phobia of horses.*

considered that his Oedipus complex became resolved when Hans's fantasies involved his having a large penis like his father's and he himself was married to his mother; his father did exist in these fantasies but in the role of grandfather.

THE OEDIPUS COMPLEX

Little Hans is a famous case study illustrating the Oedipus complex. Sigmund Freud coined this term to refer to a sexual desire for the parent of the opposite sex in both male and female children. Freud believed there were five "psychosexual" stages of development and the Oedipus complex occurred in the third stage, at around the ages of 3–6 years.

The five stages are the following:

1. THE ORAL STAGE: From birth to about 15 months, when gratification is obtained via the mouth (eating, crying etc).

2. THE ANAL STAGE: From about 15 months to 3 years, when the focus of gratification shifts from the mouth to the anus as the child experiences pleasure and control from the elimination of feces.

3. THE PHALLIC STAGE: From 3 to 6 years, when children take an increasing interest in their own genitals and show a curiosity about other people's bodies.

4. THE LATENT STAGE: From 6 years to puberty, when there is a repression of drives.

5. THE GENITAL STAGE: From puberty.

In classical Freudian psychoanalytic theory, a child's identification with the same-sex parent is the successful resolution of the Oedipus complex and is a key psychological experience that is necessary for the development of a mature sexual role and identity. He further proposed that boys and girls experience the complexes differently: boys in a form of castration anxiety and girls in a form of penis envy.

Freud used the case of Little Hans to demonstrate that the child's fear of horses was related to his Oedipus complex. Freud believed that, during the phallic stage, a boy develops strong sexual feelings toward his mother. This leads to him viewing his father as a rival and can even lead to the boy subconsciously wanting to get rid of him. However, the father is far bigger and stronger than the young boy, and so the child becomes fearful that his father, seeing the child as a rival, will castrate him. (Hans's father later reassured him that this would not happen, which seemed to help.)

Freud believed that Hans was a normal little boy undergoing normal development. Indeed, when Hans was 19, he met Freud and appeared psychologically healthy. But he will for ever be known as the little boy who was unwittingly used, in the first recorded case of psychoanalysis undertaken with a child, to demonstrate Freud's theories.

OEDIPUS *was a mythical Greek king who, in killing his father and marrying his mother, lent his name to the psychological condition, the Oedipus complex*

LITTLE HANS GREW UP TO BE HERBERT GRAF, A SUCCESSFUL OPERA PRODUCER AT NEW YORK'S METROPOLITAN OPERA, THE SALZBURG FESTIVAL, LONDON'S ROYAL OPERA HOUSE AND OTHERS. HE DIED IN 1973.

HARLOW'S MONKEY EXPERIMENTS

On page 112 we examined attachment theories that explain how children develop strong emotional bonds with their caregivers. As outlined there, John Bowlby and Mary Ainsworth were two of the most prominent theorists in the field, but there is another psychologist whose controversial experiments added greatly to our understanding of what happens when attachment does not take place. Harry Harlow's famous monkey experiments were designed to see what happens to baby monkeys (the closest to human babies, who couldn't be used for obvious reasons) when they were deprived of a loving mother.

Harry Harlow (1905–81) was an American psychologist who conducted most of his research at the University of Wisconsin–Madison. In 1932 he established a breeding colony of rhesus macaques in order to study cognitive processes. During the experiments, in which the infant monkeys were separated from their mothers, Harlow noticed that although he and his team quickly became

accomplished at taking care of the physical needs of their infant monkeys, the nursery-reared infants were clearly very different from their peers that had been reared by their mothers. They were reclusive, did not interact with other monkeys, seemed to have social deficits (such as showing excessive fear or aggression) and they clung to their cloth diapers. Harlow decided to investigate the mother–infant bond. He wanted to know whether the attachment that an infant has to its mother is due mainly to the nourishment she provides or whether the nourishment is not as important as the comfort and love offered.

Harlow tested this by creating inanimate surrogate mothers for the rhesus monkeys using wire and wood. He found that each infant became attached to its particular inanimate mother, apparently recognizing its face and preferring its own "mother" over all the other ones. Harlow next decided to investigate whether the baby monkeys preferred the clothless bare-wire mothers or the softer cloth-covered mothers — and

THE BABY MONKEYS *cuddled up to the cloth "mothers" most of the time, only leaving them for food or to explore briefly.*

how vital it was for the surrogate mother to be a source of food. For this experiment he presented the infants with both a cloth mother and a plain wire mother in two crucial scenarios. In the first scenario, the wire mother was arranged so that a bottle with food was attached to her, while the cloth mother did not hold a bottle. In the other condition it was the cloth mother who held the bottle, while the wire mother did not.

Overwhelmingly, the baby monkeys preferred spending their time cuddling up to the cloth mother. Even in the scenario where it was only the wire mother who could provide nourishment, the monkeys went to her just to feed, returning to cling to the cloth mother. They spent about 17 hours a day on the cloth mother and only 1 hour a day in total on the wire one. Harlow concluded that there was much more to the mothe-iinfant relationship than nourishment and that young monkeys and humans also require "contact comfort" or "tactile comfort" in order to develop properly.

Successive experiments showed that infants would use the cloth mother as a base from which to explore, but if they were frightened by a loud noise or a strange object (for which purpose Harlow created a scary mechanized creature — referring to it as a "diabolical object" — that moved, flapped and was very loud), they would rush back to the cloth mother. In other words, they became attached to the warmth and comfort offered by the cloth mother, rather than to the food offered by the cold, hard, wire mother.

THE BABY MONKEYS *only went to the wire mother to feed, preferring the cloth mother for comfort.*

In one experiment, Harlow placed monkeys that had been weaned from wire mothers in a new (and thus frightening) environment. When the cloth mother was there, they ran to her for comfort, but when only the wire mother was there, they ran to a cloth diaper for comfort. This again shows the importance of comfort, offered by a soft, tactile presence, over a mere provider of nutrition.

The infants raised only with the wire mother did not develop normally; they did not grow as well, were unable to interact, seemed to be very nervous and could not mate easily as adults. The females that did mate were inadequate mothers.

Harlow's experiments (published in 1958 in a paper called "The Nature of Love") were controversial. They included rearing infant monkeys in isolation chambers for up to 24 months, from which they emerged severely disturbed. Some even credit the rise of the animal liberation movement in the United States to public reaction to these experiments.

Harlow's studies also changed the way that child-rearing was viewed. Previously, many people had believed that children required physical care in the main and that excessive emotional care would "spoil" them. The mother's role was seen as simply a provider of food, not comfort. In addition, Harlow was ahead of his time when he postulated that the child's emotional needs might also be met by their father, not just by their mother. Harlow's experiments changed the way children were reared in nurseries, orphanages, and hospitals — the warmth and physical comfort from a caregiver became just as vital as the food they provide.

Another example of changes that can be associated with Harlow's studies is the development of "kangaroo care." This approach means that premature babies, who spend most of their early days attached to machines in cribs, are allowed to have as much skin-to-skin contact with their mothers as possible.

PSYCHOLOGY EXPERIMENTS
THE BOBO DOLL EXPERIMENT

In the 1960s, as televisions became standard household items, many social commentators started to become worried about the influences that were being beamed into our homes (concerns that have probably not diminished much since then). The hugely influential series of studies known as the Bobo doll experiment aimed to address the question of whether children learn to be aggressive by seeing others being aggressive. Could violent and aggressive television shows and films make children more aggressive?

The studies were conducted by Albert Bandura, whom we met on page 32 (where he was cited as the fourth-most influential psychologist of the 20th century) and on page 101 in connection with his social learning theory. Bandura was of the view that most behavior was learned rather than caused by genetic factors and he wanted to show that aggression can be learned rather than being the result of innate personality factors. The Bobo doll was an inflatable figure, about 5ft (1.5m) tall, that was designed to bounce back to upright when it was knocked over.

Bandura and his colleagues selected children aged 3–6 years to take part in the experiments. They tried to select children without obviously aggressive traits by asking the children's teachers to rate their personalities. There were three groups in this study: a control group, an "aggressive" group and a "non-aggressive" group. Each child was taken, on their own, into a room containing a variety of toys, including a Bobo doll.

In the control group they were simply allowed to play. In the aggressive group, while the child was playing, an adult would be interacting with the Bobo doll in the corner – attacking the doll with a hammer. In the non-aggressive group, the adult would also be there but would be playing calmly with the toys.

The child was then subjected to a manipulation designed to induce feelings of aggression – they were shown some lovely toys but told that the toys were reserved for other children, so they were not allowed to play with them. After that, the child was taken into another room containing a variety of toys, including the

Bobo doll and a hammer and was observed. As expected, a child who had seen the adult attacking the doll would also behave aggressively.

The studies showed that young children who see an adult behaving aggressively are likely to copy this behavior, perhaps because the adult normalizes it. The studies also challenged the accepted view at the time that rewards and punishments were the most important contribution to learning.

The studies are thought to have implications for the role that screen violence might play in making children grow into aggressive adults. However, there have been numerous criticisms of the Bobo doll experiments that cast some doubts on the conclusions drawn.

THE CHILDREN who witnessed adults behaving aggressively toward the Bobo doll were more likely to emulate their behavior and display violence themselves.

The criticisms include the following:

THE BODO DOLL EXPERIMENT *could also suggest a link between playing violent video games and violent behavior.*

● As the doll bounced back up, the children may have seen the hitting of it as a game rather than an act of violence.

● Hitting a doll is very different to hitting a real person and the one may not suggest the other.

● The setting of the study was laboratory-based and thus might not generalize to real life. In addition, the children who took part in the study were all from the same nursery and thus had similar backgrounds, which might reduce the validity of the experiment in terms of its generalizability.

● No follow-up studies were conducted so it is not known whether the "aggressive" children remained aggressive in other spheres or for a longer time period than the "non-aggressive" children. (This has ethical implications, of course — see page 183.)

For these reasons, the questions that Bandura tried to address are still being widely debated and the impact of violent video games, for example, on children's development is still not entirely understood.

BLUE EYES–BROWN EYES EXPERIMENT

On an April evening in 1968, American teacher Jane Elliott switched on her television and was shocked to hear of the assassination of Martin Luther King, Jr. He had led the civil rights movement in the United States from the mid-1950s and was instrumental in ending the legal segregation of African–American citizens in the South and other areas of the United States. His assassination led to widespread debates about racism and, as a teacher, Jane Elliott felt this was something she should bring to her classroom.

The following day, she had a class discussion about Martin Luther King and racism. But she felt that she was not really getting through to her pupils and that they failed to grasp the issues; most of Elliott's 8-year-old students were, like her, white and had lived in Riceville, a small town in Iowa where few black people lived,

MARTIN LUTHER KING, JR'S *assassination led teacher Jane Elliott to devise her famous blue eyes-brown eyes experiment.*

their whole lives. She felt that just having a class discussion about racism would not be enough for the class to really understand how easily racism can grow and what effects it can have.

So Elliott devised an intriguing experiment that she hoped would show the children what racism was like and how easy it was to become racist. Since all the children were white, she needed to use something other than skin color to create the two "races" — she selected eye color. Proclaiming that all the blue-eyed children were superior to the brown-eyed, Elliott explained to the class that from then on, those with blue eyes would get extra privileges such as extra helpings at lunch, access to the new playground equipment and extra playtime at break. The blue-eyed children were also told to sit in the front of the classroom, with the brown-eyed children at the back. The blue-eyed children were only permitted to interact and play with other blue-eyed children and they were encouraged to ignore their brown-eyed peers. Elliott even stopped the blue-eyed children from using the same drinking fountain as the brown-eyed ones.

She was interested to see how the children would react to the unfair system she was imposing, based on something as random as eye color. At first, the children did not want to accept that the blue-eyed children were in anyway superior to the brown-eyed ones. To address this, Elliott came up with a plausible explanation to justify the differences; she lied to the children by claiming that the melanin that causes eyes to be blue is also linked to higher intelligence. She made the brown-eyed children wear special collars to denote their lowly status.

Before long, the children adapted to their new roles as either "superior" or "inferior" and they quickly adopted discriminatory behaviors. Those who were labeled superior soon acted in superior ways; they became arrogant, bossy and were rather nasty to their "inferior" classmates. They did better in class tests and they even managed to accomplish math and reading tasks that had seemed beyond their ability previously. Some even began to use the term "brown eyes" in a derogatory way, to insult their "inferior" peers. Elliott famously stated that her lovely, cooperative, kind young charges became nasty, discriminating bigots in around 15 minutes.

The "inferior" classmates also changed – into timid and subservient children who scored lower on tests and even during break-time kept to their own group. Even those children who had previously been popular and "dominant" in the class hierarchy seemed to accept their inferior status in the experiment. Even their academic performance suffered.

As news of the experiment spread, Elliott began to appear on television shows and started to repeat the exercise during professional training days for adults aimed at highlighting prejudice (thus becoming one of the first to invent the concept of diversity-training). In 1971, the American Broadcasting Company (ABC) aired a documentary about Elliott called *The Eye of the Storm*, making her even better known nationally. Subsequently, William Peters wrote two books — *A Class Divided* and *A Class Divided: Then and Now* — about her and the exercise.

In 1985 the schoolchildren featured in *The Eye of the Storm* (for which Elliott received the coveted Hillman Prize, which is a journalism award for those who pursue social justice) were reunited for a PBS Frontline documentary, *A Class Divided*. A televised edition of the exercise entitled *The Event: How Racist Are You?* was shown in the UK in 2009.

THE MARSHMALLOW EXPERIMENTS

Here is one classic psychology study that you can try out for yourself, if you have children under the age of 5 and a bag of marshmallows. Simply present your child with a lovely, squishy, pink or white marshmallow and tell them that they can either have this now or, if they wait half an hour, they can instead have two. Which will they choose, instant or delayed gratification?

This was the basis of the marshmallow experiments that took place at Stanford University in the late 1960s and early 1970s led by psychologist Walter Mischel. The simple studies had far-reaching consequences, because a child's performance on this test at age 4 is said to predict how they will behave in the future.

In Mischel's original experiment, he had preschoolers sit on their own in an empty room and offered them the choice of having a marshmallow (or Oreo cookie or pretzel, according to preference) right away or if they waited until he returned, having two as a reward for waiting. The child was left alone with the marshmallow for 15 minutes. Mischel wanted to test their self-control and see what happened as a result of their conflict between immediate gratification and delayed gratification. He found that many children tried very hard to fight the temptation and to hold out for the double reward; they turned their chairs away so they couldn't see the marshmallow, sang songs, covered their eyes, stroked the marshmallow and used other distancing or distracting techniques. Other children simply ate the marshmallow straight away. Of the 600 children studied, only 200 children managed to resist temptation until the investigator returned.

What was particularly stunning about the original marshmallow studies was that Mischel followed these children over the following 50 years — and was shocked at what he discovered. In general, the delayed-gratification group of children (who had had the self-control to wait for two marshmallows) had lower BMI (body mass index, which indicates obesity), a lower rate of addiction (such as to smoking), a lower divorce rate and higher SAT (intelligence) scores over the course of their life. They were more likely to be able to deal with stress, overcome frustrations and pursue goals.

Walter Mischel's studies have been tremendously influential. You can buy "Don't Eat the Marshmallow!" T-shirts and books such as *Don't Eat the Marshmallow — Yet! The Secret to Sweet Success in Work and Life*. The television series *Sesame Street* created episodes where the Cookie Monster learns delayed gratification so he can join the Cookie Connoisseurs' Club. Investment companies have even used the marshmallow test to encourage retirement planning.

SESAME STREET'S COOKIE MONSTER *was obliged to savor the smell and texture of a cookie before gobbling it down — an act that required huge amounts of self-control in order to obtain far greater (but delayed) gratification — as part of his initiation into the Cookie Connisseurs' Club.*

IF YOUR CHILD "FAILS" THE MARSHMALLOW TEST

Don't panic if your child gobbles up the marshmallow immediately — their life is not doomed! Some commentators argue that the test is flawed in some respects because the children don't know how long they have to wait for the investigator to return — and even if they did know, 15 minutes is difficult for a child of 4 years to estimate. Perhaps their strategy of a known reward now is better than that of a bigger reward at some unknown point in the future.

Some studies have also shown that children who have experienced upheaval or unpredictability in their lives tended to eat the first marshmallow and that this is perfectly rational for them since only the first marshmallow is certain. This then has nothing to do with willpower.

Another point to consider is how many other treats your child has access to. A child who knows that they will be getting a cupcake or chocolate cookie soon may see no reason to wait for an extra sweet now. Some children may also have learned that promises are not always kept or that treats can be taken away (for example, by siblings or older children), so they might grab what they can now while they have the chance. None of these is to do with self-control or willpower; in fact, they suggest that the child may be making the more rational choice.

THE ROBBERS CAVE STUDY

In 1954, a summer camp in Robbers Cave State Park, Oklahoma, was attended by 22 boys, aged 11, who did not know that they were about to take part in what was to become one of the most famous experiments in intergroup conflict and prejudice. The researcher was the Turkish–American social psychologist Muzafer Sherif (1906–88).

Prior to the trip, the boys, who were from similar backgrounds but did not know each other, were split into two groups. During the three-week camp, they encountered camp staff who, unbeknown to them, were researchers. When the boys arrived at the camp the two groups were kept totally separate from each other and, in fact, were unaware of the existence of the other group. Bonds were encouraged among the members of a group through exercises that required the pursuit of common goals and through activities like hiking and swimming. Each group developed its own culture, friendships and norms in this first week. They developed

THE ROBBERS CAVE STUDY *utilized a real summer camp for 11-year-old boys in Oklahoma in 1954.*

leaders and a strong identity and they also chose names for their groups — The Eagles and The Rattlers.

At this point, Sherif allowed the groups to become aware of each other's existence and he began to develop friction and competition between the two groups. Competitive activities (such as baseball and tug-of-war) were arranged, with a trophy being awarded to the winning team. There were also individual prizes for the winning group such as a medal and a pocket knife — but no consolation prizes for the "losers." Sherif also created situations in which one group would enjoy benefits at the expense of the other group. For example, when both groups were attending a picnic, one group was delayed and when they arrived, found that the other group had eaten all of the food.

The campers made great efforts to improve their abilities and to proclaim their own group as the superior one. They became territorial over what they perceived to be their own areas, such as the places where they had gone swimming or had built dens, making comments such as "they'd better not come here." They tried to plant their flags in strategic places to mark out their territory and started to make disparaging comments about the other team. There was clearly an immediate division between "us" and "them."

However, as the competition wore on, the negative attitudes toward the other group became more extreme; flags were burnt, cabins ransacked, beds overturned and property stolen. They expressed very negative attitudes toward members of the opposing team — and very favourable attitudes toward those in their own group. They refused to eat in the same room and the groups became so physically aggressive toward each other that the camp staff were forced to intervene.

The Robbers Cave study showed how easy it is for prejudice and intergroup conflict to develop between well-adjusted, middle-class and well-brought-up boys. The studies were seen as an analogy for

THE INTENSE RIVALRIES of the Robbers Cave study might also shed light on other intergroup rivalries such as those between football clubs — and how such rivalry can descend into aggression.

conflict across the globe, demonstrating how competition can easily escalate into aggression. The experiment is even thought to shed light on racial tensions and explains how, in times of scarce resources such as employment (and thus competition for those resources), tensions often increase.

Sherif was also interested in whether methods could be employed that would reduce the conflict that he had created at Robbers Cave. He tried to do this by giving the two groups activities to share, such as watching movies, but this had little effect on reducing the intergroup conflict. He then took a new approach, which was to provide problems for the boys to solve; for example, he sabotaged the water supply

and encouraged the boys to find a way to fix it. This approach was far more successful and the boys did work together to solve the problem. Sherif created several more such "problems" for the boys to solve and the boys worked together toward their goals. They began eating together again and even chose to return home at the end of the camp in the same bus.

Sherif claimed that this showed how intergroup conflict can be reduced via the need for cooperation to achieve shared goals. His studies have had far-reaching implications over the years since his findings were first published.

ADRENALIN STUDY

On page 102 we met emotion theorists Stanley Schachter and Jerome E. Singer and learned about their two-factor theory of emotion. They proved their theory with the so-called adrenalin or suproxin study, which has become a staple of psychology textbooks.

Imagine, once again, that you have agreed to take part in a psychology study at your local university, but this time you are asked if you will consent to being given an injection, by a doctor, of a vitamin called suproxin. The researchers explain to you that they want to test the effects of this vitamin on vision. You agree to proceed.

After you are given the injection, you are led to a waiting room while the vitamin enters your bloodstream. While you are waiting, another participant enters and, after a while, starts getting angry about the wait. Do you get angry, too?

The answer to that will depend on what you have been told about the side effects of the "vitamin" injection (which, in the original study, was not a vitamin at all).

In Schachter and Singer's 1962 study, this is exactly what happened. The "vitamin" was actually a shot of adrenalin. As many people are aware, adrenalin produces a range of symptoms, such as raised blood pressure, increased heart rate, sweaty palms and shallow breathing. Produced naturally by the body as part of the fight-or-flight response (see page 136),

THE PARTICIPANTS THOUGHT *they were just waiting for the study to start, not realizing that what happened in the waiting room was the study.*

adrenalin is designed to increase the rate at which oxygen-rich blood sends energy around the body in order to stay and fight or to run away from a threat.

The researchers then varied what information they gave to the participants about the effects of the injection:

INFORMED GROUP: If you had been in this group, you would have been told exactly what symptoms to expect from the "vitamin" injection.

IGNORANT GROUP: As a member of this group, you would have been told nothing about any side effects from the injection.

MISINFORMED GROUP: Here, you would have been warned about side effects, but given the wrong information about what these would be; for example, you might have been told that the injection would make you itch or give you a headache. The aim of the study was not, of course, to study vision. The real purpose was to see what happens if physiological changes that are compatible with a strong emotion are secretly induced. Would people label these changes as an emotional response if they had no other explanation for them? And conversely, if they did have an explanation for the changes in their body, would they have no reason to label them as an emotional response?

The results showed that when the participants were placed with the angry accomplice in the waiting room (of course, he was a stooge), those in the informed group tended not to get angry. Those in the ignorant and misinformed groups, however, were more likely to feel some anger.

The reason for these findings (which were replicated using a "happy" stooge to try to induce happiness, too) is that when people have a ready explanation for any arousal (in this case, the ready explanation for the informed group was the injection), they will not attribute that arousal to an emotion. In the absence of an explanation for the arousal that they are experiencing (in the ignorant group and misinformed group), they will cast around for a reason to account for their physical sensations. Seeing someone else being angry over something that they too are experiencing (such as a long wait), they conclude that they must be feeling angry as well.

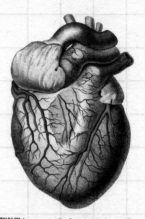

ADRENALIN *increases the heart rate to send more oxygen-rich blood pumping around the body.*

This effect, when we mistakenly think that the source of our arousal is an emotion rather than something else, is called the misattribution of arousal (see right). It can work the opposite way, too, when we ignore an emotional experience because we think there is a physical explanation for the sensations we experience. This often happens with people who suffer from panic attacks (see page 201). They believe that the physical symptoms they are experiencing are caused by some catastrophic event in their body (say, a heart attack) and fail to consider the alternative and correct explanation — that they are produced by the emotion of anxiety.

MISATTRIBUTION OF AROUSAL

At one time or another, most of us will have experienced the symptoms of a racing heart, palpitations, a dry mouth, sweaty palms and a feeling of breathlessness. We will attribute these sensations to different causes, depending on the circumstances.

For example, if you have just run for a bus, you will put them down to the exertion of running. If you have just narrowly escaped being hit by a bus, you will attribute the sensations to a feeling of shock.

This shows how we look for a ready explanation in order to account for physical sensations.

SOCIAL PRIMING STUDY

Compared with many of the other experiments discussed in this section, this one is relatively modern. In 1996 John Bargh and his colleagues at New York University wanted to test whether exposing elderly people to words associated with being old would make them walk slower and in a more "elderly" way. The study involved asking elderly participants to indicate which word was the odd one out within a puzzle of scrambled words, a number of which, when rearranged, form a sentence. Unbeknown to the participants, the word left out of the sentence was related to the concept of "being old."

Cunningly, the experimenters watched the participants walk away from the laboratory at the end and compared their speed with that of a control group who were not exposed to "elderly" words. The experimenters who were doing

SLOW, WEAK, FRAGILE, AGED

the measuring did not know which participants had been "primed" and which had not (they were "blind" to the study's conditions). The participants exposed to the "elderly" words walked out more slowly. Furthermore, the effect was claimed to occur without awareness, as participants were found not to have noticed the link between the words and their walking speed.

This is a test of "social priming," which refers to the way an environment or context (such as what we read or see, smell or feel) can activate current or even later behavior. Bargh's study showed that making people think about aging and thus activating the "trait construct," or stereotype that older people walk more slowly actually makes them feel older and act older. What is more, this priming occurs without conscious awareness.

It should be noted that Bargh's studies created quite a stir in the psychological arena because some psychologists tried to replicate the findings and failed. This has led to ongoing debates about social priming, with many arguing that social priming effects are exaggerated.

TRY IT:
EXPERIMENT WITH SOCIAL PRIMING

Try your own social priming experiment. You can subconsciously prime people to feel kind or not by giving them something to read about kindness or perhaps telling them a story about an act of kindness that you performed recently. Now ask them to sponsor you or donate to a charity box. Repeat the study with a different group of friends but this time give them something neutral to read or tell them a neutral story. Again, ask them to donate money, either to a charity box or by sponsoring you. It is likely that the people that you "primed" by suggesting kindness will donate more.

In fact, you can even prime people to be kind by *telling* them that they are kind. Try this: ask for donations to a charity box in two different conditions — in one condition you tell the person that you are asking them because you know they are kind and in the other condition you say nothing. Who will give the most?

"LOST IN THE MALL" FALSE-MEMORY STUDY

The American cognitive psychologist Elizabeth Loftus (b. 1944) has carried out pioneering work on false memories and this 1995 study is one of her best known. In this study, Loftus and her colleagues gave 24 participants a number of stories to read describing childhood events that supposedly had happened to them — the participants were told that the stories had been provided by their family members (whose details they submitted in advance). The participants were asked to try to remember as much detail about these stories as possible for the study, which they were told was examining memory of childhood events.

What the participants did not know was that only three of the stories were provided by their family members — the fourth one was an invented tale about how the participant had got lost in a shopping mall at around the age of 5 years. The story described how they were missing for quite a long time and were eventually found by an elderly person and reunited

safely with their family. To make the story sound as genuine as possible, real details from the participant's life were incorporated — for example, locations and the actual mall that they were likely to have frequented as a child.

After they had read the stories, the participants were required to recall what they remembered from the stories in written format. They were then interviewed and questioned about the events in the stories. The study showed that 25 percent of the participants claimed that they could remember the false event actually happening to them, although the memory was weaker than for real events and they used fewer words to describe it than for the events that really happened.

After the study ended, the participants were told that one of the four stories had not actually happened to them and were asked to identify which the false story might have been. A fifth of them were unable to correctly identify which one of the stories was false.

Loftus used this study to demonstrate the existence of false memories and how such memories can be created (specifically, by incorporating them into events that really did happen). With the passing of time, people find it increasingly difficult to distinguish between real and false memories. This study shows how suggestible and unreliable memories can be, and it has had huge implications on a range of areas such as eyewitness testimony in crimes and memories of childhood sexual abuse.

For more about false memory see page 92.

DO YOU REMEMBER MEETING BUGS BUNNY AT DISNEYLAND?

One criticism of Loftus's "lost in the mall" study was that it was possible that a participant really was lost in a mall at a young age — these events are not that uncommon. They might thus have been recalling partly real memories. Loftus countered this argument with a later study in which she asked people whether they remembered shaking hands with Bugs Bunny at Disneyland as a child. This is an impossible event, since this character is a Warner Bros. creation and thus would not feature at a Disney park. Yet 16 percent of participants did claim to recall shaking hands with Bugs Bunny at Disneyland.

TRY THIS:
TEST YOUR SUSCEPTIBILITY TO FALSE MEMORIES

To find out how susceptible you are to suggested false memories, memorize as many words as you can from this list (give yourself 15 seconds), then cover it up and answer the questions that follow.

REST	BED	NAP
PEACE	DROWSY	BLANKET
DOZE	TIRED	AWAKE
SNOOZE	YAWN	SLUMBER
SNORE	WAKE	DREAM

Cover up the list!

You will now see a list of words and you have to tick the ones that you can remember being in the list:

REST　　　**HOUSE**　　　**CHAIR**

BED　　　**SLEEP**　　　**CURTAINS**

MILK　　　**CARPET**　　　**YAWN**

Now read the following:

Did you tick "sleep"? And "curtains"? If you did, then you have remembered these falsely — they were not there. Your mind will have associated all the words with sleep and thus "remembered" seeing a word that was not actually there. ("Sleep" is the most common word for people to falsely recall seeing from the list.) The whole test is part of what is known as the Deese–Roediger–McDermott (DRM) paradigm for testing false memory.

THE HALO EFFECT

This is a psychological phenomenon whereby a person's views about a brand, product or individual are colored by the person's overall impression of it — as if there were a halo surrounding it. This general impression overrides ratings about specific attributes. The halo effect can be used to explain why a close friend can do something that we consider to be amusing, while someone we do not know doing the same thing might be viewed as rude or offensive.

The term "halo effect" was first coined by psychologist Edward Thorndike (see page 35) in his 1920 paper "The Constant Error in Psychological Ratings." The effect was tested empirically in a classic experiment by psychologists Richard Nisbett and Timothy Wilson in 1977. Nisbett and Wilson asked college students to rate a professor who was giving a videotaped lecture in one of two conditions that manipulated how friendly and likable the professor appeared. In the first condition, the professor was friendly and approachable, and answered questions from the audience in a helpful, cheerful manner. In the second condition,

he was cold and aloof, and appeared uninterested and detached when answering the audience's queries. The participants were told to rate the professor on a range of attributes (such as mannerisms) and were then asked how much they liked the lecturer. Their ratings for how much they liked the professor strongly affected the ratings on his individual attributes — if they liked him, they thought his attributes were better than if they did not like him (even though the attributes they were rating him on stayed constant).

This halo effect has had massive implications in marketing and advertising. For example, associating a well-known and well-liked celebrity with a brand of jeans can create a halo effect such that the jeans are perceived to share the qualities of the celebrity. The halo effect can also explain why jury members are less likely to convict an attractive defendant, why well-behaved pupils are likely to be rated as more intelligent by teachers and why work colleagues who are enthusiastic and affable are likely to be seen as producing better-quality work than less personable (but more effective) workers.

BEWARE THE HORNS

The halo effect can work in reverse, too. If a celebrity has endorsed a product and the company is enjoying a sales upsurge as a result of the halo effect, it can all go wrong if the celebrity in question gets bad press for using drugs, violence or other antisocial behavior. Suddenly, thanks to the "horns effect," things associated with the celebrity may now be seen as negative, the opposite of the halo effect. For example, supermodel Kate Moss, who was the "face" for a number of famous brands, had modeling contracts cancelled in 2005 when a picture of her allegedly using cocaine was published — this is the horns effect in action. (Moss did recover from this career blip and is now thought to be more successful than ever.)

BURBERRY
9 EAST 57TH STREET NEW YORK

TRY THIS:
ELEVATOR
EXPERIMENT

And now it's your turn. This is a classic experiment that you can try yourself. Find a busy elevator where there is only one way in and out (not the type where you enter on one side and exit at the other). Get in when there is just one other person there. As you do so, position yourself facing the back wall. See what happens. Does the other passenger face the back wall, too?

Now enlist a friend to help. This time, both of you turn and face the wall. There is a strong chance that the stranger will follow suit. Bring even more friends in on the experiment — the more you have, the more likely it is that the stranger will turn and face the back of the elevator, even though they know that this is odd behavior. This is the power of conformity.

This famous elevator experiment was originally conducted with social psychologist Solomon Asch (well known for his work on conformity, as described on page 145) as part of a 1962 television episode of *Candid Camera* entitled "Face the Rear."

ETHICAL ISSUES IN PSYCHOLOGY RESEARCH

When psychologists carry out research, they have a moral duty to ensure that their participants are protected from harm or distress. To this end, psychologists today are obliged to abide by thorough ethical guidelines set by their professional body (such as the British Psychological Society or American Psychological Association), their employer university or most likely, both. Most research has to gain ethical clearance before it can commence and it is likely that many of the studies cited in this section, which were carried out before ethical guidelines became so stringent, would never have got such clearance today.

Ethical guidelines generally cover the following areas:

CONSENT

Participants in psychological research should give informed consent to take part in the study. This means that, where possible, participants need to know exactly what they are consenting to. This can be awkward when a researcher has good reasons for not wanting the participant to know what the aims of the study are (see page 40), but they should still be told what they will need to do. Children will need parental consent to take part.

Consent means that the participant is voluntarily taking part in the study and there should not be any repercussions if they do *not* take part or if they withdraw. This can be a problem when studies involve students (as so many psychology

CONFIDENTIAL

studies tend to do, because they are captive audiences), who may be compelled to take part in order to collect study credits or to avoid extra assignments.

Generally, if you are asked to participate in a psychological study, you should be given the following information before you decide whether to be involved or not:

- A statement that participation is voluntary and that refusal to participate will not result in any consequences or any loss of benefits that the person is otherwise entitled to receive

- The purpose of the research (which might not always be the real purpose — see right)
- What you will be expected to do and how long it will take
- Any foreseeable risks and discomfort (for example, if the study involves looking at violent video games or material with sexual content, participants should always be informed of this in advance)
- Potential benefits of the research
- Whom to contact with any queries
- Information about your right to confidentiality and your right to withdraw from the study at any time without any consequences

As mentioned on page 183, many of the studies in this section would not meet modern ethical standards for consent. For example, there is considerable doubt that the mother of Little Albert (see page 148) consented to his taking part in the phobia study, and that is not the only reason this experiment was unethical, as we discuss on page 186. The boys in the Robbers Cave study (see page 167) did not know they were taking part in an experiment at all.

DECEPTION

If participants are to be able to give informed consent, then they need to be given complete information. Sometimes, however, deception is necessary in order to carry out the study — if the participants knew the true aim, the study would no longer be feasible. Thus, for example, in the Asch study (see page 145), if participants knew that the study was about conformity and that the other participants were, in fact, accomplices, then the study would simply not have worked. Similarly, Milgram (see page 143) could not have told participants that the shocks were not real because that would have negated the research.

Nevertheless, even if deception is deemed necessary, it should not cause distress or psychological or physical damage when participants are debriefed and the truth is known. The question is whether some of the deceptive studies described in this section of the book caused harm or distress. Did Milgram's participants, many of whom were visibly distressed when they administered the

DO YOU WANT TO TAKE PART IN PSYCHOLOGICAL STUDIES?

Most studies will be fun and informative, so if taking part in one interests you, contact your local university psychology department and offer yourself as a study participant — many universities have banks for members of the public to volunteer. They will collect your details and when they need participants who fit your demographics (such as gender and age) they will contact you.

"shocks," feel relief when they found out the shocks were fake or anger that they had suffered such anguish for nothing? Did Schachter and Singer's adrenalin participants (see page 170) feel distress that their emotions had been manipulated so easily? Did Asch's participants feel foolish that they had been led to give responses that were obviously wrong?

MINIMIZING HARM

No psychology experiment should ever leave a participant feeling worse after it than they did before. This is another major area in which many of the studies cited in this section would fail to get ethical clearance today. For example, participants in Milgram's studies (see page 143) were exposed to extremely stressful situations and many were obviously agitated, as seen by their trembling, sweating, stuttering, laughing nervously, biting their lips and digging their fingernails into the palms of their hands. Three participants had uncontrollable seizures and many begged to be allowed to stop the experiment. Milgram did claim that these effects were short-term and that participants were fully debriefed — during which they realized that no harm had come to the accomplice. He also followed them up a year later to check they had not suffered ill effects.

The Stanford prison experiment (see page 140) is another example of a study that would be unlikely to meet today's ethical requirements. (Modern replications of the study have adhered to stricter ethical standards.) Several participants were traumatized by the original study as they suffered both physical and psychological abuse. There did not seem to be a proper debrief.

Little Albert (see page 148) also clearly suffered in the interests of advancing psychological research. He was a perfectly healthy child before he was "given" a severe phobia and he never underwent any therapy to return him to his original state.

It could also be argued that the children in the Robbers Cave study (see page 167) were harmed, as they were induced into aggressive behavior. The same goes for the children in the Bobo doll study (see page 158) in which the participants were manipulated to make them act more aggressively.

ANIMAL STUDIES

It is not just humans who should be protected in psychological research — Harlow (see page 154) was criticized for the unethical way he treated the baby monkeys in his study. It was clear that the monkeys suffered emotional harm as a result of being reared in isolation and without a mother. This was evident by the way they sat huddled in a corner in a persistent state of fear and depression. The female monkeys he raised who became parents were so anxious that they often harmed their own babies. Of course, the benefits of such research to humans might well be considered to outweigh the costs, but it is still unlikely that such studies would gain ethical approval today.

PART 4

PSYCHOLOGICAL CONDITIONS & THERAPIES

FEW PEOPLE ARE NEVER TOUCHED OR AFFECTED BY A PSYCHOLOGICAL CONDITION AT SOME POINT IN THEIR LIVES. PSYCHOLOGICAL CONDITIONS INCLUDE DEPRESSION AND ANXIETY AS WELL AS PERSONALITY DISORDERS AND DEVELOPMENTAL DISORDERS THAT AFFECT CHILDREN. IT IS NOT POSSIBLE TO DISCUSS EVERY PSYCHOLOGICAL CONDITION HERE BUT THE MORE COMMONLY OCCURRING ONES ARE PRESENTED.

PSYCHOLOGICAL CONDITIONS

Psychological conditions are those mental health problems, developmental problems or disorders that affect a person's functioning or cause distress, harm or impairment to the self or others. Psychologists typically diagnose such conditions using the *Diagnostic and Statistical Manual of Mental Disorders*, published in its fifth edition in 2015 by the American Psychiatric Association, to determine whether a set of symptoms or behaviors meet the criteria for diagnosis. The DSM outlines approximately 150 different psychological disorders, including eating disorders, mood disorders, anxiety disorders, sleep disorders and personality disorders, as well as psychotic and developmental conditions.

STRESS

For people unfamiliar with a mental-health disorder, it can be hard to comprehend the symptoms and the effects, but stress is one condition that most understand only too well. The term "stress" is derived from the Latin word *strictus*, meaning "drawn tight" and, prior to the early 20th century, referred to the physical strain resulting from a force exerted on something. It was not until the 1920s and 1930s that the term became associated with mental health, when psychologists began to use it to refer to a mental strain.

Because it is seen as a negative condition, stress is something we are told to avoid at all costs. Indeed, in modern times, it is associated with a range of negative outcomes (of which more later — see page 194). In fact, stress is a response that was originally designed to protect us, not harm us. For our ancestors, facing threats such as predators and foes, the stress reaction was essential for survival, since it provided extra reserves of strength and energy with which to fight vicious enemies — or else run away fast. This stress reaction was coined the fight-or-flight response by the physiologist Walter Cannon in 1915 (see page 136). Cannon noted that when we spot a threat to our wellbeing and survival, our bodies react with a flood of hormones that prime us for either fighting or fleeing — both of which require extra strength in the arms and legs and more energy in the muscles.

STRESS *causes hormones that have a range of long- and short-term effects to flood through our bodies.*

The purpose of the fight-or-flight response is to divert as much oxygen-carrying blood (for energy) as possible from the stomach, skin and internal organs, to deliver it to the arm and leg muscles. To facilitate this, the body stops concentrating on non-essential functions (like digestion and skin maintenance), which can wait until later after the threat has receded.

The main hormones that achieve this remarkable feat are adrenalin and cortisol, both of which are released from the adrenal glands. Adrenalin works by raising the heart rate and blood pressure so that blood is pumped around the body

to the muscles faster. Cortisol acts on the liver to convert protein (glycogen) to glucose (sugar), which is a major source of energy for us. This glucose thus provides the energy for blood to be pumped faster and for us to be able to run or fight with extra strength.

Other vital chemicals are released by the hypothalamus (see page 54) in the brain. These are endorphins, which act as natural painkillers so that we feel less pain and are better able to concentrate on fighting or fleeing. This is why we might hear of people who were badly injured but able to keep running until the immediate danger is over.

THE STRESS REACTION *might have been good to help our ancestors survive but is less useful today when many of our stressors cannot be solved by either fighting or running away.*

While this fight-or-flight response might have been perfect to help our ancestors survive a potential attack by a wild animal, it is less useful for us today when the threats we face are very different. Rarely do we face the sort of stressor for which the fight-or-flight response was designed. For one thing, our stressors are more chronic than they were for our ancestors. It's unlikely they faced deadly lions several times a day and if they did, they would have moved to safer ground. In addition, the fight-or-flight response is hardly useful when it comes to facing urgent deadlines, angry bosses, screaming children, long waits in the supermarket or any of the other myriad of stressors that can plague us in the modern world.

The result is that we have a system that is designed to be invoked sporadically but is used almost constantly and thus invokes a response that is simply not appropriate. This means that we are almost constantly experiencing an energy surge, with extra glucose coursing through our muscles and blood diverted from other functions, causing a range of symptoms with which many of us will be only too familiar (see page 194).

TREATING STRESS

If you think you may be suffering from stress, the first thing to do is see your doctor. It can be treated with a range of stress-management techniques, including exercise (which uses up some of the freed energy in the bloodstream) and cognitive behavioral techniques (see page 238). An effective way to manage stress symptoms is with a technique called progressive muscle relaxation therapy, which is explained on page 308.

STRESS SYMPTOMS

SYMPTOM	WHY THE SYMPTOM ARISES
NECK ACHE	We tend to tense our neck muscles when stressed, causing pain.
ACHING LIMBS	The build-up of glucose in the limbs can make our arms and legs to feel heavy and tired. In addition, we tend to tense our muscles in preparation for fight or flight and this tension causes pain.
TIREDNESS	We feel tired because we have been burning up so much extra energy. This rapid mobilization of energy gives short-term benefits but longer-term exhaustion.
STOMACH ACHE	Blood is diverted away from this area so digestive mechanisms are reduced. This can lead to digestive problems and discomfort. Poor digestion for long periods can result in more serious stomach problems such as ulcers.
DRY MOUTH	The flow of saliva is reduced to the mouth as this is part of the non-essential digestive process.
DIZZINESS	Although we breathe more quickly when we are stressed, we tend to take more shallow breaths and thus we do not deeply breathe in as much oxygen as when we are not stressed. This can lead to a slightly reduced oxygen supply to the brain, causing dizziness.
COLD AND FLU	Stress can also result in a weakened immune system, making a stressed person more vulnerable to illnesses like colds and flu.

SYMPTOM	WHY THE SYMPTOM ARISES
HEART DISEASE	The glucose (and free fatty acids released from stored fat) left in the blood by the fight-or-flight response contributes to plaque formation, which can lead to heart disease. When we remain stressed for long periods of time or our stress levels rise often. Hypertension (raised blood pressure) may result from the heart continually working hard at pumping blood quickly, and can escalate into cardiovascular disease, heart attacks or strokes.

QUIZ:
HOW STRESSED ARE YOU?

If you have difficulty detaching yourself enough to assess your own stress levels, answering these 20 questions might help you. Think back over the last three months and decide how much each of the following statements has applied to you during that period, then give each a mark on a scale of 1–5.

① Very infrequently ② Infrequently ③ Sometimes ④ Frequently ⑤ Very frequently

① ② ⊗③ ④ ⑤   **1.** I eat more or less than I usually do.

⊗① ② ③ ④ ⑤   **2.** I suffer from indigestion or heartburn.

① ② ③ ⊗④ ⑤   **3.** I suffer from constipation, stomach aches, diarrhea, or other stomach problems.

⊗① ② ③ ④ ⑤   **4.** I suffer from sleep problems, such as difficulty getting to sleep or waking early.

⊗① ② ③ ④ ⑤   **5.** I feel tired or exhausted.

⊗① ② ③ ④ ⑤   **6.** I have headaches.

⊗① ② ③ ④ ⑤   **7.** I feel like crying or as if I might "explode."

① ② ③ ④ ⊗⑤   **8.** I can't sit still without fidgeting or getting up to pace the floor.

(X) (2) (3) (4) (5)   **9.** I feel my blood pressure rising.

(1) (2) (X) (4) (5)   **10.** I get impatient or irritable easily.

(1) (X) (3) (4) (5)   **11.** I feel unable to cope.

(X) (2) (3) (4) (5)   **12.** I have difficulty making decisions.

(X) (2) (3) (4) (5)   **13.** I have difficulty concentrating.

(1) (X) (3) (4) (5)   **14.** I move on to the next task before completing the present task.

(1) (2) (3) (X) (5)   **15.** I smoke or drink more alcohol than I used to.

(X) (2) (3) (4) (5)   **16.** I worry about so many things.

(X) (2) (3) (4) (5)   **17.** I feel tense rather than relaxed.

(X) (2) (3) (4) (5)   **18.** I feel that I don't have time for anything.

(X) (2) (3) (4) (5)   **19.** I feel panicky or fearful.

(X) (2) (3) (4) (5)   **20.** I feel more irritated than I ought to by interruptions or minor distractions.

TOTAL SCORE:

20   40   60   80   100

Very little stress   Low stress   Mild stress   High stress   Very high stress

ANXIETY

Anxiety is related to stress and people who suffer from severe anxiety are often said to have general anxiety disorder (GAD). Some degree of anxiety is normal and even desirable: if we did not get anxious about, say, exams or walking home in the dark or what our kids eat, we might not take the necessary steps to protect ourselves and our loved ones. Some anxiety is thus a sign of good functioning, allowing us to prepare and take appropriate precautions when faced with life's unpredictability, dangers and risks.

In evolutionary terms, anxiety is a particularly important emotion. It would have helped our ancestors prepare for difficulties such as predators or food shortages. It was anxiety that was responsible for our ancestors building shelters or storing food — and thus we have it to thank for our very survival as a species.

The response produced in our bodies by anxiety is similar to that produced by stress. As our anxiety increases, the hypothalamus (see page 54) in the brain

ANXIETY *produces a similar response to stress and, like stress, can affect every aspect of our bodies.*

What is the difference between stress and anxiety? In very simple terms, stress is the response we have when faced with a threat or a perceived threat, while anxiety is our response to stress. In other words, stress is usually felt in response to something specific that we feel is threatening our wellbeing in some way, and worrying about those stressors causes anxiety. Sometimes anxiety can continue even after the stressor is gone or without a known cause, when it is usually accompanied by general fear.

hard to relax. There is always something that worries them excessively — and, in fact, because worrying is a habit, they may be even more worried if they have nothing specific to worry about.

GAD is thought to affect about 5 percent of British adults and 3 percent of American adults, with women slightly more at risk than men. The condition is most common in people in their 20s, although it can affect people of any age. Psychological symptoms of GAD include:

- Feeling restless and "on edge"
- Having a constant sense of dread or impending doom
- Being totally preoccupied by worries
- Being easily distracted by worries or concerns
- An inability to work effectively because of the constantly intruding concerns
- Feeling depressed or worthless

stimulates the pituitary gland at the base of the skull to release various hormones that affect every part of our body in one way or another, just as stress does.

The difference between healthy anxiety and those who suffer from GAD is that people with GAD tend to feel generally anxious without there necessarily being a specific event or situation that is causing the anxiety. They feel anxious a lot of the time and find it

Physical symptoms of GAD include dizziness, tiredness, irregular heartbeat (palpitations), muscle aches, dry mouth, excessive sweating, shortness of breath, stomach ache, nausea, diarrhea, headache, irregular periods and difficulty falling asleep or staying asleep (insomnia).

WHY DO PEOPLE DEVELOP GENERAL ANXIETY DISORDER?

Sometimes people develop GAD following a series of stressful life events such as moving house, divorce, bereavement or redundancy. Each of these is a high-stress event on its own; a few such events happening close together can overwhelm anyone's coping abilities. They might also learn to be anxious based on their life experiences. For example, if they have had a health scare in the past or a close friend has, they may become excessively anxious when reading about health issues.

Some people may have a thinking style that lends itself to experiencing greater anxiety. For example, anxious people have a tendency to expect that the worst possible scenario will always occur and that they must constantly be on their guard in case something bad happens. They often feel that by thinking about the worse-case scenario, they are protecting themselves in some way from it happening — either because they will be better prepared or because they superstitiously believe that anticipating it will prevent it from actually happening — but if they let their guard down, the terrible scenario might be "allowed" to occur. This is why treatment often involves changing the way people think (see page 244).

HOW MUCH ANXIETY IS EXCESSIVE?

Anxiety is thought to be excessive or indicative of GAD if *any* of the following occurs:

- It is out of proportion to the source of the anxiety (for example, sufferers might worry about the same things as everyone else, such as money, but take it to a much higher level than most people).

- It persists even after whatever has caused the anxious response has gone.

- It appears for no apparent reason or when there is no specific situation that is causing anxiety (for example, overreacting to a simple event such as someone not responding to a text, resulting in imagining something terrible has happened to the person who hasn't texted).

- It is almost constant.

- It is debilitating, affecting and interfering with normal daily life.

PANIC ATTACKS

Anxiety can be so severe that panic attacks may result; the main symptoms of these include a sudden "rush of fear" that peaks very quickly. This is accompanied by a range of debilitating physical and emotional symptoms. The attack is often so terrifying for the sufferer that they will often go to great lengths to prevent another one from occurring. It is thought that between 1 percent and 3.5 percent of the population worldwide suffer from panic disorder (recurrent panic attacks), which appear to be most common among adolescents and young adults.

TREATING ANXIETY & PANIC ATTACKS

Panic attacks are generally treated with psycho-education (for example, helping the patient understand why they get these symptoms, how fear of the panic actually feeds the panic cycle and how the panic is not actually dangerous) and relaxation training.

Anxiety responds well to cognitive behavioral techniques (see page 239), such as learning to challenge unhelpful thinking styles. Patients might be asked to keep diaries outlining their anxiety and anxiety-provoking thoughts; they will then be taught to identify and challenge any unhelpful or flawed thinking. Examples of flawed thinking that sufferers of GAD often experience include:

PREDICTING THE FUTURE: This is where we invest a lot of energy predicting what will happen — and usually these predictions are of dire consequences. Often things will not turn out as badly as feared but we have wasted a lot of energy worrying about events that may never happen.

CATASTROPHIZING: Here we blow things out of proportion so that they seem to be worse than they really are.

FOCUSING ON THE NEGATIVE: This is noticing and concentrating on what went badly and ignoring things that went well.

"SHOULD-ING": This is when we get preoccupied with how we think things *should* be rather than accepting how things really are.

OVER-GENERALIZING: This is assuming that an isolated incident is representative of all future events.

WHAT-IFS: Being preoccupied with "what if" scenarios can stop us from doing things or going to places.

LABELING: This is where we give ourselves a condemning label like "I am stupid."

PSYCHOLOGICAL CONDITIONS
SLEEP DISORDERS

Sleeping difficulties are often related to anxiety and, in fact, can involve a two-way relationship: stress and anxiety can disrupt our sleep but sleep difficulties can cause stress and anxiety. Sometimes sleep problems have non-psychological causes (such as poor sleeping patterns, jet lag or noise) but the anxiety about not sleeping can cause stress — which can cause sleep to become even more elusive, trapping the sufferer in a vicious cycle of sleep deprivation and stress.

According to Britain's National Health Service, a third of people experience problems getting to sleep or staying asleep at some point in their lives. Insomnia, which is described as short-term (up to three weeks) or long-term (more than three weeks), is not only anxiety-provoking but can also lead to memory problems, depression, irritability and an increased risk of heart disease and driving-related accidents. (No wonder we worry so much about lack of sleep.)

Causes of insomnia vary, but the most common reasons for people seeking psychological help are centered around anxiety. Sleep is a deep state of relaxation, so it is difficult to fall asleep if you are not relaxed. Events in a person's life that provoke anxiety may stop them from relaxing, but anxiety about not sleeping often contributes, too. The other important condition for sleep is that the individual must be tired! This might sound odd but people with sleep difficulties often doze during the day and so may not be tired enough at night. Dozing during the day can effect circadian rhythms, which can make it harder to fall asleep at night.

TREATING SLEEP PROBLEMS

Treatment for insomnia can be pharmaceutical, with benzodiazepines such as temazepam and diazepam (best only for short-term use as the benefits wear off as tolerance builds up) or can involve psychological techniques such as relaxation therapy and sleep hygiene (for example, ensuring the room is quiet and dark, that no caffeine is consumed during the evening and that there is no daytime dozing). It may also include "paradoxical intention," which is a cognitive reframing technique in which the insomniac, instead of attempting to fall asleep at night, makes every effort to stay awake (essentially, stops trying to fall asleep). This can be effective because it relieves the "performance anxiety" arising from the perceived requirement to fall asleep.

PHOBIAS

A phobia is an extreme form of anxiety that is directed toward a particular object. It is usually marked by such a strong fear or panic attack that the sufferer will tend to avoid the object of their phobia as much as possible. The fear is usually irrational in that the feared object is unlikely to cause serious harm; thus, for example, people who fear elevators, escalators, spiders and heights are unlikely actually to come to physical harm from these. Some phobias might be based on a rational fear

A PHOBIA *severely limits normal functioning, which differentiates it from a fear.*

— for example, fear of fierce dogs might be quite sensible, so this would not be classed as a phobia. However, if that fear is generalized to all dogs, even small lapdogs, and the sufferer refused to leave the house because of this fear, then that would become a phobia.

Indeed, for a fear to be classed as a phobia, it is probably something that needs to impact severely on a person's life. A person might dislike spiders intensely, but if they are able to lead a fairly normal

WHY DO PEOPLE DEVELOP PHOBIAS?

There are many reasons why people develop a phobia. One possibility is that they might be conditioned to develop a fear, as Little Hans (see page 148) demonstrated. Thus, a bad experience with a dog or a very turbulent airplane flight could be the sort of incidents that lead to phobias of dogs or flying. We can also learn phobias from other people and it is quite common for phobias to be passed down from parent to child.

A different explanation is given by the "theory of preparedness," which suggests that some things, or stimuli, are "evolutionarily predisposed" to evoke a fear response. This makes sense when we consider that some phobias, such as spider phobia (one of the most common fears), are more widespread than others. It would be reasonable to assume that in our evolutionary past, our ancestors would have encountered plenty of deadly spiders, so a healthy fear of them could save their lives.

The theory does not explain why so many people are totally unafraid of spiders. But the theory of preparedness addresses this apparent flaw by suggesting that some people are more biologically "prepared" to have phobias than others. It is even possible that this "preparedness" trait gave an evolutionary advantage, in that more fearful people may have had better survival rates as they avoided more of the dangerous stimuli in life (fleeing from spiders might have been a healthy survival mechanism). Indeed, most specific phobias do involve situations that might have posed a threat in some way at a point in our evolutionary past — for example, needles or heights.

life, then this is probably not a phobia. If, however, their dislike is so strong that they refuse to enter certain rooms in their house or cannot take their children to the park, then this would actually be classed as a phobia.

Some people manage to live perfectly well with a phobia without it causing them problems. For example, someone with an elevator or escalator phobia (both very common) might be able simply to adapt their lives so they do not have to encounter these feared objects. They would still be classed as phobias since they are changing the way they go about their daily lives. The phobia might only become a problem if they were forced to face their fear — for example, if they got a new job on the 20th floor of an office block.

Phobias can be classified into two broad types:

- **SPECIFIC OR SIMPLE PHOBIAS**
- **COMPLEX PHOBIAS** (such as social phobia or agoraphobia)

Specific phobias can be further classified into four main categories:

- Animal phobias (fear of animals or creatures).
- Environmental phobias (fear of environmental events such as thunder, lightning, heights or the dark).
- Medical phobias (such as fear of blood, injections, vomiting or injury).
- Situational phobias (fear of certain situations like crowded places, public transport, flying or driving).

TREATING PHOBIAS

Cognitive behavior therapy (see page 241) is one of the most effective ways to treat phobias. Usually the technique of gradual desensitization is adopted. This is where the sufferer is gradually exposed to an increasing hierarchy of feared situations, using relaxation and other coping techniques.

For example, someone with an elevator phobia may be least scared of glass elevators in the presence of other people and most scared of closed elevators, alone, going up 20 floors. Treatment would therefore start with a glass elevator, in a busy shopping center. It might start even lower down the hierarchy, with standing near the elevator but not going into it. Once the phobic person can cope with that (using coping techniques such as relaxation) without fear, they might then progress to the next level of their hierarchy — which might be getting in the elevator but leaving the doors open and staying stationary (obviously, a quiet time is needed for this exercise). They would then move through their hierarchy, only moving on to the next level when the previous stage ceased to be fearful for them.

OBSESSIVE-COMPULSIVE DISORDER (OCD)

According to OCD-UK, obsessive-compulsive disorder affects 1.2 percent of the UK population; the figure for the U.S. is a little higher, at about 2 percent. It can be so debilitating and disabling that the World Health Organization (WHO) ranked OCD in the top ten of the most disabling illnesses of any kind, in terms of lost earnings and diminished quality of life. OCD is another anxiety disorder, this time characterized by intrusive thoughts that produce discomfort, apprehension, fear, or worry; the sufferer often performs repetitive behaviors aimed at reducing the associated anxiety. There are two elements to OCD — obsessions and compulsions:

REPEATED AND CONSTANT HAND-WASHING *can signify a version of OCD associated with fears of contamination.*

OBSESSIONS: These are involuntary, apparently uncontrollable thoughts, images or impulses that occur repetitively in the sufferer's mind. These obsessive thoughts are often very disturbing and distracting.

COMPULSIONS: These are the behaviors or rituals that the sufferer feels driven to perform over and over again; they are often performed in an attempt to make the obsessions go away or become more manageable.

For example, if a person is afraid of contamination with germs and is fearful of catching something, they might develop compulsive hand-washing rituals that require them to repeatedly wash their hands, in order to reduce their ongoing worry that they might have picked up a germ. However, the relief from each episode of hand-washing never lasts and the obsessive thoughts about possible contamination may soon return even stronger than ever. In order to reduce the obsessional thoughts and the associated anxiety, the hand-washer has to repeat the hand-washing ritual — and so the cycle continues.

The endless compulsive behaviors often end up creating great anxiety themselves as they become more demanding and time-consuming. Telling the sufferer to simply not "obey" their urges (by telling them to stop carrying out their compulsions) will just make them more and more anxious, leaving them in a no-win situation, trapped by the cycle of obsessions and compulsions.

Most people with obsessive-compulsive disorder fall into one of the following categories:

SOME OCD SUFFERERS are obsessively tidy and get disproportionately distraught if everything is not in its rightful place.

OCD CATEGORIES

CATEGORY	SYMPTOMS
WASHERS	Afraid of contamination, they usually have cleaning or hand-washing compulsions. They will often have to repeat the rituals over and over because they are never satisfied that they have done them "correctly." They are also likely to take extreme "precautions" against contamination such as wearing surgical gloves or using their elbows rather than their hands to open doors.
CHECKERS	Checkers repeatedly check that they have turned off ovens, lights, and locked doors. They have to keep checking over and over again that they have done something, otherwise they will obsess about the harm that might result. They may also have to touch things in a certain way or a certain number of times.
COUNTERS AND ARRANGERS	This involves superstitions about certain numbers, colors, or arrangements. Sufferers may have to do things a certain number of times (such as seven times) and if they don't, or are not sure whether they have, they have to start again until they are satisfied (which can take several hours). Tins in their cupboards may have to be arranged in a certain way (for example, with the labels facing the same way) or clothes hung in their wardrobe must be in certain ritualistic patterns.
HOARDERS	Hoarders fear that something bad will happen if they throw anything away. They compulsively hoard things that they don't need or use, or they collect unusual things that other people would throw away.

TREATING OCD

Like other anxiety conditions, OCD responds best to cognitive behavior therapy (see page 241). This involves repeated exposure to the source of the obsession. The sufferer is then asked to refrain from the compulsive behavior that they would usually perform to reduce their anxiety. For example, a compulsive hand-washer might be asked to touch the door handle in a public toilet and then refrain from washing.

The anxiety that results from not washing will build up in the same way that any anxiety builds up for phobics when facing the source of their fear — but it *will* decline on its own and of its own accord over time. This is the key learning point here: the sufferer has to learn, by experiencing it, that the extreme anxiety will gradually reduce on its own. It is because the human brain cannot maintain that level of anxiety for very long and we "habituate," or get used to, whatever is causing us to be anxious.

If the sufferer "gives in" and washes their hands before the anxiety has subsided, then the cycle is maintained and will not be broken. Only having the strength to resist hand-washing will weaken the link. The trick is to build up a hierarchy and start with something relatively easy before tackling the really challenging situations.

POST-TRAUMATIC STRESS DISORDER (PTSD)

Post-traumatic stress disorder (PTSD) is a severe anxiety disorder that can develop after someone has experienced an event that results in psychological trauma, such as the threat of death or severe injury to oneself or to someone else. It is thought that around a third of people who experience traumatic events will go on to have the condition. It can occur at any age, including during childhood, and can appear immediately after a disturbing event or weeks, months or even years later. PTSD can develop in any situation where a person feels extreme fear, horror or helplessness. The more disturbing the experience, the more likely you are to develop it and it does not usually develop after situations that are simply upsetting, such as divorce, job loss or failing exams.

Symptoms of PTSD include flashbacks, nightmares, sleeping difficulties, panic attacks, anger, depression, feeling constantly in danger and being "jumpy" (for example, reacting to car doors slamming).

TREATING PTSD

While PTSD responds to cognitive behavior therapy (see page 241), like other anxiety conditions do, a technique called eye movement desensitization and reprocessing (EMDR) is increasingly proving an effective treatment. EMDR uses a natural function of the body, rapid eye movement (REM), as its basis. The human mind employs REM during sleep to help it process daily emotional experiences. There is some evidence that the eye movements during EMDR perform a similar function to those that occur during REM sleep (when we dream), which we already know has a vital information-processing function. When trauma is extreme, this process breaks down and REM sleep does not bring the usual relief from distress. EMDR is thought to be like an advanced stage of REM processing. Using eye movement, the brain processes troubling images and feelings to resolve the issue.

EMDR requires patients to focus on three main aspects of the trauma:

- A visual image, which is usually that of the most disturbing part of the trauma

- The negative thought that they have about themselves in relation to the trauma

- The location of the disturbance in their body

Focusing on these aspects, the patient then tracks the therapist's finger across the visual field in rapid, abrupt eye movements. (Or instead of their finger, the therapist can use a "light bar" in which the patient visually tracks a light that moves back and forth across a metal bar.) After each set of such eye movements, the patient is asked to report on what they are experiencing. The alternating left–right stimulation of the brain with these eye movements during EMDR seems to stimulate the frozen or blocked information-processing system.

During the course of this procedure, the emotional impact of the traumatic memory usually lessens. This decrease may be gradual but in some cases it is sudden. The distressing memories seem to lose their intensity, so that the memories seem more like "ordinary" memories.

DEPRESSION

Everyone feels down at times but clinical depression occurs when that feeling either lasts a long time, recurs very often or makes the sufferer feel extremely low. According to Britain's Royal College of Psychiatrists, one in five people become depressed at some point in their lives, and it is thought to be the number one psychological disorder in the Western world. Up to 80 percent of those who commit suicide worldwide are sufferers of major depression.

There are four main groups of depressive symptoms:

- Those to do with emotions, such as feeling sad and miserable
- Physical symptoms, like lack of appetite or sleeping difficulties
- Thoughts/cognitions, for example "I am worthless" or "no one likes me" and very often, suicidal ideation (thoughts about and preoccupation with death and suicide)
- Those to do with behavior, such as staying in bed

DEPRESSION can be an extremely debilitating condition and can interfere with a person's day-to-day functioning.

Most depression is caused by negative and unhelpful thinking styles or cognitive distortions, which can be learned from other family members, rather than other factors such as genetics or hormone imbalance, although people may have a genetic predisposition to depression. Many of these flawed patterns of thinking are similar to those that overly anxious people feel (see page 198), except that the thoughts lead to negative feelings about the self and the future rather than to anxiety. The thinking patterns induce a feeling of passive helplessness rather than the more active worry cycles that they provoke in anxious people. Examples of these patterns of thinking include the following:

PREDICTING THE FUTURE: Depressed people tend to always assume that bad things will happen.

MIND-READING: Depressed people assume that they know what other people are thinking about them and that they are always being judged unfavourably.

CATASTROPHIZING: Depressed people often blow things out of all proportion. Things are always "terrible," rather than just "not very good."

"SHOULD-ING": "Should" statements, such as "I should have done this or that," are commonly used by depressed people to take the blame for an event. This makes the person feel even worse about themselves and adds to their depressed state.

OVER-GENERALIZING: This is the depressed person's assumption that an isolated incident is representative of all future events.

IGNORING THE POSITIVES: Depressed people often ignore or discount instances of things going well, and focus on when things go badly.

LABELING: Depressed people are more likely to give themselves negative labels like "a failure" or "boring." Labeling like this can add to their feelings of low self-worth.

TREATING DEPRESSION

Depression can be hard to treat because symptoms include hopelessness and a lack of motivation to seek help. Severely depressed people may not see the point of treatment as they do not believe it will work. In such cases, medication can be the most effective treatment.

For moderate depression, however, cognitive behavior therapy (see page 241) can be effective. This might involve identifying and challenging unhelpful thoughts and looking for alternative explanations for negative thinking. A skilled therapist can help the depressed person learn these new skills. They can also teach the patient to look for the pleasure in simple things, to boost their self-esteem and to acknowledge their strengths and the positive things in their life.

EATING DISORDERS

Eating disorders are psychological conditions characterized by abnormal eating habits such as eating too much or too little. A 2015 report commissioned by the charity Beat estimates that more than 725,000 people in the UK are affected by an eating disorder, while American figures suggest there are 11 million sufferers in the U.S. The two most common specific forms of eating disorders are the following:

EATING DISORDERS *are commonly attributed to a desire to lose weight but this is too simplistic an interpretation. Eating disorders can be triggered by many different things.*

ANOREXIA NERVOSA: Extreme food restriction to the point of self-starvation and excessive weight loss typifies this eating disorder. Around 1 in 250 women and 1 in 2,000 men worldwide will experience anorexia nervosa at some point. The condition usually develops at around the age of 16 or 17.

BULIMIA NERVOSA: This is characterized by binge-eating and purging (such as self-induced vomiting and the use of laxatives) and, possibly, over-exercising. Bulimia is around two to three times more common than anorexia nervosa and 90 percent of people with the condition are female. It usually develops around the age of 18 or 19.

There are many possible causes of eating disorders, including biological, psychological and environmental factors. For example, someone with a parent or sibling who has a history of an eating disorder is more likely than individuals without such a relative to develop an eating disorder, suggesting that there may be a genetic link (although this could be learned behavior, too). Research also shows that a mother who diets or worries excessively about her weight may trigger her child to develop an unhealthy attitude toward food, as may a relative or even a classmate who teases an individual about their weight or shape.

There may be personality factors, too. For example, some people with eating disorders may have low self-esteem, perfectionism or a high degree of approval-seeking. Body dysmorphic disorder, which is an altered way of seeing yourself, is also associated with many people with eating disorders. Studies have found that 15 percent of individuals diagnosed with this body dysmorphia also suffer from either anorexia nervosa or bulimia nervosa.

TREATING EATING DISORDERS

This can be very complex and involve various approaches such as self-help, medication, group support, psychotherapy and cognitive behavior therapy (see page 241). These therapies would help to target the unrealistic, negative thoughts that lead to the unhealthy eating behaviors of anorexia nervosa and bulimia nervosa. Emotional reasons for eating patterns are explored and the patient is helped to recognize emotional triggers and learn how to avoid or combat them. Therapies might also involve education about nutrition, healthy weight management and relaxation techniques.

BIPOLAR DISORDER

Bipolar disorder, sometimes referred to as manic depression, is not the same as the depression talked about on page 215. What makes bipolar different is that it includes not only periods of depression, but also periods of elation too; bipolar is a combination of mania and depression alternating in cycles. About 3 percent of the population worldwide have bipolar disorder at some point in their life and it typically starts between the ages of 15 and 19 years, with men and women equally susceptible.

DEPRESSIVE SYMPTOMS

- Depressed mood.

- No interest or pleasure in all, or almost all, activities previously enjoyed.

- Insomnia (inability to sleep) or hypersomnia (sleeping too much).

- Fatigue or lack of energy.

- Feelings of worthlessness or excessive or inappropriate guilt.

- Suicidal ideation (thoughts about and preoccupation with suicide).

MANIC SYMPTOMS

- Excessive happiness or energy.

- Inflated self-esteem or grandiosity (at its worse, sufferers may even lose touch with reality — in other words, become psychotic — such as imagining that they have been chosen for a special mission).

- Decreased need for sleep (such as feeling rested after only three hours of sleep).

- Very talkative, often speaking excessively quickly.

- Easily distracted.

- Impulsivity that can lead to taking actions without thinking of the consequences (like expensive shopping sprees or poor business investments).

- Hallucinations or delusions (for around half of sufferers).

The exact mechanism underlying bipolar disorder remains unclear. Genetic factors are believed to account for 60–80 percent of the risk of developing the disorder and the risk is nearly ten times higher in children or siblings of those affected with the disorder when compared with the general population.

Abnormalities in the structure or function of certain brain circuits may play a role in developing bipolar disorder, while environmental factors are also likely to play a part for people susceptible to the disorder. Thus, for example, traumatic events or stressful experiences might lead to the onset of a bipolar episode for those at risk. There may also be neuroendocrinological factors; for example, dopamine, a known neurotransmitter (see page 61) responsible for mood has been shown to increase during the manic phase.

MANY PSYCHOLOGICAL CONDITIONS ARE HEREDITARY but this is just one factor. Having a close relative with a condition does not mean that you will have it too.

PSYCHOLOGICAL CONDITIONS
SCHIZOPHRENIA

This is probably the best known of the disorders that come under the category of psychoses, which are mental-health conditions in which the sufferer is, at times, unable to distinguish between what is real and what is not. Around 1 percent of the population worldwide suffers from schizophrenia, with most cases appearing in the late teens or early adulthood. Occasionally schizophrenia can appear for the first time in middle age or even later. People with schizophrenia may see or hear things that don't exist, believe that others are trying to harm them, speak in strange or confusing ways, or feel like they're being constantly watched and they generally seem detached from the world around them. The main symptoms of schizophrenia include the following:

HALLUCINATIONS: These are sounds or sights that seem very real to the sufferer but do not, in fact, exist outside of their own mind. The most common hallucination is when the sufferer believes that they are hearing voices; these voices may provide a commentary on the their day-to-day life, carry on a conversation with them (with the sufferer responding either out loud or in their heads), issue warnings about suspicious people and events or even issue orders. While the voices are real to the sufferer, sometimes the patient might be able to understand that they only exist in their head and manage to control them — or simply learn to ignore them. But, during severe, or "acute," phases these voices can take over, becoming very controlling and sometimes quite threatening.

DELUSIONS: With this disorder, the sufferer believes something even though there is clear evidence that they are wrong. Delusions occur in more than 90 percent of those who have the disorder and often involve ideas, thoughts or fantasies that have little basis in reality. Common schizophrenic delusions include *delusions of persecution* (whereby the sufferer believes strongly that someone or some people, such as the State or even a celebrity, are out to get them); *delusions of control* (where the sufferer is convinced that their thoughts or actions are being controlled by other people, such as the police) and *delusions of grandeur* (the sufferer is convinced that they are someone really important like a secret prince, a celebrity such as Elvis Presley or even a religious figure like Jesus Christ. This delusion can also manifest itself in believing that they have unusual powers that no one else has, like the ability to make themselves invisible).

CHAOTIC BEHAVIOR: People with schizophrenia can quickly stop behaving in socially acceptable ways. Their behavior might become erratic or peculiar and they may react inappropriately in everyday settings. They might become uninhibited and be unable to exert any control over their impulses. Sudden or extreme mood changes are typical.

LACK OF INTEREST OR ENTHUSIASM: Sufferers may become uninterested in the wider world, in their hobbies or even in day-to-day activities like eating or personal hygiene.

LACK OF EMOTIONAL EXPRESSION: The sufferer may show a reduction in their normal display of emotions — either facially or vocally. For example, they may not smile or even have eye contact, and they may speak in a flat monotone without any intonation or animation.

SOCIAL WITHDRAWAL: Perhaps because of the other symptoms, sufferers begin to interact less and less with the world around them until they have withdrawn into themselves.

Schizophrenia is thought to result from a little-understood interaction between genetic, physiological and environmental factors. It is clear that there is a significant hereditary component. People with a first-degree relative (parent or sibling) who has schizophrenia have a 10 percent chance of developing the disorder, compared with a 1 percent chance in the general population. But about 60 percent of schizophrenics have no family members with the disorder, so genetic factors are not the only explanation for the development of the condition.

Some researchers believe that genetics give a person the susceptibility to the illness but that there are environmental events that trigger it. Stress, for example, with its high levels of cortisol, might be one such environmental factor that could trigger schizophrenia in susceptible people. Examples of stressful events include exposure in the womb to infection, low oxygen levels during birth, exposure to a virus during childhood, loss of or separation from parents or caregivers, bereavement or other trauma.

TREATING SCHIZOPHRENIA

The most common treatment options for schizophrenia involve medication, prescribed by a psychiatrist, but psychological therapies used alongside are often crucial, too. Such therapies can involve psycho-education, family therapy, social skill training, self-help groups and individual psychotherapies.

Abnormalities in the brain might play a role in the development of the illness. Research also suggests that schizophrenia may be caused by a change in the level of two neurotransmitters (see page 61): dopamine and serotonin. Indeed, drugs that alter the levels of neurotransmitters in the brain can relieve some of the symptoms of schizophrenia.

PERSONALITY DISORDERS

This is the collective name for a group of mental-health difficulties that are present throughout a person's life, affecting both how they relate to other people and how they think of themselves, and it also includes the actions that stem from this. They are disorders in that they cause suffering either to the person themselves or, occasionally, to those around them. About 9 percent of the population worldwide would be diagnosed with a personality disorder (PD) of some sort if they sought help but in fact many people do not realize that they have a disorder (sometimes because it is mild) and thus do not seek professional input.

It is thought that there are 10 main types of personality disorder, which can be grouped into three categories or clusters. The most common types within each of these three clusters are as follows:

SUSPICIOUS PERSONALITY DISORDERS: In this category are paranoid, schizoid or antisocial personalities. *Paranoid* personalities are characterized by being suspicious, finding it hard to trust others, always looking for signs of betrayal and feeling easily rejected. *Schizoid* personalities are "colder" emotionally, preferring not to have close relationships with others and having little interest in intimacy. *Antisocial* personalities are characterized by being uninterested in how others feel; it is the antisocial personality that is more likely to commit crimes, act impulsively, feel no guilt and thus hurt other people.

EMOTIONAL/IMPULSIVE PERSONALITY DISORDERS: Two of the most common types in this category are borderline and narcissistic. *Borderline* personalities are very impulsive, have difficulty controlling their emotions, find it hard to maintain friendships and are inordinately distressed by feelings of abandonment when these relationships fail. *Narcissistic* personalities have a very strong sense of their own importance, believe they will achieve great things, crave admiration from others and use other people for their own ends.

NARCISSISM *originates from the character from Greek mythology, Narcissus, who was in love with his own reflection.*

ANXIOUS PERSONALITY DISORDERS: There are two main types within this category: avoidant and dependent. *Avoidant* personality types worry a lot, are very anxious and tense, are very sensitive and insecure, tend to avoid close relationships because of fear of rejection and may be reluctant to try new activities. *Dependent* types are far more passive, relying on others to make decisions, are quite needy and have low confidence.

TREATING PERSONALITY DISORDERS

This usually involves psychological therapies rather than medication, although drugs can be used for conditions (such as depression) that may co-occur with the disorder.

Psychological treatments include psychotherapy, which might focus on dysfunctional thoughts; self-reflection and being aware of how one's own mind works; psychodynamic psychotherapy (which is based on the idea that many adult patterns of behavior are related to negative early-childhood experiences) to help understand how distorted thinking patterns might have developed; and cognitive behavior therapy (see page 241), which can help patients better cope with thoughts and feelings.

Like many mental-health conditions, the causes of personality disorders are unclear and there are likely to be a variety of factors, such as environmental influences and genetics, that contribute to developing the condition. The role of the family and upbringing may have an impact in the development of some traits associated with personality disorder. For example, in a study of 793 mothers and children, researchers asked the mothers if they had told their children that they did not love them or threatened to send them away. Children who had experienced such verbal abuse were three times as likely as other children to have borderline, narcissistic or paranoid personality disorders in adulthood.

Other studies have shown a link between the number and type of childhood traumas and the development of personality disorders. People with borderline personality disorder (BPD), for example, had especially high rates of childhood sexual trauma (although this does not mean that all those with borderline personality disorder have experienced sexual abuse or that all victims of sexual abuse will develop this disorder).

DEVELOPMENTAL DISORDERS

This category covers disorders for which the symptoms, which cause significant impairment in functioning, are present from an early developmental stage (usually appearing within the first two years of life). The most common ones are autism spectrum disorder (ASD) and attention deficit hyperactivity disorder (ADHD).

AUTISM SPECTRUM DISORDER (ASD)

Around one in a hundred people worldwide have autism spectrum disorder and it is more common in boys than in girls. People within it tend to fall within two main areas:

SOCIAL IMPAIRMENT: People with ASD often have difficulties in social situations because of communication deficits characterized by a lack of eye contact; a flat, monotone voice; a lack of understanding about the need to take turns; an inability to empathize; a narrow range of interests; and an inability to read social cues.

REPETITIVE AND STEREOTYPED BEHAVIORS: Children (or adults) may display repetitive actions, sometimes called stereotypy, stereotyped behaviors or stims. A common example is repeatedly flapping their arms or waving their fingers in front of their faces. People with ASD might also be obsessed with obscure objects or places, such as a certain shop, road names or even a particular word.

This disorder is a "spectrum," which means that children vary in their severity or symptoms. Sometimes the term Asperger's syndrome (also referred to as high-functioning autism spectrum disorder) is used to describe those who are less severely affected; unlike the more severe "autism," people with autism spectrum disorder have no significant delay in language development.

It is not clear what causes autism spectrum disorder. Studies have shown that genes play an important role; for example, if one identical twin has autism, then the other has around a 75 percent chance of also having it. While the role of genetics might not be disputed, the role of other factors is. A particular controversy about the cause of the disorder centers on whether there is a link between it and certain childhood vaccines, particularly the measles-mumps-rubella (MMR) vaccine. However, despite extensive research, no reliable study has shown a link between autism spectrum disorder and this vaccine (see page 232).

TREATING AUTISM SPECTRUM DISORDER

There is no effective treatment for autism and certainly no cure. Treatments that can help tend to address behavioral and learning deficits and can include educational sessions around the building of social and communication skills (such as the ability to start conversations); this is known as applied behavior analysis or ABA. Psychological therapies could also be used to enhance social interaction skills — for example, the ability to understand other people's feelings and respond to them — and cognitive skills, such as encouraging imaginative play.

RAIN MAN

There is a unique (and relatively rare) form of autism called autistic savantism, in which a person can display outstanding skills in music, art or numbers, as illustrated so well by the character played by Dustin Hoffman in the 1988 film *Rain Man*. An estimated 10 percent of the autistic population have savant abilities.

Savantism was first identified by the 19th-century British physician John Langdon Down (who first described Down's syndrome). Derived from the French word *savant*, it describes someone of great learning or knowledge. Down originally referred to his patients as "idiot savants" because of the contrast between their amazing skills and other grave disabilities.

DUSTIN HOFFMAN'S *portrayal of an autistic man in* Rain Man *brought autistic savantism into the public arena.*

KIM PEEK *was the original inspiration behind* Rain Man, *even though he was not actually autistic at all (he was diagnosed with FG syndrome in 2008).*

The original inspiration for the savant portrayed in *Rain Man* was Kim Peek, who died of a heart attack at the age of 58 in 2009. Peek, who did not in fact have autism but rather was born with damage to his cerebellum, was said to have memorized over 12,000 books, including the complete works of Shakespeare and the Bible, and had encyclopedic knowledge of U.S. area codes and major city zip codes and maps. (He could tell you precisely how to get from one U.S. city to another and then how to get around in that city, street by street.) He also had calendar-calculating abilities and could read extremely rapidly, simultaneously scanning one page with the left eye and the other page with the right eye.

Peek was actually classed as "mentally retarded" as a child but was later coined "The Living Google" because of his incredible knowledge. Despite his gifts he was unable to wash or dress unaided. Kim's first job was managing a 160-person payroll, a weekly task he performed in a few hours without a calculator. He was made redundant, but it took two full-time accountants and a new computerized system to replace him.

Kim won an award from the Christopher Reeve Foundation for helping other people with disabilities — quite an achievement when you consider he was expelled from his first school at the age of 7 after just seven minutes for being "uncontrollable."

MMR CONTROVERSY

The MMR jab combines three childhood vaccines — measles, mumps and rubella — in one injection, which is first given to children at around 12–18 months (with a booster around the age of 3–5). These diseases can cause serious, and potentially fatal complications, including meningitis, encephalitis (swelling of the brain), deafness and developmental problems.

The MMR vaccine, introduced in 1971, has virtually eradicated the diseases in the Americas, the UK and Europe. In recent years, however, cases (and deaths) of the most serious of them, measles, have occurred in these regions due in part to the autism controversy.

In 1998 a study published in the medical journal *The Lancet* suggested a link between MMR and autism. It led to widespread panic that had an effect on vaccination rates. Cases of measles rose, and included deaths. In 2006, a 13-year-old boy became the first person in 14 years to die of the disease in the UK.

A journalist, Brian Deer, investigated Wakefield's research and claimed it was flawed. He also alleged that Wakefield had conflicts of interest. A subsequent General Medical Council hearing concluded in January 2010 that Wakefield was guilty of serious professional misconduct and his medical license was revoked. *The Lancet* eventually retracted the 1998 paper.

Since then, numerous studies on MMR and autism have failed to find any link. For example, a 2014 study of over a million children in four different countries found no evidence of a link between the MMR vaccine and the development of autism in children. The article's effects linger, however, as some parents still choose not to vaccinate their children.

ATTENTION DEFICIT HYPERACTIVITY DISORDER (ADHD)

Also called attention deficit disorder (ADD), this is another developmental condition. It has the following symptoms:

INATTENTION: Examples of inattention include being easily distracted, missing details, often forgetting or losing things, frequently switching from one activity to another, being unable to maintain focus on one task or learn something new, having trouble completing homework assignments, not seeming to listen when spoken to, daydreaming, becoming easily confused and struggling to follow instructions.

HYPERACTIVITY: This includes fidgeting and squirming rather than sitting still, talking nonstop, rushing around, touching or playing with everything in sight and finding it difficult to undertake quiet tasks or activities.

IMPULSIVITY: Examples of impulsivity include being very impatient, blurting out inappropriate comments, acting without regard for consequences, having difficulty waiting for one's turn in games and often interrupting conversations or others' activities.

Not all these symptoms will be displayed by every child with this disorder — for example, some children might be predominately inattentive and others mainly hyperactive (while others can be both). The symptoms of ADHD can

CHILDREN AND ADOLESCENTS WITH ADHD *often struggle to concentrate and pay attention at school and may thus struggle to access the curriculum.*

TREATING ADHD

There is no cure for ADHD but medication is often used to manage the symptoms when these are severe. Stimulants such as methylphenidate (brand names Ritalin or Concerta) and amphetamine (Adderall) are the most common type of medication used; it might seem odd to prescribe stimulants, given that hyperactivity is often a major symptom of ADHD, but these medications work by stimulating brain circuits that help maintain attention.

Cognitive behavior therapy (see page 241) or other psychological therapies are sometimes used, as well as training in social skills. Mindfulness (see page 244) has also been shown to have some success in many cases.

obviously impact on education as well as leading to difficulties making friends, leaving children feeling isolated, stressed and depressed. While it is a lifelong condition, there is a lessening of symptoms over time, particularly with regard to hyperactivity. As adults, many people with ADHD choose careers or jobs that allow their symptoms to be less of a hindrance such as those that allow the job-holder autonomy over their activities or that do not involve a great deal of sitting concentrating (non-office jobs, entrepreneurship and jobs with fast-changing environments are often chosen).

Incidence rates vary according to the diagnostic criteria used, but the statistics suggest a massive increase in people with the condition. There is no definitive method of diagnosing ADHD and the phenomenal rise in children being given this label in recent years has led some to believe that it is being diagnosed far too readily. The Center for Disease Control's national survey of Children's Health in the United States, for example, reported an 830 percent increase in children diagnosed with ADD/ADHD from 1985 to 2011. In fact, 11 percent of American school-age children and nearly one in five boys of high-school age in the United States have been diagnosed with ADHD – this makes it the second-most frequent long-term diagnosis made in children (narrowly trailing asthma).

As in autism spectrum disorder, there

are likely to be various causes of ADHD, including genetic. Researchers at Cardiff University in Wales recently studied the genes of 366 children with ADHD, as well as 1,000 children without the condition and found that children with it were more likely to have duplications of small segments of their DNA or to have sections that were missing. Previous research has shown that siblings of a child with ADHD are between four and five times more likely to have the condition themselves — and many parents only realize they themselves have it when their children are diagnosed.

COULD YOU HAVE ADHD?

Many adults are unaware that they might have ADHD because recognition and diagnosis were much rarer in the past, and it is only when they are diagnosed that difficulties in their life begin to make sense. Some of the symptoms of adult ADHD include:

- **DIFFICULTY FOCUSING OR CONCENTRATING:** Finding that your mind wanders excessively during meetings or that you simply cannot tolerate sitting still for long are symptoms of this. It could even lead to accidents, such as when driving. For the same reason you may be poor at listening and tend to zone out when you get bored, which could cause problems at work or in relationships.

- **RESTLESSNESS:** For example, always fidgeting and being unable to sit still without feeling frustrated.

- **IMPULSIVITY:** If you make decisions or take action without thinking things through or considering the consequences, you may be impulsive.

- **DIFFICULTY COMPLETING TASKS:** People with ADHD are often great at having ideas and starting projects but often give up or get bored before they are completed. Part of the problem here is that they are easily distracted from the task in hand.

- **DISORGANIZATION:** Having a messy home or office, being consistently late or losing things could all be symptoms. This, too, can cause problems in relationships or at work.

PSYCHOLOGICAL THERAPIES

To modify feelings or change the behavior of people who are experiencing difficulties that affect their mental health, psychologists have designed the processes known as psychological therapies. These encompass a range of interventions, based on psychological theory and evidence, that help people to alter their thinking, behavior or relationships (or all of these) at the present time and/or process trauma and disturbance from the past. The aim is to alleviate emotional distress and improve functioning and wellbeing. Such therapies may be provided to adults or children with mental-health issues, to those with learning disabilities or to people with physical or neurological disability. A wide range of therapies are available and psychologists might specialize in different forms of therapy. The more common therapies and approaches are outlined here, grouped into the following categories:

"TALKING THERAPY" *with trained therapists is a common component of many psychological therapies.*

PSYCHOLOGICAL THERAPIES

TYPE OF THERAPY	EXAMPLES
COGNITIVE AND BEHAVIORAL	Behavior therapy, cognitive behavior therapy, mindfulness-based cognitive behavior therapy.
PSYCHODYNAMIC	Free association, brief psychodynamic therapy.
HUMANISTIC	Gestalt therapy, human givens therapy, person-centered therapy, solution-focused brief therapy, existential therapy.
PSYCHIATRIC	Medication, electro-convulsive therapy.
OTHER PSYCHOLOGICAL	Integrative therapy, transactional analysis, EMDR (see page 214).
NON-PSYCHOLOGICAL	Neuro-linguistic programming, hypnosis, emotional freedom techniques.

COGNITIVE BEHAVIORAL THERAPIES

These therapies are a group of approaches that are based on changing the way people think and/or the way they behave. Thoughts and behavior are often interconnected and this approach takes the view that if we can change the way we think, we will change the behaviors that are causing us difficulties.

BEHAVIOR THERAPY

Sometimes called behavior modification, this therapy aims to change human behavior that is inappropriate or unhelpful in that it is causing problems or difficulties for the patient. Conditions that respond well to behavior therapy include addictions, anxiety, phobias and obsessive-compulsive disorder (OCD).

The underlying principle behind behavior therapy is that because unhelpful behaviors have been learned, so they can be unlearned. There is no need to develop any great insight into why or how these behaviors developed — the focus is simply on learning how to do things differently. Thus, behavior therapy puts less emphasis on the past or childhood experiences and more on looking at how today's behaviors and thoughts can be modified.

Behavior therapy is based on theories of conditioning (see page 96), with various therapeutic approaches based on either classical or operant conditioning. (As explained on page 98, classical conditioning forms an association between involuntary, automatic behavior and a stimulus, while operant conditioning utilizes reinforcement.)

Examples of therapies based on classical conditioning include the following:

SYSTEMATIC DESENSITIZATION: This is a gradual exposure to a feared stimulus so that the patient can unlearn conditioned responses to those stimuli. Thus, if the fear is of spiders, the patient might start by learning to talk about or read about spiders without fear, before progressing to being in the same room as one, being close to one and eventually perhaps even holding one. The therapist teaches the patient relaxation skills that can be used at the same time as exposure to the fear-rousing stimulus and in this way the conditioned response of fear of that stimulus can be reduced. The technique is used successfully when treating phobias or panic attacks.

AVERSION THERAPY: In contrast to systematic desensitization, which attempts to break the link between a stimulus and a negative response, aversion therapy tries to create a link when such a link is desirable. For example, a patient with OCD might snap an elastic band against their wrist whenever an unwanted thought intrudes into their minds — this is attempting to condition the unwanted thoughts with a (mildly) painful stimulus. Similarly, when an alcoholic is given (with their consent) a drug that will cause them severe nausea when combined with alcohol, they learn to associate alcohol with unpleasant feelings, which leads to a reduction in the drinking.

ALCOHOLISM *can sometimes be treated successfully with aversion therapy, by using a drug that causes nausea when combined with alcohol.*

FLOODING: Here the patient is exposed to their very worst fear for a considerable amount of time, until their high level of anxiety disappears. The theory is that we cannot maintain very high levels of arousal indefinitely — eventually exhaustion sets in and the anxiety and panic will subside on its own. A patient with claustrophobia, for example, who is locked in an elevator, will eventually stop being anxious. There is a danger with this therapy, however, that if the person refuses to continue the treatment (and, of course, they are free to stop whenever they wish), they could be left with a worse fear than when they started.

FLOODING should be used with great caution as exposing someone to their worst fear could do more harm than good.

Therapies based on operant conditioning include the following:

TOKEN ECONOMIES: Using positive reinforcement, this involves the patient being offered "tokens" (such as points, stars or stickers that can be exchanged for privileges, prizes or other rewards) when the desired behavior occurs. This is commonly used with people who have learning difficulties, to help "shape" desirable behaviors by modifying one part of the behavior at a time rather than the whole behavior all at once. However, it can also be used with anyone whose behavior we are trying to change, such as trying to improve pupils' school attendance or adults' time-keeping at work. The aim is for the new behaviors learned in this way to be maintained even when the rewards stop.

MODELING: This relies on learning through observation and imitation, and can be used as a part of mentoring or buddying schemes for children or with people with learning difficulties. The patient observes someone else performing the appropriate behavior and copies them, thereby learning to perform the required behavior themselves. For example, a child who is afraid of dogs may watch a parent playing happily with dogs and learn that there is little to fear.

COGNITIVE BEHAVIOR THERAPY (CBT)

This is a blend of two therapies — behavior therapy (see page 238) and cognitive therapy, which was developed by psychotherapist Aaron T. Beck in the

A GOOD MODELING BEHAVIOR to show a child with a fear of dogs would be for them to see a parent interact happily with dogs.

1960s. Cognitive therapy aims to change the way people think, while behavior therapy focuses on people's actions. Cognitive behavior therapy, then, looks at the relationship between how people think and how these thoughts affect actions; it is a therapy that aims to change both thoughts and behavior.

Its central premise is that a person's thoughts strongly affect how they feel and behave, and that people have problems such as depression or anxiety because their thought processes are "maladaptive" (unhelpful) or negative. The main aim of cognitive behavior therapy is to help the patient identify any negative or unhelpful thoughts and to change them into more positive or helpful thoughts. Many people get into habitual patterns of thinking — such as always thinking pessimistic thoughts, which in turn mean that they feel bad and act in ways that are not helpful, so this therapy technique aims to help them recognize that they are doing this and to suggest ways that they might adopt more optimistic thinking patterns in some situations.

Imagine that you see someone you recognize in the street — perhaps an acquaintance or old friend — but they appear to ignore you. If you have unhelpful thinking patterns, you might react by thinking, "They ignored me! They obviously don't like me! In fact, I don't have many friends at all. Not many people like me. I must be such an unlikable person. In fact, I think I'll just go home. I was on my way to meet friends for coffee but I should do them all a favour and stay away — they probably only invited me out of pity." Cognitive behavior therapy would help you to identify your "thinking errors" (thoughts that are flawed or without basis) in this situation, which are as follows:

"They ignored me!" (You are making an assumption here — perhaps there is another explanation, such as that they didn't see you or were distracted). "They obviously don't like me!" (Again, you are making an assumption; also, this is an example of "mind-reading" since you cannot read their mind nor can you know that they don't like you.) "In fact, I don't have many friends at all." (Here, one event has now been generalized to other events your life.) "Not many people like me." (More assumptions and mind-reading — how do you know this?) "I must be such an unlikable person." (This is negative labeling and "all-or-nothing" thinking, as you are assuming that you are either likable or not, instead of accepting that you might be likable to some people on some occasions, but not all the people all the time). "In fact, I think I'll just go home — I was on my way to meet friends for coffee but I should do them all a favour and stay away." (These thought patterns have now impacted on your behavior.) "They probably only invited me out of pity." (Again, assumptions and mind-reading are occurring here.)

Cognitive behavior therapy will help the client to challenge these thinking errors, perhaps by suggesting that they look for evidence for their assumptions or find alternative explanations for them. In this way, the therapy is very much focused on the here and now rather than on the problems' possible causes, which may lie in the past. Of course, many negative thinking patterns are developed throughout childhood, so the past cannot be ignored — but this therapy is more focused on solving today's problems than on helping the client understand why they are the way they are.

What is particularly distinctive about maladaptive thinking is that thoughts are often very negative. People can get trapped in a vicious cycle of thinking negatively and these thoughts often have specific qualities:

- They are often distorted so they do not match reality.
- They have a negative impact in that they make the patient feel bad or depressed.
- The thoughts seem reasonable and plausible so the possibility of questioning them does not occur to the patient.
- They appear involuntarily, which means that they are very hard to control.

The maladaptive thoughts often reflect low self-esteem, self-criticism and self-blame, as well as negative interpretation of events, and low expectations for the future. The role of cognitive behavior therapy is to challenge these thoughts. One way to achieve this is to ask the patient to keep a "thought diary" in which they record the thoughts that occur in response to certain events and then they bring the diaries to the sessions, when the therapist will challenge them. (Eventually the patient will learn to challenge their thoughts themselves.) In the example we've just looked at, you would perhaps respond to the questions as follows:

THERAPIST'S QUESTION	PATIENT'S RESPONSE
WHAT IS THE EVIDENCE FOR YOUR BELIEF THAT NO ONE LIKES YOU?	Well, only that this person ignored me. In fact, the evidence doesn't really point to everyone disliking me. I could test it out by seeing how many people say hello or good morning to me at work or somewhere that people know me. If two or three people do, then perhaps I am not as disliked as I imagine.
WHAT IS THE EFFECT OF THINKING THE WAY YOU DO?	It makes me depressed and sends me into a negative spiral, so I end up not wanting to go anywhere and just thinking that the world is against me. It may even lead to a self-fulfilling prophecy — the more I withdraw, the less people will want to interact with me, which i then interpret as no one liking me.
WHAT ALTERNATIVE VIEWS COULD THERE BE?	Maybe she didn't see me or was distracted by her own problems. Or even if she was ignoring me, that doesn't mean everyone dislikes me.
WHAT THINKING ERRORS ARE YOU MAKING?	Assuming that I know what other people think, extrapolating one event to everything else (just because one person may or may not like me does not mean I am unlikable), labeling myself. I'm focusing only on the negatives (being "ignored") and ignoring the positives (that I am meeting friends for coffee).

These processes take time to accomplish but skilled cognitive behavior therapists should be able to help a person change how they react and think, so that they feel and behave in more positive ways.

MINDFULNESS-BASED COGNITIVE BEHAVIOR THERAPY

Mindfulness therapy is a relatively new approach that helps clients pay attention to the present moment without judgment, using techniques like meditation, breathing and yoga. Mindfulness training can help individuals become more aware of thoughts, feelings and their bodies so that these are no longer overwhelming.

Mindfulness-based stress reduction (MBSR) is a mindfulness-based cognitive therapy program developed by Jon Kabat-Zinn at the University of Massachusetts Medical School. It uses a combination of mindfulness meditation, body awareness and yoga. Mindfulness-based cognitive behavior therapy (MBCT) is a psychological therapy designed to aid in preventing a relapse of depression, employing traditional cognitive behavior therapy (CBT) methods combined with mindfulness and mindfulness meditation.

MINDFULNESS THERAPY *is extremely popular and can include mindfulness-based stress reduction and acceptance and commitment therapy.*

A particular type of mindfulness is acceptance and commitment therapy (ACT), which is based on two key ideas: accepting what is out of your personal control and committing to make changes to improve. The focus is on creating a rich and meaningful life without actually trying to reduce symptoms, because sometimes those symptoms need to be accepted in order to enhance one's existence.

PSYCHODYNAMIC THERAPIES

CARL JUNG *was a Swiss psychologist and psychiatrist who had a major impact on the development of psychodynamic therapy.*

Unlike the therapies discussed so far, the focus of psychodynamic therapies is often on the past. A key factor here is on the subconscious and various techniques in this group of therapies are designed to bring unconscious processes to the forefront of the mind. Many of these subconscious processes will have been laid down in childhood, so understanding

how and why they appeared seems to be a key to unlocking them. Therefore, the goals are to increase self-awareness and understanding of how the past can impact on the present.

The roots of psychodynamic therapy lie in Freud's psychoanalytic approach (see page 14) and it is thus the oldest of the modern therapies. However, the work of other proponents of the psychoanalytic approach, such as Carl Jung, Alfred Adler, Otto Rank and Melanie Klein, also impact on the methodology. Psychodynamic therapists believe that our unconscious mind suppresses painful feelings and memories, using defenses, such as denial and projections (see page 250). Although these defenses do offer protection in the short-term, in the longer term they are often harmful and prevent us from dealing with difficult situations and resolving them.

ID, EGO & SUPEREGO

Freud believed that personality is structured into three parts: the id, the ego and the superego, all developing at different stages in our lives.

1. **THE ID:** Consisting of all the inherited (biological) components of personality, this is regarded as the most primitive and instinctive of the three elements. Driven by a "pleasure principle," the id demands immediate gratification that results from food, water, sex and other basic needs.

2. **THE EGO:** In contrast to the instinct-driven id, the ego is more mature and tries to control and manage the id. Rather than operating on a pleasure principle like the id, it is driven by a "reality principle," and tries to work out realistic ways of satisfying the needs of the id, without attracting negative consequences — for example, by trying to keep the id's drives at bay until a more socially acceptable time (say, postponing chats with friend until after work). The ego takes into account the social expectations, norms, etiquette and rules of society.

3. **THE SUPEREGO:** The superego serves as a conscience and incorporates values and morals that are learned from our parents and others. It uses guilt to exert its effect on the ego.

Freud claimed that the three components are in constant conflict, each battling to exert their influence on actions and behavior.

ANNA FREUD *was the sixth child of Sigmund Freud (pictured together here). She became an important psychotherapist in her own right, building on the work of her father — for example, in her development of his ideas of the ego and defenses.*

The basic assumptions underlying the psychodynamic approach are as follows:

- Any mental-health problems, like much of our behavior, have their root in the unconscious mind.
- The principle of psychic determinism suggests that all behavior has a cause or reason, such as unconscious traumas, desires or conflicts.
- It is our childhood experiences that are responsible for our behavior and feelings as adults (including our psychological problems).
- Different parts of the unconscious mind — the id, ego and superego (see page 247) — are in constant struggle with each other.
- To avoid the unpleasant consequences of conflict between the id, ego and superego, we develop various defenses.

FREE ASSOCIATION

One of the main techniques used in psychoanalytic therapy is free association; here the client is encouraged to talk freely to the therapist, saying the first things that come to mind without any attempt to control or inhibit ideas and thoughts. This uncovers defenses and is thus thought to allow true feelings to emerge. Sometimes the therapist will say words (such as "father" or the name of the patient's spouse) and the patient is urged to say the first things that spring to mind without worrying about how bizarre or silly they might sound — although there does have to be a trust in the therapist for this. So, for example, a patient might claim to have a great relationship with their parents, but during free association might blurt out hidden feelings around issues of feeling let down by them. The therapist helps the client identify the new feelings that have emerged and uses them to lead to new behaviors or healthier ways of thinking.

BRIEF PSYCHODYNAMIC THERAPY

Psychodynamic therapies can take a long time — years sometimes. However, a briefer form has been developed that is suitable in some cases — usually where there is one clearly identified issue to deal with that the therapist believes can be identified and tackled quickly (although it is still likely to require at least 25 sessions).

PSYCHOLOGICAL DEFENSE MECHANISMS

In order to cope with and reduce anxiety, people often use defense mechanisms, which are usually automatic and unconscious. In 1936, Anna Freud (daughter of Sigmund Freud) identified a number of defense mechanisms that appeared in the works of her famous father. These include the following:

REPRESSION: This is a subconscious attempt to keep unpleasant thoughts, memories and feelings out of mind and even memory. Thus, we might repress memories of a traumatic incident to the extent that we even seem to "forget" we experienced it, not realizing that even repressed memories can impact on how we feel or act today.

PROJECTION: Instead of acknowledging unacceptable thoughts or feelings, we attribute them to someone else or "project" the thoughts or feelings onto them. For example, we might accuse our partner of being angry when it is we who are angry.

REACTION FORMATION: Here, a person might attempt to distance themselves from unacceptable thoughts or feelings by behaving in a way that is directly opposite to their real inclinations. Thus we might loathe a particular person but go out of our way to be especially nice to them instead.

RATIONALIZATION: This is an attempt to use incorrect explanations to justify unacceptable behavior, thoughts or feelings. For example, if you steal pens from work, you justify this by rationalizing that everyone does this or that you work so hard you deserve a few freebies.

DISPLACEMENT: Here we might transfer feelings about a person or event onto someone or something else. Thus, if we have a bad day at work and then come home and have a row with our partner, that is displacement.

DENIAL: If a person refuses to acknowledge something that is obvious to most other people, they are in denial. For example, someone might be in denial that they need help for stress or depression, because then they might be forced to acknowledge a perceived weakness.

REGRESSION: When a person reverts back to a more immature state of psychological development, which is felt to be safer and less demanding, it is known as regression. Thus we might turn to comfort foods from our childhood when we are feeling low.

SUBLIMATION: This is the channelling of unacceptable thoughts and feelings into socially acceptable behavior. For example, feeling angry and aggressive can be channelled into sporting activities.

BUILDING TRUST BETWEEN THERAPIST & CLIENT

It is essential the client trusts that the therapist is appropriately qualified to treat their problem and that they will act ethically at all times. This includes adhering to strict confidentiality (which includes not discussing the client with spouses, partners or other family members without permission) and not recommending treatment or therapy beyond what is required. The client also needs to trust that the therapist will not judge them or be dismissive. The therapist builds trust with the client by using active listening skills, giving feedback and being respectful (for example, returning calls promptly, seeing clients on time, dressing professionally and being prepared).

PSYCHOLOGICAL THERAPIES
HUMANISTIC THERAPIES

Humanistic therapy is the name given to a group of approaches that focus on the role of free will, self-development and growth in human development. Humanistic therapies tend to focus on the present — looking at where the patient is in the here and now, rather than considering how they got there or worrying about what the future might hold. They aim to help individuals recognize their strengths, creativity and choices with a focus on "self-actualization" (reaching one's potential). Fundamental assumptions underlying humanistic psychology include the following:

- Experiencing (thinking, sensing, perceiving, feeling, remembering) is key.
- Individuals should acknowledge free will and take personal responsibility for self-growth and fulfilment.
- Self-actualization (a person's need to reach maximum potential) is something for which everyone strives.
- People are inherently good and will experience growth if provided with suitable conditions, especially during childhood.

There are various schools of humanistic therapy and the therapies covered here are the most common.

GESTALT THERAPY

Developed by Fritz Perls, Laura Perls and Paul Goodman in the 1940s and 1950s, Gestalt therapy focuses on the whole of an individual's experience, including their thoughts, feelings and actions in the here and now; thus, unlike psychodynamic therapies, it is less concerned with the past, except with how the past impacts on the present. Gestalt therapy concentrates on the skills and techniques that a person needs to develop in order to be more aware of their own feelings, thoughts, ideas and beliefs. This can be achieved with a range of techniques such as the following:

ROLE-PLAY: With this technique, the therapist might play the role of the individual who is the source of difficulties with the patient, such as a spouse or parent. The patient is then asked to interact with them in this role. Alternatively, it could be the patient who takes on the role of the other person so that they can experience different feelings and emotions that will aid their own self-awareness.

THE "EMPTY CHAIR" TECHNIQUE: Here an empty chair is placed opposite the client, who is asked to imagine that it is occupied by someone significant, such as their parent, spouse or even themselves. They start off by interacting with this imaginary person — talking to them and asking questions. Then they swap chairs so that they are sitting in the empty chair and become the other person; the roles are reversed as the interaction continues. The aim is to help the client become aware of suppressed feelings that might be fuelling conflicts or distress.

THE "EMPTY CHAIR" TECHNIQUE *is where the client is asked to imagine that the empty chair is occupied by someone significant and they are then asked to "interact" with this person.*

HUMAN GIVENS THERAPY

The human givens approach believes that we will be happier if we are more aware of and more sensitive to our innate needs and resources. All humans have a common set of innate physical and emotional needs, coupled with appropriate physical and emotional resources (see below). We deploy our "given resources" in order to meet our "given needs" in our daily lives. It is thought that when these innate needs are met, we will be happy and satisfied, but when the needs (especially our emotional needs) are not met, we become stressed or depressed. The therapy separates needs and resources as follows:

NEEDS	RESOURCES
• SECURITY	• MEMORY
• AUTONOMY AND CONTROL	• RAPPORT
• STATUS	• IMAGINATION
• PRIVACY	• INSTINCTS AND EMOTIONS
• ATTENTION	• A RATIONAL MIND
• CONNECTION TO THE WIDER COMMUNITY	• A METAPHORICAL MIND
• INTIMACY	• AN OBSERVING SELF
• COMPETENCE AND ACHIEVEMENT	• A DREAMING BRAIN
• MEANING AND PURPOSE	

A human-givens therapist then utilizes techniques such as relaxation, visualization, guided imagery and metaphors to help their client recognize any unmet emotional needs and then to find ways to meet these needs using their own resources.

PERSON-CENTERED THERAPY

Also known as client-centered counseling or Rogerian therapy, person-centered therapy is a humanistic approach developed by Carl Rogers (see page 33) during the 1940s and 1950s. Rather than seeing therapy as an expert treating a patient, it views the therapist and client as equal partners in trying to solve a problem. Rogers strongly believed that in order for a client's condition to improve, the therapist should be warm, genuine and understanding. With this approach, clients take responsibility for changing their life, rather than the therapist doing so. Instead of the emphasis being on unconscious motives, as in psychodynamic therapy, the client is presumed to know what they feel. Rogers claimed that the client is the best expert on themselves.

There are three "core conditions" that underlie client-centered therapy:

- The therapist is "congruent" with the client, which means that they interact in a genuine and authentic way (rather than maintaining the more neutral facade of the psychodynamic therapist).
- The therapist offers the client

HELPING CLIENTS TO HELP THEMSELVES

Carl Rogers was deliberate in his use of the term "client" rather than "patient," as he felt that this implied a more equal relationship than the "sick" patient being cured by the all-knowing doctor. Unlike psychodynamic therapy, which focuses on trying to interpret unconscious issues that would appear to have caused the patient's problems, the person-centered approach is far less directive. The therapist does not tell the client what to do, judge them, or offer answers to problems. Instead, the therapist helps the client work out issues and solutions themselves.

"unconditional positive regard," by demonstrating deep concern for the client and showing acceptance and non-judgmental attitudes.

- The therapist also displays "empathetic understanding" to the client.

According to Rogers, when these three conditions are apparent in a therapist, clients will feel free to express themselves without having to worry about what the therapist thinks of them or whether they are being judged. Here, the therapist does not attempt to change the client's thinking in any way (unlike in cognitive behavior therapy). Because of this client-led approach, clients are free to explore the issues that are most important to them rather than those considered important by the therapist. This allows clients to recognize alternative ways of thinking for themselves that will then go on to promote personal growth. The therapist's role is to facilitate this process by providing the appropriate non-judgmental and non-directed environment in which clients can be free to engage in self-exploration.

It should be noted that the person- or client-centered approach, while having its roots in humanistic therapies, is sometimes adopted with other therapies too, such as cognitive behavior therapy or even psychodynamic therapy.

DR. CARL ROGERS *conducts a group therapy session in 1966 where he provides unconditional positive regard and empathetic understanding to all involved.*

SOLUTION-FOCUSED BRIEF THERAPY

Also known as solution-focused therapy (SFBT) or brief therapy, this approach focuses on building solutions rather than analyzing problems, like in other approaches. Typically, the therapy involves only three to five sessions, far less than most other therapies. (Cognitive behavior therapy may involve up to 12 sessions, while psychodynamic therapies can last years.) Other therapists can spend a great deal of time thinking, talking and analyzing problems, while the problems simply continue. The aim with solution-focused brief therapy, however, is to use the client's strengths and skills to work on developing solutions, rather than investing too much time and energy analyzing the problem. Since its origins in the mid-1980s, this therapy has proved to be an effective intervention across the whole range of problems.

During sessions the therapist asks questions that encourage the client to find their own solutions to problems. Techniques include the following:

EXCEPTION QUESTIONS: Most people find that problems do not always seem as bad at all times — sometimes we feel better or have brief periods of respite. Often those better times are caused by our utilizing our own coping resources. Exception questions, such as "tell me about a time when this problem didn't bother you as much" or "tell me about a time when you felt happy," allow people to recognize these times and to think about what resources they employed to improve the situation. By exploring how these exceptions to the current difficult times happened and highlighting the strengths and resources that were used to move into an "exception

WITH THE MIRACLE QUESTION TECHNIQUE *clients are asked to imagine what life would be like if their current problem was miraculously solved overnight.*

period," a therapist can help the client to find their own solution.

SCALING QUESTIONS: A scale from 0 to 10 is used to help the client identify where they currently are with regard to a problem and where they would like to be. This helps to identify aims and goals and also to know when objectives are met. Scaling can also be used to rate problems in terms of their difficulties.

THE MIRACLE QUESTION: Here the client is asked to imagine that a miracle occurs at night while they are asleep that solves the current problem. They are asked to consider how they will know that the problem is solved when they wake up in the morning — what will be different? What will life be like? This helps the client see clearly how a future without the problem might look. It is this vision that motivates the client, allowing them to see how a solution could be achieved in small, practical steps.

EXISTENTIAL THERAPY

Looking to explore difficulties from a more philosophical perspective, existential therapy explores issues such as the meaning of life, rather than taking a technique-based approach. It does not delve into the past, but focuses on the here and now. Emotional and psychological difficulties are viewed as inner conflict caused by a person's confrontation with fundamental aspects of existence — the inevitability of death, freedom, responsibility, existential isolation and meaninglessness.

Existential therapy has its roots in both humanistic and psychoanalytical approaches but is also heavily influenced by philosophers from the 1800s (for example, Friedrich Nietzsche). During therapy, the client is helped to confront the four givens (or "ultimate concerns"), which are their role in the wider world, their social world, their inner world and their ideal world. Existential therapy aims to help clients confront the bigger anxieties (about life and its meaning) and to recognize the freedom of choice we have as to how we live our lives (and the responsibility that those choices bring). Existential therapists help their clients to take ownership of their lives and their decisions and to recognize that their lives are meaningful.

PSYCHIATRIC APPROACHES

Sometimes mental-health and psychological conditions are treated by psychiatrists and other medical practitioners, either instead of psychologists or in conjunction with them.

MEDICATION

This can help with a range of conditions, including schizophrenia, bipolar disorder, anxiety and depression. Antidepressants, for example, are commonly prescribed by physicians in response to a patient presenting with depression, because often it is quicker, cheaper and easier to prescribe medication than to try to access psychological therapies for the patient. (Waiting lists can be long and psychological therapies time-consuming and thus costly.) They can also offer a kick-start to help people get back on their feet and perhaps enable them to access other therapies.

Antidepressants are thought to work by increasing levels of neurotransmitters (see page 61) in the brain. Certain neurotransmitters, such as serotonin and noradrenaline, can improve mood and emotion, although this process is not fully understood. Antidepressants include the following:

SELECTIVE SEROTONIN REUPTAKE INHIBITORS
(SSRIs): These are the most widely prescribed antidepressants, since they cause fewer side effects (and an overdose is also less likely to be serious.) First developed in the late 1980s, they work by blocking the reuptake of serotonin into the nerve cell that released it, which prolongs its action in the brain. They include fluoxetine (brand name, Prozac), citalopram (Celexa), paroxetine (Paxil) and sertraline (Zoloft).

SEROTONIN-NORADRENALINE REUPTAKE INHIBITORS
(SNRIs): An alternative to SSRIs (they work on the neurotransmitter noradrenaline as well as on serotonin), some people respond better to this class of drugs. Examples include duloxetine (Cymbalta) and venlafaxine (Effexor).

NORADRENALINE AND SPECIFIC SEROTONERGIC ANTIDEPRESSANTS (NASSAs): These may be effective for some people who are unable to take SSRIs. The main NASSA prescribed in the US is mirtazapine (Remeron).

TRICYCLIC ANTIDEPRESSANTS (TCAs): An older type of antidepressant, TCAs tend no longer to be recommended as a first-line treatment for depression because they can be more dangerous if an overdose is taken. Examples include amitriptyline (Elavil), clomipramine (Anafranil), imipramine (Tofranil), lofepramine (Gamanil) and nortriptyline (Pamelor).

Any of these antidepressants may have side effects such as nausea, sleep problems, blurred vision, palpitations and headaches. They can even make anxiety worse before it gets better. Antidepressants can also cause withdrawal symptoms so stopping taking them should not be done suddenly.

Antidepressants can also be used to treat anxiety, but other drugs of choice for anxiety conditions include tranquilizers — benzodiazepines such as diazepam (Valium), alprazolam (Xanax), chlordiazepoxide (Librium), lorazepam (Ativan) and oxazepam (Serax) — and beta-blockers (such as Propranolol).

MENTAL HEALTH AND THERAPY IN FILMS AND CULTURE

Sadly, the way mental-health problems are depicted in films such as *Silence of the Lambs*, *Final Analysis*, *The Shining* or *Psycho* is often unrealistic, negative and sadly cliché, with the mentally ill too often portrayed as mad, bad and dangerous. In the Batman film, *The Dark Knight*, for example, Batman describes the Joker as a schizophrenic clown, as if those with schizophrenia are invariably violent and their savagery is triggered by events such as a full moon, Halloween or Friday the 13th. Alternatively, people with mental illness are often cured in an improbably short time frame or become the romantic love interest for their therapist.

Therapists, too, are frequently portrayed in an unrealistic way, with men being eccentric, mad, incompetent (*What About Bob?*) or evil (*Dressed to Kill* and *One Flew Over the Cuckoo's Nest*). Similarly, female therapists are portrayed as repressed until they fall in love with their male patients (usually symbolized by the removal of glasses and the letting down of tightly tied hair).

There are some recent exceptions — Daniel Craig's portrayal in *Some Voices* and Russell Crowe's in *A Beautiful Mind* are thought to reflect more realistic portrayals of schizophrenia.

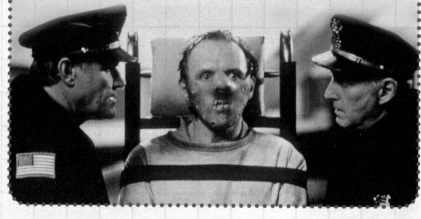

ELECTRO-CONVULSIVE THERAPY (ECT)

Although this therapy is not commonly used today, it is worth a mention here as it used to be employed quite routinely for severe depression and other mental-health disorders.

The treatment was developed in the 1930s when doctors noticed that some people with depression or schizophrenia who also had epilepsy seemed to feel better after having a convulsion. Building on this, electro-convulsive therapy was developed whereby an electrical current was passed through the brain to produce seizure. It is generally offered today only if medications for treating severe depression have not helped or the patient cannot tolerate the side effects. However, ECT is not without the risk of its own side effects (such as headaches, confusion, injury due to muscle clenching, and memory problems), which is why it is only used in rare cases nowadays. More effective treatments have been developed and its use has declined by about half. It is still endorsed however in the UK and the US (where it is administered to 100,000 people each year) as well as in other countries including Austria, Canada, Australia, Denmark, Netherlands, Germany and India.

ECT was a popular treatment in the past but its side effects (especially memory loss) have meant it has fallen out of favour today.

OTHER THERAPIES

Some of the therapies covered here share characteristics with more than one approach and so have been included in the category to which they are most closely aligned. However, other therapies don't fit comfortably into any single category. These include eye movement desensitization and reprocessing (EMDR), which is covered on page 214, integrative therapy and transactional analysis.

INTEGRATIVE THERAPY

This is a combined approach to psychotherapy that utilizes different elements of specific therapies to suit the various needs of individual clients. It has its roots in humanistic approaches but is based on the belief that there are different ways to work with a client, depending on their personality and issues. The client is regarded as an individual and the therapy should be tailored to them rather than to fit a certain type of therapy. Integrative approaches see the person as a whole and believe that, in order to heal, the whole of an individual must be taken into account – their emotional, cognitive, behavioral

DR. ERIC BERNE *was the founder of transactional analysis, which is a useful technique for understanding communication difficulties between people.*

and physiological systems – as well as the social world they exist in and interactions with their environment.

TRANSACTIONAL ANALYSIS (TA)

Founded by Eric Berne in the 1950s–1960s, transactional analysis is a technique that draws on elements of humanistic, existential, psychodynamic and cognitive behavioral therapies. The therapy views the human personality as being made up of three parts – adult, parent, and child. Our interactions with way we do. When we make judgments about people or the world around us, we are going into parent mode and become quite forceful, telling others what they should or should not be doing. By contrast, the healthy adult role allows us to be more rational and thoughtful in the way we view and interact with the world. Finally, when we behave as we did when we were children, becoming rebellious, stubborn, sulky or obedient, we are accessing our inner child. Often we move into these roles automatically with different people and this can cause unhappiness, conflict or distress. Transactional analysis helps people break away from the script and learn to stay in adult mode more often.

others are governed by which of the three roles we are taking at that time and which role the other person is taking.

For example, problems might arise if when talking to someone of authority, a person goes into child mode instead of adult mode. As part of this child role, the person becomes angry, sulky or rebellious, which affects the interaction/relationship with the person of authority. Transactional analysis helps the client understand why they default to this mode or "script" and what they can do to change the script so they stay in adult mode.

Transactional analysis thus helps to explain why we think, feel and behave the

TRANSACTIONAL ANALYSIS *helps us understand when we are in "inner child" mode or when someone we are interacting with is in that mode. It can help us stay in adult mode and encourage our conversational partner to do the same.*

NON-PSYCHOLOGICAL THERAPIES

There are a number of "complementary" therapies that are sometimes thought of as psychological therapies but are not based on psychological theory and research. Some have no scientific evidence at all to support them — for example, they are not based on double-blind studies (see page 40) — while others have only anecdotal evidence of success. Some have simply not been subjected to the rigorous scientific testing required by psychologists. Still others are useful only in some cases and thus have not been proved generalizable to the wider population.

This is not to say that the therapies discussed in this section do not work. Many clients and practitioners attest to their efficacy and the therapies may, indeed, have great results for some people.

NEURO-LINGUISTIC PROGRAMMING (NLP)

This was developed by Richard Bandler and John Grinder (both are trainers with backgrounds in psychology) in California in the 1970s. It is based on the belief that three aspects of human functioning are linked: the neurological processes, the linguistic (language) processes, and behavior patterns learned through experience. Neuro-linguistic programming is alleged to influence brain behavior through the use of language so that a person is able to change the way their brain responds to stimuli (programming) so that they can develop new and more adaptive behaviors (behaviors that help rather than hinder the individual).

The techniques used are based partly on behavioral modification and rely on the client's knowing what outcome they want to achieve and on having sufficient self-awareness and flexibility of behavior that they can adapt their behavior until they attain that outcome. In order to move people toward these goals, it teaches a series of linguistic and behavioral patterns that have proved highly effective with this. Thus, neuro-linguistic programming is about learning specific skills in order to break free of old habits and self-destructive patterns and behaviors, to create more appropriate behaviors and to make positive changes that will lead to better interactions with others and more self-awareness.

The technique is burgeoning as practitioners and clients claim great successes in treating a range of problems. However, there are very few truly credible studies supporting it as a therapy at the moment and as a result it may not be widely available. This is not to imply that NLP is not effective, but many regard it as a model rather than a therapy; indeed many psychologists and therapists draw on aspects of NLP without calling themselves NLP practitioners.

HYPNOSIS

Hypnosis is considered by many to be not so much a therapy as a state of deep relaxation. It involves entering an altered state of consciousness during which the client focuses their attention totally on the therapist and is thus receptive to suggestions and instructions from them. Under hypnosis, the person is so relaxed that their subconscious processes can be accessed.

While there is anecdotal evidence for the success of hypnosis in treating a range of conditions, there is a lack of credible scientific studies to suggest that it should be regarded as anything more than a complementary therapy. Again, this does not mean that it is not effective for some. Its success in many cases might be due to its use of suggestibility or even to the placebo effect. There is certainly some evidence to support its use in stopping smoking, losing weight and other conditions — but not enough to recommend its wider use in clinical practice.

EMOTIONAL FREEDOM TECHNIQUES (EFT)

This relatively new alternative therapy does not yet have a body of clinical evidence that would allow it to become mainstream. Also known as tapping therapy, it is a form of acupressure, except that, instead of using needles, tapping with the fingertips is employed. The aim of the tapping is to input kinetic energy onto specific meridians, during which a person thinks about their specific problem and voices positive affirmations. The procedure is said to clear the emotional block from a person's bioenergy system and is being used to treat a range of conditions, from phobias to post-traumatic stress disorder. Unfortunately, there are few, if any, published scientific studies to verify its effectiveness.

PART 5

EVERYDAY USES OF PSYCHOLOGY

PSYCHOLOGY IS NOT JUST A FASCINATING DISCIPLINE THAT INTRIGUES ANYONE INTERESTED IN HUMAN BEHAVIOR; IT HAS DIRECT PRACTICAL APPLICATION, TOO. APPLYING PSYCHOLOGICAL PRINCIPLES TO MANY EVERYDAY SITUATIONS CAN MAKE A DIFFERENCE AND EVEN CHANGE YOUR LIFE.

THE SOLUTIONS

STOP SMOKING

Smoking is not only about nicotine addiction but also habit, conditioning (see page 98) and the "dopamine-reward pathway." Awareness of these can help reduce the cravings. Nicotine stimulates the production of the feel-good chemical dopamine in the brain and reinforces the act of smoking so that it becomes a habit, while abstinence from nicotine is punished, since it leads to unpleasant withdrawal symptoms and cravings.

In addition, so-called secondary reinforcers add weight to the whole learning process. For example, going outside for a cigarette break, having a coffee, the smell of smoke, the feeling of holding the cigarette — all these become associated with the sensations of smoking and thus become secondary reinforcers for the primary reward of the nicotine. They are thus cues, or triggers, to smoke.

Since this conditioning process is outside conscious awareness, the smoker simply feels a powerful desire to smoke, which varies according to the presence of the cues and triggers. This is why nicotine-replacement therapy does not always work — it addresses only the nicotine addiction and not the secondary reinforcing pull of the other cues. (E-cigarettes, however, can provide the nicotine hit and the secondary reinforcement — but in a safer way than nicotine.)

There are various ways you can use psychology to fight this addiction:

FIND A SUBSTITUTE: Breaking the association between the reinforcers and smoking will reduce the craving to smoke, so introducing some other dopamine-producing activity in place of the nicotine can help a person to quit smoking. This is why some people put on weight when they stop smoking — they replace the cigarettes with snacks or other items that provide a dopamine hit. Healthier ways to replace the dopamine hit include doing something new, taking up a hobby, achieving something or going out with friends. Spend time with your family and put a photo of your children or partner on the cigarette box as motivation to stay healthy.

KEEPING HANDS BUSY *can break one trigger of smoking because cravings include the whole of the smoking experience. Eliminating each trigger or finding a substitute can contribute to breaking the cycle of addiction.*

AVOID THE TRIGGERS: Don't go for coffee breaks or do whatever you associate with having a cigarette.

INTRODUCE A PUNISHMENT: Make yourself do something you don't enjoy (for example, 30 push-ups) whenever you are smoking, so you will associate it with immediate negative consequences.

HOW TO USE PSYCHOLOGY TO...
FEEL LESS PAIN

The next time you are due for an
uncomfortable procedure, such as dental
treatment, reduce the pain you feel using
the following tips:

USE DISTRACTION: Focusing attention on pain
makes the pain worse. Patients who are
hypochondriacs are thought to be
over-vigilant about bodily sensations. It
has been found that by focusing on these
sensations will amplify them to the point
of feeling painful. Conversely, distracting
patients is highly effective in reducing
their pain. This is why many dentists have
TVs that a patient can watch during
treatment. So, if the circumstances allow,
take a book, watch a film, listen to music
or chat to a friend or family member.

TRY NOT TO GET ANXIOUS: Anxiety, fear and loss
of control contribute to pain. Treating
anxiety and providing psychological
support has been shown to reduce pain
and the need for painkillers.

INCREASE YOUR CONTROL OVER THE EVENT: When
we feel in control we feel more able to cope
with the pain — a lot of pain is connected
with fear of the unknown. Requesting that
you be kept informed of what is being
done at all times and that you are given
the opportunity of stopping when you
wish may make all the difference in your
perception of pain.

ADJUST YOUR EXPECTATIONS: If you are
expecting to find something painful, you
are more likely to find it so than if you are
not expecting it. For example, studies have
shown that minor whiplash injuries can
affect people differently, depending on
their expectations.

SMILE: When we smile, our brains think we are happy. People who frown during an unpleasant procedure report feeling more pain than those who do not, according to a study published in May 2008 in the *Journal of Pain*. Researchers applied heat to the forearms of 29 participants who were asked to make unhappy, neutral, or relaxed faces during the procedure. Those who exhibited negative expressions reported being in more pain than those in the other two groups. It could well be that in order to feel less pain, all we need to do is stop showing pain on our faces.

THE PAIN OF DENTAL WORK *can be reduced by trying not to get anxious, asking to be told what is happening in order to feel in control and using distraction.*

HOW TO USE PSYCHOLOGY TO...
BE A GREAT LEADER

There are many theories about this, but these days most lean toward one clear ideal — to be a great leader, according to leadership guru James MacGregor Burns in 1978, you need to be a "transformational leader." This is someone who transforms their followers from simply obeying them in order to gain rewards (such as recognition or pay) to buying into their whole ethos for greater good.

In other words, people want to help a transformational leader achieve their goals because they believe in them, not just because they are told to. They believe in the transformational leader's mission, they feel part of their vision and they want to do everything they can to help their leader achieve that. This is very different from the old-style "transactional leader" whose followers simply did as they were asked in order not to be fired or because they felt obliged to.

So, how to be a transformational leader? Here are four ways to achieve this:

BE A GREAT ROLE MODEL: Set high standards and follow them yourself. Never ask your followers to do anything you would not do yourself. Get your hands dirty. Act morally and ethically.

MOTIVATE PEOPLE: Create a vision and communicate that vision to your followers. Be optimistic about goals and your belief in a better world.

CARE ABOUT YOUR FOLLOWERS: Treat each follower as an individual with individual needs and motivations. Praise and acknowledge them for their contributions. Provide training or input according to each person's needs.

ENCOURAGE YOUR FOLLOWERS TO HAVE THEIR OWN IDEAS: Listen to them and welcome their input. This includes letting them disagree with you. Encourage them to come up with creative solutions to problems rather than always finding them for yourself.

HOW TO USE PSYCHOLOGY TO...
INCREASE YOUR IQ

If you have to complete an IQ test for a job, there are various things you can do to improve your score. Modern psychologists have shown in published research that IQ can be raised — and that these improvements in IQ are permanent.

As explained on page 67, there are two kinds of intelligence: crystallized and fluid. Crystallized intelligence refers to what you know; it is based on learned knowledge. Fluid intelligence is more about your capacity to learn new information, retain it and then use that new knowledge as a foundation to solve a problem or learn a new skill.

Here are some ways you can improve both types of IQ:

READ MORE: A language-rich environment can increase a person's intellectual acumen. Read widely and choose cognitively "stretching" material in which you may encounter unfamiliar words (be sure to look them up, to enrich your vocabulary).

WORK ON YOUR MEMORY: IQ and memory are often closely linked, so use the strategies on page 277 to improve your memory.

EXERCISE: Research shows that people who engage in regular exercise have higher IQ scores and better memories. For example, in 2013, researchers at Boston University School of Medicine in the United States showed that physical activity is highly beneficial for brain health and cognitive skill. A study carried out in 2009 that examined 1.2 million Swedish men proved that cardiovascular fitness can raise your intelligence significantly.

EAT WELL: Eating healthy food is also good for the brain. Scientists in 2014 showed that some foods are better for it than others: vegetables, such as broccoli and spinach, along with tomatoes, some berries and omega-3 fatty acids found in oily fish, improve memory and overall brain functioning. Protein contains high levels of amino acids, which in turn cause neurons to produce the neurotransmitters norepinephrine and dopamine (see page 52), which are associated with mental alertness.

PRACTISE TAKING IQ TESTS: It is said that what IQ tests really measure is your ability to take IQ tests — and this can be improved with practice.

LEARN NEW SKILLS: This gives your brain a work-out. Chess, martial arts, juggling, line dancing ... whatever it is, challenging yourself by learning new things will make your brain more agile. Each new skill creates new synaptic connections, which build up into new neural activity, priming your brain for even more learning.

HAVE A THIRST FOR KNOWLEDGE: Audiobooks, podcasts, internet lectures, documentaries — all are great ways to acquire a broader knowledge of the world, which will help your IQ grow.

CHALLENGE YOURSELF: Do puzzles, quizzes, spelling tests and the like. Problem-solve, build things, construct kits, abandon the satnav and rely on your own skills — all these will help strengthen your cognitive skills.

LEARNING TO PLAY CHESS *is a great way to challenge yourself and help to increase your IQ.*

HOW TO USE PSYCHOLOGY TO...
IMPROVE YOUR MEMORY

You can improve your working memory by giving your brain a memory workout. Look at the following list of words for 60 seconds, then cover it up and write down the words that you remember:

JACKET, WATER, LETTER, RAIN, RULER, CURTAIN, BOX, PAPER, GLASS, SWEATER, STAPLER, ZIPPER, DIARY, BANANA, SHOE, PEN, BRACELET, PHOTO, CHAIR, TIN

Now, try to improve your memory by practicing memorizing things through making connections between random objects, such as jacket–water (imagine putting on a jacket to protect yourself from someone throwing a bucket of water). Now connect water–letter (imagine you have written a letter that is washed away by water) and continue in this way in order to learn a whole chain of words or objects.

Using the same technique, look at the following new list and spend the 60 seconds making connections between the words.

BIRD, SCHOOL, EYE, CAFÉ, SHARK, BREAD, CORN, BLOOD, MONEY, NEWSPAPER, CAT, FLOWER, SUN, INJURY, CALENDAR, TODDLER, BLUE, COMMENT, FRIDGE, BILL

Now when you write down what you can recall, you should find it much easier.

NAME ASSOCIATIONS: You can use these techniques to remember names, too — just associate the name with something that will connect the name to that person (for example, Robin: "a rotund gentleman who looks like a robin redbreast"; Chris: "tall and lanky just like another Chris I know"; Anna: "has blonde hair the color of a banana"). Or you can link new memories with old ones by associating the new information with something that happened to you in the past (for example, Claire: "she has a graceful dancer's neck — this reminds me of an old school friend called Claire with whom I performed a dance in a school show").

FORMAT CHANGES: Using "elaboration" (assigning meaningful information to something) and "rehearsal" (repetition) to push information into long-term memory stores is another good technique for improving your memory. One way to do this is to translate the information into different formats so that it reaches your long-term memory via different routes. For example, a long list to memorize can be sung to a familiar tune (audio route) or made into a drawing (visual–spatial route). Using different colors with written material or saying things in different accents or voices can help with audio material, too.

CHUNKS AND ASSOCIATIONS: Other techniques involve chunking sets of information into groups of seven (see page 89), using mnemonics (the most effective are those that use humor or novelty, but see right) and associating the material with a pleasant smell or sound. (For example, spray perfume when you learn, then again when you want to recall. Similarly, playing a certain type of music while you learn should allow you to recall the material whenever you hear or hum that music.) Holding a certain object while learning will work in a similar way, as the material will be recalled more easily when that object is held in the future.

MNEMONICS

A mnemonic is any learning device that aids memory. Typically, it takes the initials of each item that is to be remembered and makes it into a memorable word — for example, RICE for the instructions for treating a sprain (Rest the injured area, Ice the sprain, Compress with a wrap or bandage, Elevate the injured area).

Other common types of mnemonic use the initials of a string of items to make a memorable sentence, such as "Richard Of York Gave Battle In Vain" to recall the colors of the rainbow (Red, Orange, Yellow, Green, Blue, Indigo, Violet) and HOMES to remember the Great Lakes (Huron, Ontario, Michigan, Erie, Superior).

There are also rhyming mnemonics to help recall information such as "I before E except after C" to remember spellings or "red sky at night, shepherd's delight, Red sky at morning, sailors take warning." to remember what red sky in the evening signifies (respectively, high pressure and stable air; low pressure and unstable air).

Songs are useful for remembering something, especially for children. For example, once learned, the ABC song is never forgotten.

There are mnemonics to help with remembering complex information, such as in the sciences — for example, to recall the digits of pi. For example, counting the letters in each word of the easily remembered "May I have a large container of coffee?" yields the sequence 3,1,4,1,5,9,2,6, which is pi.

A much more difficult song, however, is The Periodic Table Song, which covers all 118 elements of the periodic table. Learn this one and you are well on your way to an excellent memory!

MAKE BETTER DECISIONS

Psychologists have identified a number of heuristics, or mental short cuts (sometimes called rule-of-thumb strategies), that would seem to help us make decisions and judgments efficiently but that can actually interfere with our ability to make good decisions. Heuristics are when we focus on one aspect of a problem and ignore other aspects that may disprove our conclusion. They allow us to make quick decisions without having to weigh everything up all the time, which would be too time-consuming — but they can let us down by allowing us to ignore the logical or rational decision. To ensure you don't fall into their traps, be aware of the following:

AVAILABILITY HEURISTIC: This is where we make a judgment based on how easily an event comes to mind. For example, after a plane crash many people may assume that flying is more dangerous than it actually is simply because the crash is fresh in their minds. The statistics have not changed (it's no less safe to fly than before the crash) but the headlines bring the topic to the forefront, increasing the availability of information. This can influence decisions about whether or not to fly — but they are poor decisions not based on fact.

OVERCONFIDENCE: We tend to be overconfident about our own knowledge or skills. For example, if asked, most people would rate themselves to be above average in kindness. In fact, a survey in 2014 showed that over 85 percent of respondents rated themselves above average on this attribute but statistically half of them have to be below average in kindness. Thus many were simply overconfident and

THE AVAILABILITY HEURISTIC *is why we fear plane crashes more than car crashes; plane crashes are very rare events, which is why when they do happen, they are in the news and this makes them more available in our minds.*

overstated their skill. This also applies to other attributes, such as how good a sense of humor we have or how beautiful our children are compared with the average. This overconfidence in our judgments can affect perceptions of risk, which means that many of us misjudge a risk with complete confidence. ("It will never happen to me"/"It is bound to happen to me"). We tend to be even more overconfident when placing faith in experts, so that if an "expert" states an opinion, we are more likely to accept it as fact. All of this can cause biases in our rational decision-making processes.

ANCHORING AND ADJUSTING: When making decisions, we tend to "anchor" onto a prevalent piece of information and then adjust away from that piece of information until we reach a decision that seems reasonable to us — (see right). Credit card companies take advantage of our fondness for this mental short cut; have you noticed how they keep trying to increase your spending by raising your credit limit? This is because we see the figure and that serves as an anchor at which to aim our monthly spending.

ANCHORING AND ADJUSTING

What is the length of the River Nile? Write down your estimate between 1,000 and 15,000 miles (or between 1,600 and 24,000 km).

Now estimate it again, but between 500 and 5,000 miles (or between 800 and 8,000 km).

The chances are that your first estimate was bigger, because you used the numbers given as "anchors" to work from (or adjust to).

CREATE A GREAT FIRST IMPRESSION

There are many techniques from psychology that can help us impress people at a first meeting — this is especially useful in a job interview. Most people make judgments within just a few seconds (so-called "thin-slicing") so it is vital to get it right. Here are some ways to do that:

CREATE A HALO EFFECT: As explained on page 180, the halo effect is a cognitive bias whereby an overall view of someone is colored by one prominent attribute — as if one positive characteristic that stands out produces a halo around them. Create a halo effect by the clothes you wear, your general appearance, a smart handshake, a broad smile and confident body language. Even if you say something stupid after this, the halo effect you have created should cover you!

LOOK FOR AREAS OF COMMONALITY: As mentioned on page 300, we like people who are similar to ourselves (possibly because we feel comfortable with what is familiar) — this is the so-called "similarity attraction hypothesis." The sooner you can demonstrate that you have things in common, the more similar you will appear, and thus the more likable. These things could be hobbies, interests, a recent film you saw or even opinions. If you find that you disagree or do not share an interest, steer the conversation toward something that reflects more commonality.

BE OPEN: We generally like people who are expressive and enthusiastic — this tendency is called the "expressivity halo" — because it makes us feel that we can understand and read that person better. We also trust people who let us in rather than shut us out. Therefore, being expressive and open about your life, feelings, and attitudes can add to your aura of trustworthiness.

LISTEN WELL: Everyone likes to talk about themselves, so be sure to allow the other person to speak. And when they do, listen, rather than being preoccupied with the impression you are creating or what you are going to say next. Actively listening creates the impression that you are interested in what they are saying — and we all like people who find us fascinating.

A FIRST IMPRESSION is made very quickly so make sure it is good — you will not get a second chance to make a first impression!

HOW TO USE PSYCHOLOGY TO...
BECOME MORE CREATIVE

Can't think of a solution to a problem? Or trying to come up with a new and novel idea for something? Psychology can help you get those creative juices flowing with some surprising suggestions:

THE VALUE OF BOREDOM: It has long been suggested that boredom can boost creativity. When people are bored, they find it difficult to focus their attention on the task, and their thought processes shift to other areas that can provide more stimulation. When they cannot physically escape the boring task, their attention often shifts from external focus on the task to inner focus — thoughts, feelings and experiences — which provide the stimulation that is missing from the boring task. The inner focus could involve searching for new ways to carry out the boring task in order to make it more engaging or thinking about unrelated problems. Also known as daydreaming, this attention-shifting is a common by-product of boredom. Indeed, previous research has shown that individuals use daydreaming to regulate boredom-induced tension, which suggests that it is an effective coping strategy for dealing with boredom. In other words, being bored facilitates the daydreaming that is the key to creativity.

DYNAMIC MEMORY: Daydreaming is a part of dynamic memory — the ability to re-evaluate information and possible solutions by re-examining a problem or unresolved scenario. The act of daydreaming can thus provide individuals with the opportunity to reconsider an issue that is preoccupying their mind. They can do so as often as they wish, in varied ways, and each time incorporating new information and possible solutions. Daydreaming allows seemingly illogical ideas and impractical solutions to be explored, and through this an innovative or more suitable solution to a problem may be found. In other words, boredom and daydreaming can lead to creative problem-solving, which suggests a link between daydreaming and creativity.

HOW TO USE PSYCHOLOGY TO...
FEEL HAPPIER

There are several psychological tricks we can do to enhance feelings of happiness:

BE GRATEFUL: Studies have shown that there is a strong relationship between gratitude and wellbeing. This might be because people who experience a lot of gratitude are likely to have more positive experiences in their lives. But feeling grateful also means acknowledging that someone has done something nice or helpful for us, meaning that we have to acknowledge at some level that we are worthy of that goodwill. This can make us feel valued and cared for, and in turn enhances our self-worth. It has also been suggested that grateful people are more appreciative of life's simple pleasures.

KEEP COUNTING YOUR BLESSINGS: Learn to be grateful by keeping a "count my blessings" journal where you note all the events that you have to be grateful for each day.

PERFORM GOOD DEEDS: A Japanese study in 2006 showed that kind people experience more happiness and have happier memories than less kind people. The research showed that simply noting and counting our own acts of kindness for a week can make us happier. This could be because we are reminding ourselves of how nice we are and enhancing our own self-esteem. Even just the thought of helping others makes us happier and there are physiological reasons for this. Brain scans have shown that thinking about helping others activates the brain's mesolimbic pathway, which produces the feel-good chemical dopamine.

BE FORGIVING: Judging people negatively and bearing grudges cause negativity and lead to resentment and bitterness, sapping our feelings of wellbeing. Try to see things from the point of view of the other person and give them the benefit of the doubt; it will make you happier.

SEEK PLEASURABLE AND MEANINGFUL ACTIVITIES: Look for small, enjoyable things you can do every day — enjoy a coffee, meet friends, walk in the sunshine. Note and appreciate these small acts of pleasure so that you can see how enjoyable life is. Choose activities in which you can be "in the flow" — when you are thoroughly absorbed in a meaningful task that challenges your abilities (this is rarely achieved via screen time).

HOW TO USE PSYCHOLOGY TO...
BUILD A BETTER WEBSITE

Every part of your web page will have a psychological impact on your potential customers. Here are some tips for using psychology to make the most of it:

TRUST INDICATORS: Customers are more likely to buy from you if they trust you. Sprinkling trust indicators – such as professional affiliations, endorsements, customer feedback, testimonials and guarantees – across your website can thus improve sales.

PROOF THAT YOU ARE JUST LIKE YOUR CUSTOMER: Many sites have a "Who are we?" page where they tell the story of the business. Because people are more likely to like someone who is like them, showing on your web page someone to whom the customer can relate will help your sales. If you are targeting young mothers, for example, displaying a photo of yourself as a young mother, with a story explaining how being a mother sparked the idea for the product, is a great idea.

USE OF COLOR: Certain colors are thought to arouse particular emotions. For example, blue is often seen as a trustworthy color (just look at how many banks use this color for their logos and branding), yellow as an optimistic color and red as a fiery, exciting one. Choose colors that reflect the image you want to convey.

SOCIAL COMPARISON THEORY: When people make decisions, they often look to other people to see how to behave. If other people are buying your product, then they are likely to do so, too. This is why "recommend a friend" works so well, as does encouraging customers to report their purchases on social media.

PSYCHOLOGY affects more aspects of consumers' impressions of a website than you might think.

SOMETHING FOR FREE: Give your potential customers advice, a fun quiz or useful facts so that the principle of reciprocity kicks in, whereby they want to return the favour and do something for you (buy your product).

THE RIGHT FONT: The best font to use is one that is legible. Studies have shown that if you give people directions in a fancy font and in a normal font, people estimate that the journey will take far longer when they are reading the directions in the fancy font. Similarly, restaurant menus in fancy fonts are perceived by customers to reflect more time-consuming food preparation (which might be good in an upmarket restaurant but not in a fast-food joint).

HOW TO USE PSYCHOLOGY TO...
LOSE WEIGHT

The Health Belief Model (HBM) is a psychological model used to explain and predict health behaviors based on an individual's attitudes and beliefs about the health-enhancing value of the change they plan (diet, exercise) weighed against the perceived costs of that change (time, money, quality of life). A range of factors are involved. According to the HBM, your chances of sticking to your new diet depend on the following factors:

YOUR PERCEIVED SUSCEPTIBILITY: This refers to how likely you think it is that you will experience negative effects from not sticking to your diet (for example, how much you really believe your health will suffer or self-esteem be reduced).

PERCEIVED SEVERITY OF THIS OUTCOME: This is how serious you think these negative outcomes would be (for example, a belief that you might develop high cholesterol would be less severe than believing you might develop heart disease).

THE HEALTH BELIEF MODEL suggests that you will have success in your new diet if you think there are strong negatives, which outweigh the costs of the diet, associated with not dieting and if you feel confident in your ability to succeed with the diet plan.

PERCEIVED BARRIERS/COSTS OF THE NEW DIET:
These include financial costs as well as psychological barriers (such as the reduced quality of life that you might associate with the new diet).

PERCEIVED BENEFITS: The benefits (for example, looking better or being healthier) have to outweigh the perceived costs.

CUES TO ACTION: These are the things that can stimulate change, such as a far-from-flattering photo of yourself.

SELF-EFFICACY: This means how much you believe in your ability to actually stick to this diet. If you know that you quit the last ten diets you started and you don't really have much confidence this time, then you are doomed to failure.

You are therefore most likely to stick to your new diet if the following apply to you:

- You are convinced that horrible and serious things will happen to you if you don't.
- You have thought about how to manage the psychological costs of the new diet (for example, by including treats and pleasurable foods).
- You believe that there are immense tangible benefits to losing weight (such

as looking and feeling good), which outweigh the costs.
- You have had a "cue to action" (such as a health scare or having to buy a new work wardrobe because your old one no longer fits).
- You have confidence in your ability to diet (perhaps because you are trying something new or have strong social support).

Armed with this knowledge, you can increase your likelihood of sticking to the diet by manipulating the variables in the model. Have a health check to get a real estimate of the serious consequences of a continued fat- and sugar-laden diet. Make a list of all the benefits of losing weight. Minimize the psychological costs of the new plan. Take a spectacularly unflattering photo of yourself and stick it to the fridge (yes, this does work). Finally, develop a strong belief in your ability to stick to the diet for a given period of time by following a realistic eating plan (one that incorporates real food rather than liquid meals and has occasional treats built in, plus social support).

HOW TO USE PSYCHOLOGY TO...
POTTY-TRAIN YOUR TODDLER

This involves simple conditioning and shaping of behavior (see page 98). The conditioning schedule you use should be continuous reinforcement — in other words, you should reward your child each time they "perform" on the potty. The following techniques should help:

SHAPING THEIR BEHAVIOR: You will need to shape their behavior by rewarding them for carrying out behaviors that are a step toward the ultimate goal. For some toddlers, this will involve a reward each time they sit on the potty, while for others who are particularly wary it means rewarding them for going near it, for touching it or for sitting on it fully clothed.

FROM ACCIDENTAL TO DELIBERATE: Once you have shaped their behavior so that they are happy to sit there, diaper-free, you might then need to reward their staying there for a length of time. The goal is to "catch" the random behavior that you hope will eventually occur, when they "perform" by coincidence while sitting there. At this point the reward should be instant and gratifying, so that your child wants to repeat the experience in order to gain another such enjoyable response. This process should continue until your child is more or less producing on demand.

NEGATIVE BEHAVIOR: Your toddler might still be wetting or soiling their underwear, however, but conditioning has advice for this, too. Some parents favour the punishment route, but punishment is less effective than using reward schedules. Negative reinforcement may work — the child who wets themself feels uncomfortable so will want to remove that physical discomfort by using the potty. Otherwise, just ignore the negative behavior while continuing to reward the positive.

REWARDS: In terms of what rewards to use, chocolate and candy work well but are not so good for the teeth or body. Sticker charts use the concept of a token economy (see page 240) and can be very successful. Of course, a healthy serving of celebratory

kisses and praise can be a powerful reward
in itself, as can extra attention from
parents or having a story read to them
while they are sitting there. Eventually,
rewards are internalized and no longer
needed. Potty-trained children who wet
themselves accidentally receive
punishment enough from the discomfort
without needing the external rewards for
using the potty.

HOW TO USE PSYCHOLOGY TO...
COPE WITH TEENAGE TANTRUMS

Any parent of a teenager will know about the trauma of the teenage tantrum, but applying some of the following psychology tips might just ease you through the teenage years with a little less angst:

AVOID "NEGATIVE EFFECT RECIPROCITY": This rather grand term simply means that when your teen starts throwing insults and accusations at you, resist the very human urge to give as good as you get. It is human instinct to defend yourself by attacking, but it is counterproductive with anyone, especially with a teenager. Remember that your teen may be testing you, so don't feed their insecurities by giving them a reason to doubt your love.

STAY IN ADULT MODE: Transactional analysis, as explained on page 264, is an approach that assumes that we can take on one of three roles — adult, parent or child — in any of our transactions or interactions. Being in child mode means that you are acting like a child — for example, being petulant, illogical or emotional and displaying other behaviors that you might expect of a 5-year-old. Adults can easily

slip into this role. Your teen will probably be exhibiting "child" behavior while desperately trying to be "adult." Your taking the adult role means that you are trying to maintain an equal relationship with your adversary, whereas taking the parent role is about demonstrating your superiority in terms of power and knowledge. Most teenage conflict revolves around the parent being in parent mode and the teen being in child mode, whereas successful outcomes are more likely if both you and your teen can be in adult mode. But how do you turn your belligerent teen into an "adult"? The best way is for you to stay in adult mode; once you go into parent mode, it is very hard for your teen to move out of the responsive child mode. You can do this by staying calm, avoiding negative effect reciprocity (see previous tip), not treating them like a child, avoiding being patronizing or condescending, and looking for rational solutions rather than emotional point-scoring.

DO SOMETHING ODD: Another de-escalation technique that will throw an angry teen is to do something odd or out of the ordinary. For example, suddenly grab a banana from the fruit bowl, use it as a microphone and yodel your favourite *Sound of Music* number. Or leap, twinkle-toed, on the kitchen floor and give your best Fred Astaire/Ginger Rogers impression. Anything that is likely to stop your teen in their tracks (and is within your ability to be spontaneously silly) should interrupt the anger cycle long enough to defuse the situation.

TEENAGE TANTRUMS *are a fairly typical part of development as the child becomes an independent person but often lacks the maturity to control their emotions.*

HOW TO USE PSYCHOLOGY TO...
RECOGNIZE IF SOMEONE IS LYING

Many people think that they know what to look for to spot a liar, such as blink rate or gaze aversion (being unable to look you in the eye) — but in most cases, they are wrong. For example, most liars know that gaze-avoidance is thought of as a good cue to deception, so they make great efforts to keep eye contact when they lie.

Here, then, are five more dependable ways to spot a liar. These are the cues that are the hardest for a liar to fake:

INCREASED REPETITION OF COMMON WORDS AND PHRASES: Liars have enough to concentrate on with remembering their lies, so they tend to resort to tried and tested phrases to reduce their "cognitive load." Thus, you might find that with increased questioning they tell their story in exactly the same way; truth tellers are often more able to use variety in their verbal expressions.

MISMATCH OF WORDS WITH BODY LANGUAGE: Liars might say one thing but their body language or facial expression contradicts them. For example, saying, "Yes, I love your new hairstyle" but folded arms, a slight shake of the head or a toneless voice is a giveaway.

INABILITY TO TELL A STORY IN A NON-LINEAR WAY: This means that although they can tell their fake tale from beginning to end, they struggle more if asked to tell it out of sync. Trap them, then, by asking them about bits of the story in a different order and see if they struggle to answer you.

AVOIDANCE OF THE "I" WORD: In false accounts, people tend to avoid using the pronouns "I," "me," "my" and "mine" in an attempt to distance themselves from their account. The "I" may become "we." For example, "I went out for a drink with some lads — I didn't even speak to a girl!" might indicate more truth than "we went out for a drink — it was just a lads' night out."

USE OF PASSIVE RATHER THAN ACTIVE VOICE: In the sentence "Tennis is played by Jane every day" this is the passive voice, while "Jane plays tennis every day" is the active voice. The passive voice can indicate that the liar is trying to distance themselves from their shifty tale.

LIE DETECTOR TESTS *are not as reliable in detecting lies as people might think; they only measure "arousal" and people can learn to control their physiological arousal when they lie. Conversely, many people can appear very anxious even when they are not lying, which can be picked up as arousal by a lie detector.*

HOW TO USE PSYCHOLOGY TO...
HAGGLE

People who haggle can save themselves a lot of money. Here's how to be one of them:

WATCH YOUR LANGUAGE: Use confident language that is neither hesitant nor negative. Hesitant phrases such as "I mean," "you know" and "isn't it?" reduce your credibility as a negotiator and weaken your arguments. Tag phrases, such as "don't you think?" and "you know?" will also weaken your case.

AVOID EMOTIONAL LEAKAGE: We are pretty good at controlling our facial expressions but less good at the parts of our body further from the brain — our hands and feet can typically give us away. So, don't tap your fingers or jiggle your foot when you see a product that you love.

WATCH OUT FOR SALES PLOYS: Tricks like "foot in the door" (where the salesperson gets you to admit you like something about the product), "alternative close" (asking you, for example, which color you prefer), "limited availability offers" (must end today!) or "perceived scarcity" (only two left!) all use clever psychology to play to our fear of missing out, our need to appear consistent or a reluctance to offend.

TAKE SOMEONE WITH YOU: While you drive the bargain, they can observe the seller's body language and watch out for signs that the seller might be lying — for example, if there are discrepancies between the seller's words and body language or if they suddenly start avoiding eye contact.

PLAY GOOD COP/BAD COP: Having someone with you also allows you to play the oldest trick in the book, good cop/bad cop. There are a few variants of this but, generally, one of you will point out the flaws in the product while the other's enthusiasm reassures the seller that you are still interested. Research suggests that it should actually be called "bad cop/good cop" as it is more effective when the "bad cop" starts off.

THE KEY SKILL to learning to haggle is not to be afraid of "no"; once you have the confidence to give it a go, you can learn to be a super haggler!

MAKE PEOPLE KINDER

Wouldn't it be great if we could use psychology to encourage people to be kinder? In fact, there are several ways that applying a bit of psychology can do this:

MODELING AND SOCIAL PROOF: One way is to use modeling; if we are kind, others are likely to copy us and be kind, too. This is why letting another car pull in front of you when you are driving encourages other drivers to do so, too. We like to look to others as affirmation of how to behave; this is known as social proof or informational social influence. Salespeople use this by suggesting that other people have already purchased the product they are selling so that you are more likely to copy them (which is why we are urged by sellers to announce on social media that we have bought their product). Dubious salespeople selling in crowds are using this technique when the salesperson's accomplice, pretending to be a member of the public, buys their goods — when we see others doing it, we are more inclined to copy.

VICARIOUS LEARNING: We can use the same principles to teach our children to be kinder. Researchers have shown that people are more likely to perform random acts of kindness (such as doing something nice for a stranger) if, as children, they witnessed their own parents doing such things. This is an obvious example of vicarious learning, whereby we learn how to behave from the example of others around us.

PLAYING TO AN AUDIENCE: Having an audience also increases kind acts. This is because being publicly recognized as a kind individual often enhances our self-image and thus makes us feel good about ourselves. So if we want to encourage acts of kindness from others, we should make sure that there are very public

PSYCHOLOGY can be used to encourage people to be kinder in their busy, everyday lives.

opportunities for them to carry them out. Interestingly, merely giving people the illusion that they are being observed (for example, by hanging up posters of faces) can generate significant increases in pro-social acts such as charitable giving.

SELF-SERVING PROPHECIES: Telling people how kind they are can also increase their kindness. People do seem to react to the power of self-serving prophecies; if they are told (even at random) that they are more kind than other people, they will then go on to engage in more random acts of kindness. So, if you want your children to be kind, tell them that they are and the chances are that they will become so.

HOW TO USE PSYCHOLOGY TO...
MAKE SOMEONE LIKE YOU

There are lots of psychological tricks that can be employed to encourage other people to like you:

EMULATE THEM SUBTLY: Basic psychology tells us that we like people who resemble us. This is because we like ourselves, so if someone seems to be similar to us, it makes sense that we should like them, too. Therefore, to help someone like you, make yourself more like them by copying their mannerisms, mirroring their body language and expressing similar views.

FIND REASONS TO PRAISE THEM: We are also drawn to people who make us feel good. So, meaningful praise helps (but be wary of meaningless compliments).

ENTERTAIN THEM: Everyone enjoys being around people who are entertaining and stimulating, which means that having interesting experiences and stories to relate is useful. Humans crave novelty, therefore make sure you have new and novel things to talk about.

ASK FOR A SMALL FAVOUR: This makes them feel good and boosts their self-esteem in a subtle way as they have been able to help you. They will also feel that they must like you if they did a favour for you.

SHOW AN INTEREST IN THEM: Everyone likes to talk about themselves, so allowing them to do this while making interested noises will endear you to them — as will asking questions about their life and interests.

BE POSITIVE: No one likes to be surrounded by negativity, so resist the temptation to moan and complain about life too much.

MIRRORING *someone's body language in a subtle way can subconsciously influence their liking of you.*

MAKE SOMEONE FALL IN LOVE WITH YOU

Remember the Schachter and Singer two-factor theory of emotion from page 102? It suggests that if we notice physiological arousal, we look around to see what the cause of that arousal might be. We can use this to encourage someone to take a romantic interest in ourselves. All we need to do is to induce that arousal in the following ways:

FRIGHTEN THEM: One way to do this is to scare the living daylights out of your date. Horror movies, bungee jumping or white-knuckle roller-coasters are great for giving your date's feelings a nudge in the right direction. When they become physiologically aroused through the fear, they will look at you, snuggle into your arms for protection or clutch your hand and hopefully misattribute their arousal to your advantage. Instead of realizing that they are aroused because of fear, they might well assume they are aroused because they love you so much. This works especially well if they are the sort of person who refuses to admit to feeling afraid — their denial will lend itself to misattribution in your favour.

EXCITE THEM: If fear doesn't rock their boat, excitement should work just as well: climb a mountain, go canoeing or indulge in some other exciting activity on a date. If the object of your desire is an office colleague, working together on a high-pressured project with stressful deadlines should do the trick, too — as could winning a thrilling contract or some other workplace achievement (which helps to explain why office romances are so common).

CONDITION THEM: Other psychological tricks at your disposal include using conditioning: associate yourself in their mind with all things good and positive. If you can make them feel good as well, the conditioning will be stronger.

BE LESS AVAILABLE: You could also try the "scarcity principle"; people crave what they can't have, so don't be too available. Instead, show how much in demand you are with other people.

HOW TO USE PSYCHOLOGY TO...
STOP BEING SO ANGRY

If you are the sort of person who gets angry too much and too often, there are a number of techniques you can employ to reduce your anger:

AVOID THE ANGER TRIGGERS: There is often a pattern to the things that typically make us angry. Identify what makes you angry — probably as a result of habit or conditioning — and work out which of these triggers can be avoided and which can't. By avoiding those that you can, you will at least reduce the frequency of anger triggers in your life.

DISTANCE YOURSELF FROM THE PROVOCATION: It is not always possible to avoid anger triggers, but it may be feasible to distance yourself from them, either physically or temporally. Physical distancing techniques include moving further away (for example, from someone who is being rude or disrespectful to you) or going for a walk to cool down. Temporally distancing yourself is just about using time rather than space as a barrier between yourself and the event that could elicit the anger. For example, you might ask for time to think

over an issue, to avoid saying something in anger that you might later regret.

DISRUPT YOUR ANGER RESPONSE: If we cannot avoid the trigger and cannot moderate it, the only course of action left is within ourselves — cognitive (mental) strategies. We cannot change the event but we can change the way we react to it. One way to do this is by changing the way we interpret anger-inducing events. Another approach is to reduce the significance of the event to us, by disrupting our anger response, such as by engaging in incompatible behavior. Anger is a state of arousal and it is impossible to experience this if you are relaxed. Therefore, find an activity that makes you feel relaxed — it will not be easy for you to feel anger at the same intensity.

PUT YOURSELF IN THE OTHER PERSON'S SHOES: Increase your compassion by imagining that the person with whom you are angry is going through a very difficult time themselves. Similarly, improve your empathy by searching to find something that you might have in common with the person.

USE THOUGHT-STOPPING: This is another cognitive technique that involves you "catching" the anger-response processes and interrupting them. When we are angry, we tend to go over and over in our heads what has happened and this causes the anger cues to be reinforced continually. Therefore, when you feel your anger rising, interrupt your anger response by telling yourself to "stop" the thoughts from going around your head.

HAVE A LAUGH: Humor is another cognitive technique that relies on the introduction of something incompatible with the anger response. The basic premise of using humor is that we cannot feel both angry and amused at the same time; laughter will thus replace rage. Humor can also be used to put events into perspective by interrupting the appraisal part of the anger response; when we can laugh at something, we interpret the event differently. This is why people may say to you, "You'll laugh about this one day." What is more, laughing can interrupt the anger response by providing an emotional release from the tension. And it can be used as a distractor — if something makes you laugh, you might forget why you were angry in the first place.

LIFE IS FULL OF FRUSTRATIONS *that can stop us achieving our goals — learning to cope with these will make us happier and less stressed.*

HOW TO USE PSYCHOLOGY TO...
DEFUSE SOMEONE ELSE'S ANGER

Often it is the anger of other people that is more of a problem than our own, but psychology has plenty of tips for dealing with this, too:

ACKNOWLEDGE THE EMOTION: This is the first step to dealing with other people's anger. Show the other person that you understand that they are angry, and why. Often, people get more and more angry simply because they feel the need to demonstrate just how cross they are. Acknowledging that you have recognized how angry they are can take the wind out of their sails and they no longer need to keep showing you the intensity of their feelings.

KEEP YOUR VOICE LOW AND CALM: Concentrating on the tone and pitch of your voice will help to reduce the intensity of the other person's anger. If you were to respond to them by shouting and matching their intensity, you will only increase their rage — because the louder you get, the louder they will become to match your level.

SIT DOWN TOGETHER: Consider getting the angry person to sit down somewhere with you; it is harder to get excessively angry from a seated position. People tend to stand up when they are very angry so trying to keep people seated can counter this automatic response.

BE CONCILIATORY: Very angry people can be beyond rationality, so be wary of asking too many questions at this stage. Just make conciliatory comments, such as "I understand," "that must have been distressing," "that sounds like a real inconvenience" or "it sounds like you have been sent on a bit of a wild goose chase."

APOLOGIZE: If appropriate, agree with them and apologize. It is amazing how difficult some people find this.

STANDING UP *when you are angry can often lead to the anger escalating as it is much easier to use aggressive body language when standing — so getting someone to sit down and calm down can help to diffuse the anger.*

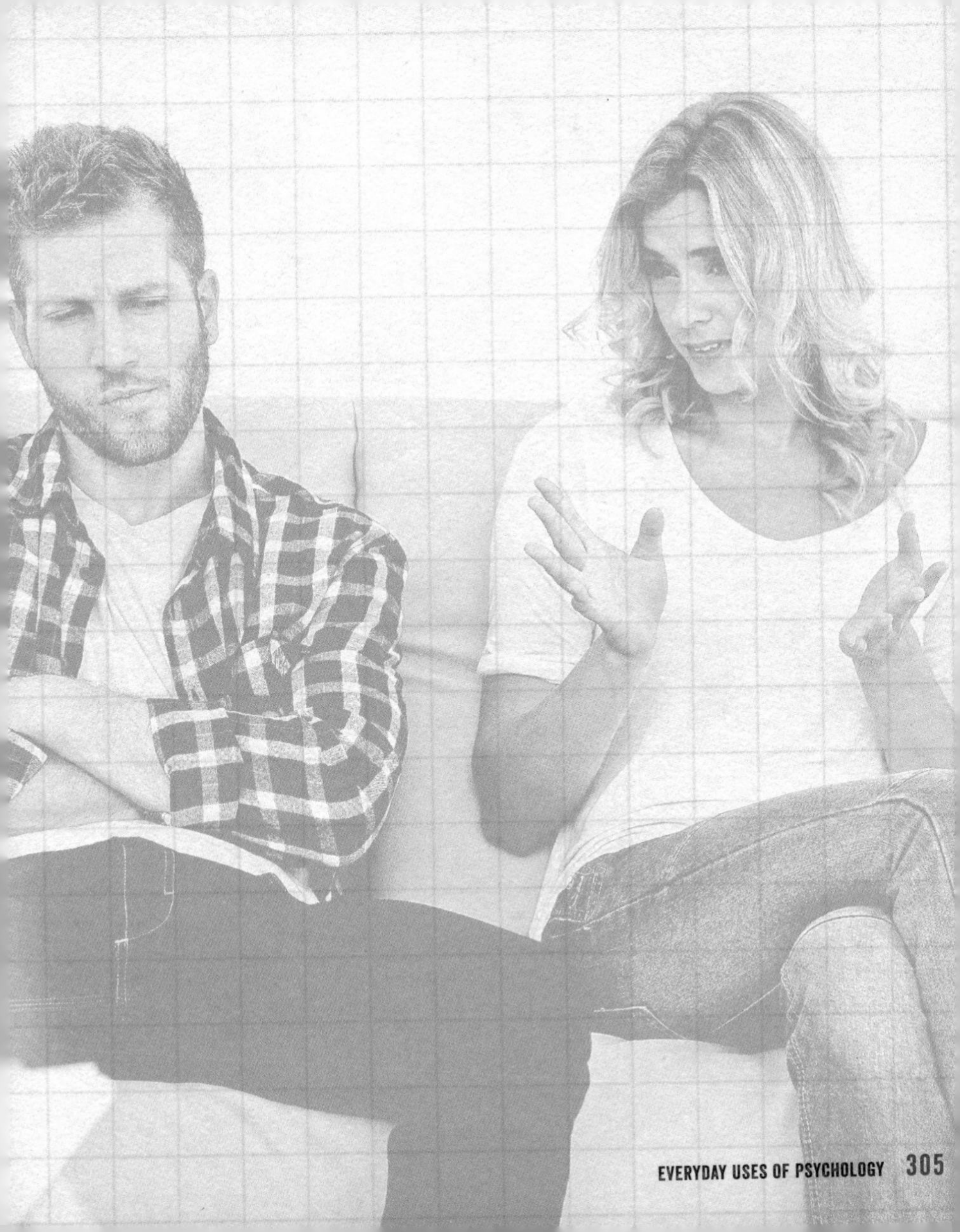

CONCLUSION

AS WE REACH THE END OF THIS EPIC JOURNEY THROUGH THE HUMAN MIND, I HOPE YOU HAVE DISCOVERED HOW ENDLESSLY FASCINATING THE STUDY OF PSYCHOLOGY IS. MY AIM HAS BEEN TO SHOW YOU WHAT IS REALLY IMPORTANT ABOUT THE SCIENCE OF MIND AND BEHAVIOR: THE MAIN THEORIES, EXPERIMENTS, METHODS AND PEOPLE. AS A PSYCHOLOGIST WHO IS PASSIONATE ABOUT THE FIELD, I HAVE TRIED TO GIVE YOU A FULSOME FLAVOR OF ALL THAT IS MAGICAL ABOUT HOW THE HUMAN MIND WORKS.

HOW YOU USE THIS KNOWLEDGE NOW IS UP TO YOU. YOU MIGHT BE KEEN TO LEARN MORE, READ MORE OR EVEN PURSUE A CAREER IN PSYCHOLOGY. ALTERNATIVELY, YOU MIGHT SIMPLY WANT TO UNDERSTAND YOURSELF OR OTHERS A LITTLE BIT MORE CLEARLY. OR YOU MIGHT WISH TO SEEK HELP FOR SPECIFIC ISSUES IN RELATION TO YOURSELF OR YOUR LOVED ONES (SEE RESOURCES SECTION FOR GUIDANCE). WHATEVER YOUR MOTIVATIONS FOR PICKING UP THIS BOOK, I HOPE YOU HAVE ENJOYED THE RIDE AND GAINED INSIGHTS AND A NEW UNDERSTANDING OF PSYCHOLOGY.

RESOURCES & REFERENCES

PROGRESSIVE MUSCLE RELAXATION THERAPY
(FOR RELAXATION AND STRESS REDUCTION)

This technique helps the user to learn the difference between tension in the body and relaxation. Many relaxation techniques rely on telling people to "relax" but this is actually quite hard to do. Progressive muscle relaxation therapy (PMRT) works by teaching you to tense each muscle in turn and then to relax it, so that you can really feel the difference between tension and relaxation. Try it yourself:

1. Sit comfortably in an armchair or you can even lie on the bed. Close your eyes for best effect (but not if it makes you uncomfortable).

PMRT *is proven to lower blood pressure but is a skill that should be learned and practiced in order for it to be effective.*

2. Concentrate on your breathing — breathe in and out very slowly. Every time you breathe out, think to yourself the word "relax." Do this several times.

3. Curl and tense your toes tightly so that it feels very uncomfortable. Notice how tensing your toes makes your calves and even your thighs uncomfortable, too. Notice how tensing just your toes can spread the tension through your body. Now relax your toes and enjoy the feeling of relaxation this produces. Feel the difference between tension in your toes and relaxation. And every time you breathe out, think to yourself the word "relax." Repeat this step.

4. Move on to your thighs. Tense them tightly so that it feels very uncomfortable. Notice how tensing your thighs spreads the tension throughout your body — your stomach feels tense, and even your arms. Now relax your thighs and enjoy the feeling of relaxation and warmth that this produces. Feel the

difference between tension in your thighs and relaxation. And every time you breathe out, think to yourself the word "relax." Repeat this step.

5. Move on to your stomach. Tense it tightly so it feels very uncomfortable. Notice how tensing your stomach muscles spreads the tension throughout your body. Now relax your stomach and enjoy the feeling of relaxation and warmth that this produces. Feel the difference between tension in your stomach and relaxation. And every time you breathe out, think to yourself the word "relax." Repeat this step.

6. Tense and relax each muscle group in turn: your fingers (clench into tight fists), shoulders (shrug them to your neck), eyes (squeeze them tightly closed) and face (scrunch up your mouth). Finally, tense your whole body and relax it.

PART 1

American Psychological Association careers advice: www.apa.org/careers/index.aspx

Canadian Psychological Association careers advice: www.cpa.ca/students/career/

"The 100 Most Eminent Psychologists of the 20th Century," *Review of General Psychology*, 2002 (vol. 6, no. 2), www.creativity.ipras.ru/texts/top100.pdf

Designing and Reporting Experiments in Psychology by Peter Harris, Open University Press, 3rd edition, 2008

As Nature Made Him: The Boy Who Was Raised as a Girl, by John Colapinto, HarperCollins, paperback edition, 2001

Original newspaper coverage of Kitty Genovese murder: www.nytimes.com/1964/03/27/37-who-saw-murder-didnt-call-the-police.html?_r=0

Minnesota Center for Twin & Family Research: www.mctfr.psych.umn.edu/research/UM%20research.html

Epilepsy Foundation of America: www.epilepsy.com

Epilepsy Canada: www.epilepsy.ca

An Introduction to Psychological Assessment and Psychometrics by Keith Coaley, Sage Publications, 2nd edition, 2014

You're Hired! Psychometric Tests: Proven Tactics to Help You Pass by Ceri Roderick and James Meachin, Trotman, 2010

PART 2

Opening Skinner's Box: Great Psychological Experiments of the Twentieth Century by Lauren Slater, Bloomsbury Publishing, paperback edition, 2005

"Pareidolia: Why We See Faces in Hills, the Moon and Toasties," *BBC News Magazine*, 31 May 2013, www.bbc.co.uk/news/magazine-22686500

Basic Vision: An Introduction To Visual Perception by Robert Snowden, Peter Thompson and Tom Troscianko, Oxford University Press, 2nd edition, 2012

How to Develop a Brilliant Memory Week by Week: 50 Proven Ways to Enhance Your Memory by Dominic O'Brien, Watkins Publishing, 2014

"Why Does the Human Brain Create False Memories?" by Melissa Hogenboom, BBC News, 29 September 2013, www.bbc.co.uk/news/science-environment-24286258

Video of Skinner box: www.youtube.com/watch?v=D-RS80DVvrg

Video of love or fear study: www.youtube.com/watch?v=P0aMEkGlcQE

Intelligence: All That Matters by Stuart Ritchie, Hodder & Stoughton, 2015

How Intelligent Are You? The Universal IQ Tests by Victor Serebriakoff (Honorary President of World MENSA), Robinson, reissue 2014

Video of Konrad Lorenz's experiment, National Geographic Society: https://www.youtube.com/watch?v=2UIU9XH-mUI; https://www.youtube.com/watch?v=eqZmW7uIPW4

Video of Mary Ainsworth's "strange situation" experiment:
www.youtube.com/watch?v=QTsewNrHUHU

Video of Piaget's conservation tasks:
www.youtube.com/watch?v=gnArvcWaH6I

Dual Language Development and Disorders: A handbook on bilingualism & second language learning by J Paradis, F Genesee and M Crago, Paul H Brookes Publishing, 2011.

Groupthink: Psychological Studies of Policy Decisions and Fiascoes by Irving L Janis, Houghton Mifflin, 2nd hardback edition, 1983

A Theory of Cognitive Dissonance by Leon Festinger, Stanford University Press, 1957

PART 3

Video of BBC documentary "The Stanford Prison Experiments":
www.youtube.com/watch?v=gb4Q2o2oT1Q

Video of Milgram's studies (original footage):
www.youtube.com/watch?v=xOYLCy5PVgM

Video of autokinetic effect studies (original footage of Sherif's studies, upon which Asch's were based):
www.youtube.com/watch?v=0DoIxN6B4PQ

Video of Asch conformity study (original footage):
www.youtube.com/watch?v=NyDDyT1lDhA

Video of Harlow's monkeys (original footage):
www.youtube.com/watch?v=_O60TYAIgC4

Video of "The Brain: A Secret History – Emotions; Bandura Bobo Doll Experiment," DebateFilms:
www.youtube.com/watch?v=zerCK0lRjp8

Video of Jane Elliott's blue eyes–brown eyes experiment:
https://www.youtube.com/watch?v=Nqv9k3jbtYU

The Marshmallow Test: Understanding Self-control and How To Master It by Walter Mischel, Corgi, paperback edition, 2015

The Robbers Cave Experiment: Intergroup Conflict and Cooperation (orig. pub. as *Intergroup Conflict and Group Relations*) by Muzafer Sherif, O J Harvey, B Jack White, William R Hood and Carolyn W Sherif, Wesleyan University Press, Wesleyan edition, 1988

'Cognitive, Social, and Physiological Determinants of Emotional State', *Psychological Review*, by S. Schachter and J. Singer, 1962

"Disputed Results a Fresh Blow for Social Psychology" by Alison Abbott (article about social priming), *Nature*, 30 April 2013, http://www.nature.com/news/disputed-results-a-fresh-blow-for-social-psychology-1.12902 and http://www.scientificamerican.com/article/disputed-results-a-fresh-blow-for-social-psychology/

Video of "False Memory: Lost in the Mall," ShortCutsTv:
www.youtube.com/watch?v=VTF7FUAoGWw

PART 4

Video of "Managing Stress: Brainsmart," BBC:
www.youtube.com/watch?v=hnpQrMqDoqE

Overcome Phobias and Panic Attacks: Teach Yourself by Sandi Mann, Hodder & Stoughton, 2013

Sleep Education: www.sleepeducation.org/sleep-disorders-by-category

Alliance for Eating Disorders Awareness:
www.allianceforeatingdisorders.com

National Eating Disorders Information Center
(Canada): www.nedic.ca

National Institute of Mental Health (US):
www.nimh.nih.gov/index.shtml

Canadian Mental Health Association: www.cmha.ca

Schizophrenia Society of Canada:
www.schizophrenia.ca

Schizophrenia and Related Disorders Alliance of
America: www.sardaa.org

Autism Society of America:
www.autism-society.org

Autism Canada: www.autismcanada.org

"No Link Between MMR and Autism, Major Study
Concludes" by Sarah Boseley, *The Guardian*, 21
April 2015, htts://www.theguardian.com/
society/2015/apr/21/no-link-between-mmr-and-
autism-major-study-concludes

CHADD - The National Resource on ADHD (USA)
www.chadd.org

Canadian ADHD Resource Alliance: www.caddra.ca

*An Introduction to Cognitive Behavior Therapy:
Skills and Applications* by David Westbrook, Sage
Publications, 2nd edition, 2011

*Mindfulness: A Practical Guide to Finding Peace in
a Frantic World* by Mark Williams and Danny
Penman, Piatkus, 2011

American Psychoanalytic Association:
www.apsa.org

Canadian Psychoanalytic Society:
www.en.psychoanalysis.ca/

Gestalt Therapy: 100 Key Points and Techniques by
Dave Mann, Routledge, 2010

Person-Centred Therapy: 100 Key Points by Paul
Wilkins, Routledge, 2nd edition, 2015

*Existential Therapy: 100 Key Points and
Techniques* by Susan Iacovou and Karen
Weixel-Dixon, Routledge, 2015

*Games People Play: The Psychology of Human
Relationships* by Eric Berne, Penguin, reissued 2010

PART 5

*Stop Smoking with CBT: The Most Powerful Way to
Beat Your Addiction* by Max Pemberton, Vermilion,
2015

*Paying it Forward: How One Cup of Coffee Could
Change the World* by Sandi Mann, HarperCollins,
2014, Kindle edition, 2015

"A Normal Psychology of Chronic Pain" by
Christopher Eccleston, *The Psychologist*, June
2011, vol. 24, http://thepsychologist.bps.org.uk/
volume-24/edition-6/normal-psychology-chronic-
pain

*Lead from the Heart: Transformational Leadership
for the 21st Century* by Mark C. Crowley, Balboa
Press, 2011

Manage Your Anger: Teach Yourself by Sandi
Mann, Hodder & Stoughton, 2012

*How to Develop a Brilliant Memory Week by Week:
50 Proven Ways to Enhance Your Memory* by
Dominic O'Brien, Watkins Publishing, 2014

"Seven Ways to Improve Your IQ," *Men's Health*, 12 November 2015, http://www.menshealth.co.uk/healthy/brain-training/seven-ways-to-improve-your-iq

"5 Cognitive Behavioral Strategies for Losing Weight that Work" by Christy Matta, www.psychcentral.com/blog/archives/2013/09/18/5-cognitive-behavioral-strategies-for-losing-weight-that-work/

Would I Lie to You? by Paul Seager and Sandi Mann, Albert Bridge Books, 2013

Video on how to haggle: www.youtube.com/watch?v=sgZ0kUtUqgg

Surviving the Terrible Teens: How to Have a Teenager and Stay Sane by Sandi Mann, Paul Seager and Jonny Wineberg, Crimson Publishing, 2008

Action for Happiness: www.actionforhappiness.org

HOW TO FIND PROFESSIONAL HELP

Depending on where you live, your doctor or medical clinic should be able to provide you with a referral to psychological services. Keep in mind that demand can be high and there might be a waiting list. Also, charges may not be covered under national, state or provincial health plans. However, many employers provide extended health plans that do include psychological services. Check first so you do not have surprise bills.

If you do not have any coverage and cannot afford fees, there might be local clinics where you can find help, and sometimes colleges and universities run clinics by prospective professionals. Here are some of the best ways to find a local therapist:

UNITED STATES: The best place to look for a local licensed psychologist is with the American Psychological Association,

http://locator.apa.org/or in directories such as GoodTherapy http://www.goodtherapy.org/find-psychologists.html or *Psychology Today* https://therapists.psychologytoday.com/rms/ (this site covers Canada, too). Some of these allow you to search according to criteria that include location, areas of specialization, language, insurance and more.

CANADA: The best place to start in Canada is with the provincial and territorial listings with the Canadian Psychological Association at (www.cpa.ca/public/findingapsychologist).

Another way of finding a good practitioner is by word of mouth. Unfortunately, many people don't like to talk about mental-health issues, but those who do often find others in similar positions. You may well find a friend who can personally recommend a therapist who has helped them and whom they trust and like. Keep in mind, however, that some psychologists will not agree to see a client that is a relative or friend of someone they are already treating.

INDEX

PICTURE CREDITS

Alamy AF Archive 230, 262; Andrew Paterson 27; bilwissedition Ltd. & Co. KG 135; Blend Images 18; Cultura Creative (RF) 220; Cultura RM 113; D Hurst 160 main; Daria Zuykova 239; David Taylor 240; Elena Elisseeva 22; Gianni Dagli Orti/The Art Archive 153; Graham Hughes 175; Granger, NYC. 246; moodboard 162; PhotoAlto 81; Pictorial Press Ltd. 177, 263; Sergio Azenha 133; SPUTNIK 96; Tanya Lacey 300; The Natural History Museum 14. **Dreamstime.com** Andor Bujdoso 208; Andrea Crisante 2; Aphinan Jarong 44; Bluraz 242; Drserg 59; John Helgason 158; Minaret2010 204; Noam Armonn 45; Otmar Winterleitner 198; Syda Productions 192; Travnikovstudio 121; Viorel Dudau 226; Wavebreakmedia Ltd 171. **Getty Images** Al Fenn/The LIFE Picture Collection 139; Andreas Solaro/AFP 15; Anthony Barboza 129; Art Media/Print Collector 225; Bettmann 35, 172; BSIP/UIG via Getty Images 4 right, 61; Chris Parsons 4 background; DEA/G. DAGLI ORTI 9; fotografixx 39; Frank van Delft 241; Jan Rieckhoff/ullstein bild via Getty Images 145; Kraig Scarbinsky 120; Lars Baron/Bongarts 169; Louis Monier/Gamma-Rapho via Getty Images 30; Matthew Ward 210; Michael Rougier/The LIFE Picture Collection 33, 257; Nina Leen/The LIFE Picture Collection 157; Norbert Michalke 47; Paul Hudson 77; PeopleImages 116; Peter Dazeley 291; PhotoAlto/Ale Ventura 71; Roberto Serra - Iguana Press 104; Sam Edwards 85; Science & Society Picture Library 66; Science Photo Library - PASIEKA 62; SCIEPRO 9 left, 60; Serny Pernebjer 258; Sigmund Freud Copyrights/ullstein bild via Getty Images 247; Three Lions 41; Time Life Pictures/Mansell/The LIFE Picture Collection 31; Underwood Archives 123; Westend61 122; ZEPHYR/Science Photo Library 55. **iStock** 4x6 20, 21; AfricaImages 191; ajkkafe 173; annedde 17; Antagain 205; Anton Gvozdikov 98; baona 221; CSA-Plastock 149 right; David Hanlon 275; fbatista72 105; Floortje 232, 261; Grady Reese 167; Hans Laubel 140; ideabug 28; iStoc km/hoto_RAW 92; Jacob Wackerhausen 124; John Gollop 12, 88; kupicoo 26; Liubomir Turcanu 76; Mark Papas 100; miappv 36; Neustockimages 184; Ni Qin 276; OJO_Images 25; okeyphotos 168; PeopleImages 83; poligonchik 178; Roman Samokhin 97; Sashkinw 182; SelectStock 64; Shaun Lombard 207; skynesher 245; teekid 147; temmuz can arsiray 206; tetmc 233; visualspace 99; Volker Göllner 146; Wavebreakmedia 236, 252; ZU_09 9 right. **NASA** 130. **Octopus Publishing Group** Russell Sadur 73. **Press Association Images** AP 264; AP Photo/New School for Social Research 32. **REX Shutterstock** 79; Action Press 165; Blend Images 254; Everett Collection 161; ITV 231; Novastock 49. **Science Photo Library** Omikron 214; Wellcome Dept of Cognitive Neurology 48, 155, 156. **Shutterstock** 297; 4x6 119; 578foot 284; albund 294; Alena Ozerova 308; Alexander Raths 209; altanaka 229; Andrey Armyagov 86; Antonio Guillem 215, 293; Axel Bueckert 219; Benoit Daoust 180; bontom 301; CandyBox Images 194; Carolyn Franks 190 right; Chaikom 38, 69; Cherednychenko Ihor 222; Chimpinski 183; David Asch 143; Daxiao Productions 288; Dm_Cherry 95; fantom_rd 265; file404 70; Frank Wasserfuehrer 213; Gam1983 307, 310, 312; Hein Nouwens 11 right; hxdbzxy 176; igor. stevanovic 212; Incredible_movements 57; indigolotos 166; iodrakon 144; jcjgphotography 270; Johan Larson 102; Juan Gaertner 54; kart31 114; Kisialiou Yury 248; Kozlenko 164; LifetimeStock 50; Lisa Alisa 189; Ljupco Smokovski 174, 298; lynea 11 left; Maksym Poriechkin 282; Mariyana M 118; Master1305 250; Morphart Creation 53 left; natrot 170; niderlander 187; nikolarisim 56; pathdoc 201; Pavelk 103; PHOTOCREO Michal Bednarek 280; pimpic 107; PongMoji 279; Pressmaster 314; Rawpixel.com 43, 94, 125, 185, 287; Ruslan Ivantsov 160; Sebastian Kaulitzki 53 right; shahreen 106; Shymko Svitlana 193; sondem 271; style-photography 101; Sumate Gulabutdee 289; Syda Productions 303; T.Dallas 138; Tatiana Shepeleva 75; Timof 117; ved prakash sharma 286; Vereshchagin Dmitry 273; vita khorzhevska 285; Voran 281; vtwinpixel 200; watchara 268; wavebreakmedia 110, 269, 304; winnond 203; xpixel 52; Yuravector 148; yurgo 63; Yuriy Rudyy 217, 218. **Stanford Historical Photograph Collection (SC1071)** 141, 142. **The Advertising Archives** 181. **TopFoto** ullsteinbild 67.